T0330300

Financial Fraud Prevention and Detection

Founded in 1807, John Wiley & Sons is the oldest independent publishing company in the United States. With offices in North America, Europe, Asia, and Australia, Wiley is globally committed to developing and marketing print and electronic products and services for our customers' professional and personal knowledge and understanding.

The Wiley Corporate F&A series provides information, tools, and insights to corporate professionals responsible for issues affecting the profitability of their company, from accounting and finance to internal controls and performance management.

Financial Fraud Prevention and Detection

Governance and Effective Practices

MICHAEL R. YOUNG

WILEY

Library of Congress Cataloging-in-Publication Data:

ISBN 9781118617632 (Hardcover)
ISBN 9781118762097 (ebk)
ISBN 9781118761632 (ebk)

Printed in the United States of America

10 9 8 7 6 5 4 3 2 1

To Leslie

Contents

viii   ▣   Contents

Preface

A LMOST ANY PUBLIC COMPANY can become a petri dish for fraudulent financial reporting. It can seep into a company's financial reporting system undetected. Once inside, it can silently grow. It can spread to involve more and more people. It can end up infecting any number of accounts. It can become so pervasive that even those responsible for the fraud don't know how bad it has gotten.

Over the last 15 years, the financial community has taken great strides against financial fraud. Sarbanes-Oxley has created enhanced mechanisms for fraud deterrence. Dodd-Frank has added enhanced incentives for whistleblowers. Companies have worked hard to improve their financial reporting cultures.

But to paraphrase Mark Twain, reports of the death of financial fraud are greatly exaggerated. In fact, an ostensible decline in financial fraud may have as much to do with the economic climate—and in particular the 2008 Financial Crisis—than with changes in the law. When times are tough, financial fraud will naturally decline because the pressure for spectacular results has dissipated. It is when the good times return that the risk of fraud increases.

This book seeks to assist in the battle against financial fraud. It warns of the insidiousness with which financial fraud starts and grows. It gives practical, concrete advice on fraud prevention. It addresses fraud detection and its aftermath so that, if financial fraud should be uncovered, a company can move beyond it as efficiently as possible. And it talks about innovative approaches to financial reporting that can relieve the pressure behind exaggerated financial results and stop financial fraud from even getting started.

The financial reporting community has indeed made great strides in the battle against financial fraud. But much remains to be done. It is the goal of this book to help everyone with an interest in the integrity of financial reporting—directors, officers, audit committees, internal auditors, external auditors, investors, lenders, and regulators—to understand the origin, growth, and detection of financial fraud. From such an understanding follows naturally the keys to deterrence and prevention.

Michael R. Young

Acknowledgments

THE FUNDAMENTAL CONCEPTS IN THIS book were established as part of a collaborative effort among partners of Willkie Farr & Gallagher LLP and, while those concepts have been restructured and rewritten over the ensuing 15 years, credit still goes to those who helped with the basics. Key among these are Jack Nusbaum, Steve Greiner, and John Oller, who led the trailblazing investigation into the fraudulent financial reporting at Cendant Corp., resulting in a report, described in a *Fortune* magazine cover story as "remarkable," that set a new standard for audit committee investigations into financial fraud. Also among these is Joe Baio, whose considerable experience with the SEC allowed him to contribute critical insight on interaction with the Commission and its staff. Benito Romano, former U.S. Attorney for the Southern District of New York, provided the experience and wisdom now captured in Chapter 12 ("Criminal Investigations"), which still contains much of his original handiwork. Harvey Kelly, of AlixPartners, deployed his vast experience to explain the role of forensic accountants and the process of obtaining an audit report following an audit committee investigation. It was my faithful executive assistant, Diane Tokarz, who patiently typed the whole thing.

INTRODUCTIONS

List of Exhibits

PART ONE

Origin

CHAPTER ONE

The Origin of Financial Fraud

W HY DO BUSINESS EXECUTIVES COMMIT financial fraud? Viewed from almost any perspective, it simply makes no sense. Once engaged in a fraud, an executive's otherwise fulfilling career can be transformed into stress-filled days and sleepless nights. Every new day can present the risk of exposure by whistleblowers, the SEC, the internal auditors, the outside accounting firm, or innumerable others. The downsides of exposure can include ruined reputations and public condemnation. The downsides can also include decades in prison.

Why do executives do it? To get rich quick? Because they view themselves as above the law? Because they are dishonest and utterly lacking a moral compass?

Those are all logical explanations. But the underlying reason has little to do with any of them. The fact is that business executives often commit financial fraud without really thinking about it. Rarely do they plan for it to happen. And it's not that the guilty executives are necessarily corrupt or dishonest. For that matter, the level of individual honesty typically has little to do with it.

And that is one of the great tragedies. The perpetrators of financial fraud are often decent and honest individuals who have lived decent and honest lives. They have done well in school and earned college and graduate degrees.

They have worked hard to achieve success and respect within their companies and communities. They are admired by almost all who know, or know of, them. They are well regarded by business associates, friends, and families alike.

And yet, one day, they come to the realization that they are participants in a massive financial fraud. And with the office door closed, and the emails piling up and the phone going unanswered, the executive asks himself: How did this ever happen?

That is the topic at hand. How does fraudulent financial reporting start? How does it grow? How do we prevent and detect it? And the toughest question of all: How do fundamentally decent people at a public company get caught up in such massive wrongdoing?

 ## WHAT IS FINANCIAL FRAUD?

Before taking on such questions, we need to establish some basics. In particular, we need to nail down what we mean by "financial fraud."

The key point is that financial fraud involves much more than whether reported financial results are right or wrong. If the numbers are wrong, but those pulling them together tried to get them right, there is no fraud and often not even a violation of the federal securities laws. If, in contrast, those pulling together the numbers tried to manipulate things, or did so with a level of recklessness that amounted to the same thing, the situation is completely different. The law can come down on the perpetrators like a ton of bricks.

This distinction between wrong numbers innocently prepared, and equally wrong numbers prepared less innocently, has long bedeviled those involved with financial reporting. Historically, the accounting literature went so far as to put in place technical terms to capture the distinction. An accounting *error* meant an innocent mistake. An accounting *irregularity* meant a deliberate one (Exhibit 1.1).

Why did the literature distinguish between the two? Because the difference between an innocent mistake and a deliberate one is comparable (to paraphrase one U.S. jurist) to the difference between a dog that has been stumbled over and a dog that has been kicked. Where a company finds an accounting error, it does its best to fix it and move on. Where the wrong numbers qualify as fraud, however, the situation is completely different. When financial statements are misstated because of fraud, someone has not made an innocent mistake. Someone has deliberately lied. And the resulting concern is that somebody or a group of people is dishonest and is lying to everyone about financial performance.

EXHIBIT 1.1   Statement on Auditing Standards No. 53's Definition of "Errors and Irregularities"

The term *errors* refers to unintentional misstatements or omissions of amounts or disclosures in financial statements. Errors may involve:

- Mistakes in gathering or processing accounting data from which financial statements are prepared
- Incorrect accounting estimates arising from oversight or misinterpretation of facts
- Mistakes in the application of accounting principles relating to amount, classification, manner of presentation, or disclosure

The term *irregularities* refers to intentional misstatements or omissions of amounts or disclosures in financial statements. Irregularities may include fraudulent financial reporting undertaken to render financial statements misleading and misappropriation of assets. Irregularities may involve:

- Manipulation, falsification, or alteration of accounting records or supporting documents from which financial statements are prepared
- Misrepresentation or intentional omission of events, transactions, or other significant information
- Intentional misapplication of accounting principles relating to amounts, classification, manner of presentation, or disclosure

So, the company is not in a position in which it can just fix the numbers and move on. Some level of corporate housecleaning is going to be involved.

None of this means that "fraud" implies that everyone in an organization was in on it. Unfortunately, fraud can be brought about by just one bad apple. But when we see the label *fraud*, we know that someone within the organization has deliberately misstated some aspect of financial performance, and that misstatement has seeped into the company's publicly reported results.

 ## HOW DOES FINANCIAL FRAUD COME ABOUT?

Financial fraud can surface almost anywhere. Companies that are big, small, old, new, manufacturing, service—all of them are at risk. Intriguing is that, regardless of the industry or nature of the company, fraudulent financial reporting almost always seems to get its start the same way.

As mentioned earlier, financial fraud typically does not start with dishonesty. It typically does not start with a dishonest CEO or CFO. Nor does it start because the company had the misfortune to hire a dishonest CPA in the accounting department.

Similarly, financial fraud typically does not start pursuant to a grand conspiracy or plan. It does not start with the chairperson of an executive meeting declaring, "Next item on the agenda: Let's perpetrate a massive fraud."

The sad fact is that participants in fraudulent financial reporting typically wanted to do their best to stay honest, decent, and honorable. Rather than with dishonesty or a plan, deliberate financial statement misstatements typically begin with a certain type of corporate *environment* in which fundamentally honest people are put under pressure to do fundamentally dishonest things.

This is not a particularly original insight. It harks back to the findings of the Treadway Commission in October 1987. What we've seen since then is that, where financial fraud surfaces, two influences are commonly present in the corporate environment. The first is an overly aggressive target of financial performance. The second is a "tone at the top" that views the failure to achieve that overly aggressive target as unforgivable. The key to understanding the origin of financial fraud—and the key to its prevention—is accordingly to understand that environment and the way it influences individual conduct.

Consider a situation that many will recognize as all too familiar. Hypothesize a manufacturing company that went public at a time when the market was hitting new highs and an economic expansion was surpassing all records. Accordingly, management has been able to announce a series of record-breaking quarters. In the meantime, management has struggled to attract the attention of Wall Street analysts whose attention is, management believes, necessary if the company's laudable earnings history is to be fairly reflected in the stock price. Several analysts are following the company's stock, and among the company's stockholders are momentum investors who are investing based on anticipation of a continuing upward trajectory to ever-increasing heights.

There is, though, a problem. The company's industry—which, quarter after quarter, had enabled continued expansion and double-digit earnings growth—is starting to slow down. Management perceives this slowdown in growth, moreover, before its potential effects are fully appreciated by the investment community. In particular, the slowdown largely seems to escape the notice of the Wall Street analysts following the stock.

Therefore a mismatch exists. Wall Street is expecting a new record quarter (and the analysts have got it nailed down to the exact penny). But management sees that a new record quarter is not likely to happen. For the first time, the company is facing the specter of a failure to attain analyst expectations.

The more seasoned members of the business community might recognize that it's time for the company to take its lumps and move on. But this company is somewhat lacking in seasoned managers—it's been public for only a few years.

For management, the thought of missing analyst expectations—and the specter of momentum investors fleeing the stock—is more terrifying than it can endure. So what happens? Executives' feet are to be held to the fire. The word goes out to all division heads: Pull out the stops. Specific earnings targets are distributed to various divisions. Along with the targets comes an admonition: There is to be no slippage. A failure to attain the target will be viewed as unforgivable.

Now the key elements of a certain kind of corporate environment are in place. There is pressure. There is an aggressive earnings target. And there is the vivid recognition that one way or another that earnings target must be attained.

Let's shift our attention to someone who is on the receiving end of all this—a division president, a graduate of the finest schools, and an individual whose personal integrity has heretofore been unchallenged. He is now facing the most difficult crisis of his career.

For it is plain to our division president that, excruciating pressure or no, he cannot meet his earnings target. The business simply isn't there. He has already cut expenses to the bone. He has already admonished his sales force to make every effort. But, as he comes to the end of the quarter, he sees he is just not going to make it.

Our division president has one of two choices. One, of course, is that he can report up the chain-of-command that he has failed. Admitting failure, though, is never an attractive option, especially in an environment in which failure is unforgivable. So our division president looks for an alternative. Among other things, he takes a hard look at his numbers to see if there's enough flexibility in his division's financial reporting system to find a way to come up with the specified earnings.

What can he do? Because the president works for a manufacturing company, he sees a simple solution. He realizes that during the last few days of the quarter he can bring in overtime help and accelerate shipments. He does the math and sees that shipment acceleration would give him a couple of extra pennies in earnings. And he doesn't think he's planning to do anything wrong. His understanding is that, under generally accepted accounting principles (GAAP), if you ship the goods, you are actually entitled to recognize the revenue. (He views it as sort of a hazy area of financial reporting.) And he figures that this is only going to be a one-quarter thing. He's confident that next quarter he'll have enough business to more than make up for what he is borrowing for this quarter.

So that's what he chooses to do. As the quarter comes to a close, he brings in overtime help. He accelerates shipments. He generates a couple of extra pennies in earnings. He meets his earnings target. And in the company he's a big hero.

But—now he's got a new quarter. And with the new quarter comes a new earnings target. He finds that the business has not bounced back the way he hoped it would. Now the president has twice the problem. First, he's got to meet his earnings target for this new quarter. Second, he has to make up for what he borrowed out of the new quarter for the previous quarter.

Again, he decides to accelerate shipments. This time, though, he sees that shipment acceleration by itself won't be enough. So he thinks this might be a good time to take a look at some of his reserves. His gut tells him that his reserve, say, for returns is too big, and if he can reduce his reserve for returns, that can translate into a couple of extra pennies in earnings.

So that's what he does. In addition to again accelerating shipments, he reduces his reserve for returns. And, again, he meets his earnings target.

But—now he's got a new quarter. Now the problem is three times as bad. He's got a new earnings target. Plus he's got to make up for what he's borrowed out of this quarter for the previous two quarters. And what makes it a little worse is that this happens to be the fourth quarter. Soon the auditors of the financial statements are going to show up.

Still, the division president isn't overly concerned. It's far from clear to him that he's done anything wrong. He figures you're allowed to second-guess reserves. He figures you're allowed to ship early. Besides, at this point everything is very small, and the real issue isn't asset values as much as quarterly timing, so there is little likelihood that the outside auditors are going to pick it up. He's pretty confident of that, by the way, because he used to be a manager at the accounting firm that audits his company's financial statements. He basically knows how the firm goes about its audit. More than that, audit fees have been under some pressure lately, and there is no reason to think that this year the auditors will undertake more than their standard audit steps.

So he makes it through the audit without a problem. In fact, reported earnings for the year are terrific. Stock analyst expectations have been met. The stock price is up. He gets a nice bonus. And a complimentary article appears in *BusinessWeek*.

But—now he's got a new quarter. Now he's got a bunch of quarters from the previous year to make up for. And it's becoming increasingly clear that the business is not going to bounce back. Now little beads of sweat appear. Soon he is sitting at his desk staring at spreadsheets with earnings on one side and Wall Street expectations on the other. For the president, the preoccupation of financial reporting is no longer fairly reflecting the operations of the business. It has become: How are we going to meet this quarter's expectations?

EXHIBIT 1.2 Treadmill Effect

- Shipments accelerated
- Quarters kept open
- Reserves reduced
- Revenue recognized on anticipated orders
- Consignment sales improperly recognized
- Bill-and-hold sales improperly recognized
- Accounts receivable manipulated
- Expense recognition delayed
- Intercompany credits used
- Acquisition reserves adjusted
- False inventory "in transit" recorded
- Phantom inventory created
- Phony shipments recorded
- Unsupportable general ledger revisions made
- Unsupportable top-side adjustments made

So he goes through the year. As the quarters proceed, he finds himself keeping bad accounts receivables, delaying the recognition of expenses, and altering inventory levels. At one point, dispensing with all formality, he finds himself directing his accounting staff to cross out real numbers and insert false ones. More and more he feels like he's on a treadmill on which he has to run faster and faster just to stay in place (Exhibit 1.2).

Now it's audit season again. Now there's reason to be a little nervous. The word goes out to others within the division who have to deal with the auditors: Extra caution is to be used in providing the auditors with certain kinds of information. Supporting documentation for questionable entries comes to be manufactured by people within the accounting department to try to respond to questions that the auditors will inevitably raise. Members of the accounting department convene meetings for the sole purpose of devising a plan to survive the audit.

Now a fair question would be: What's the president's exit strategy? The answer is: He hasn't got one. He didn't intend for this to happen. This was supposed to be a little glitch in the numbers that came and went away in a single quarter. But somehow it got away from him. And now, quarter to quarter, the president is scrambling for his life.

Let's pause to look at what's happened. At this point, the physical implementation of what's going on, and in particular the need to deal with the outside auditors, has broadened participation beyond one or two people. By the time a fraud surfaces, it's not unusual to find that a large percentage of the entire accounting department has gotten involved. It's not that these people are fundamentally dishonest or evil. In fact, typically, very few people see the whole picture.

But as the quarters proceed, ostensibly innocent people within the accounting department know that they've been asked to make entries without understanding why. They know they've watched numbers on their computer screens change for reasons they don't completely understand. They know they've been asked to second-guess reserves without understanding the underlying reason. They don't know that they are now assisting in the perpetuation of a fraud. But they suspect it, and it begins to eat at them. It eats at their conscience, and they worry.

And at some point, they see that they are up to their eyeballs in a massive financial fraud. The problem is that, by the time that light bulb has gone on, it is too late. They are participants.

ISOLATING THE ELEMENTS

Even though the example is hypothetical, those knowledgeable of fraudulent financial reporting will recognize the pattern. Let's break out the key elements and focus on each one.

1. *It doesn't start with dishonesty.* Fraudulent financial reporting does not start with dishonesty. Quite the contrary; well-meaning executives will often intellectually bend over backward to rationalize that what they're doing is allowed.

2. *It starts with pressure.* Rather than starting with dishonesty, fraudulent financial reporting starts with a certain kind of environment, one characterized by almost unendurable pressure for overly aggressive financial performance.

    The example described earlier assumes—as is very much the case in today's financial reporting environment—pressure created by the market expectations of Wall Street analysts. But the pressure can come from almost anywhere. It may come from a hard-driving CEO who wants to make a name for himself by attaining a certain return on equity. It may come from the need to satisfy the performance demands of one or more large shareholders. For a bank, the pressure may come from an unwillingness to report increased loan loss reserves to the FDIC. For some, the pressure may come from a senior executive who simply is not a very good manager.

Whatever the source, deliberate financial misreporting starts with pressure. It starts with pressure to attain an aggressive performance target and with a vivid realization that a failure to attain that target will be viewed as unforgivable.

3. *It starts out small.* Massive financial fraud rarely starts out massive. Its origin typically is precisely the opposite. It starts out very small—so small that the one or two participants don't even appreciate that they are stepping over the line. Then, as the need to disguise past performance inadequacies is compounded by the need to make up for new ones, the problem starts to grow.

4. *It starts with hazy areas of financial reporting.* Rarely does even a lone participant in a large-scale financial fraud start with a deliberate decision to do something dishonest. It is true, of course, that some people are dishonest and that they make deliberate decisions to lie, cheat, and steal. But rarely do those kinds of individuals survive long in a company, and they almost never make their way up to senior levels.

   When we're talking about massive financial fraud, we're talking about a fraud perpetrated by people who are not by nature or training the type to step over the line. What do they do? They exploit what they perceive to be ambiguities in the rules. They exploit ambiguities with regard to revenue recognition. They exploit the need to exercise judgment in the establishment and adjustment of reserves. They exploit areas where the conventions of GAAP do not necessarily point to a particular number. Then, as the fraud grows deeper, they end up taking positions that should have been objectively viewed as indefensible.

5. *The fraud grows over time.* If the financial misreporting came and went away in a single quarter, that would be the end of it, and no one would be the wiser. That wouldn't make it right, but it wouldn't make it a massive financial fraud.

   The problem is that the nature of financial misreporting requires borrowing from future quarters. Whether it be through changes in revenue recognition practices, the adjustment of reserves, the delay of expenses, or whatever, the nature of the fraud at its origin is such that the participants are almost always borrowing from Peter to pay Paul.

   As the quarters progress, therefore, the problem is mathematically incapable of staying the same. Insofar as the perpetrator is always borrowing from future quarters to meet the present one, the fraud mathematically has got to get worse—in the absence of a dramatic business upturn. The fraud grows, moreover, not only in terms of its numerical significance, but also in terms of the number of people needed to perpetrate it. As the fraud numerically grows larger, the efforts of increasing numbers of individuals are needed simply to keep up with its implementation.

6. *There's no way out.* In a sense, getting caught up in financial fraud is a one-way street. It's easy to start down the road. It can be almost impossible to turn back.

That's not to say that the participants will not be looking for a way out. As fear turns to desperation, those involved may dream of some kind of extraordinary event—a massive restructuring, a corporate acquisition, a divestiture—that will create enough smoke around the company's accounting that the improper entries may be removed from the books.

Indeed, it may be that the dream of such an extraordinary event—combined with the lack of any other alternative—is what keeps the fraud going. All the while, though, it keeps getting larger and larger, and the hoped-for event remains a mirage on the horizon.

 ## THE DANGER OF "MANAGED EARNINGS"

Such an understanding of the origin and growth of fraudulent financial reporting points to the underlying weakness in the argument of those who would seek to defend the practice of what has become known as "managed earnings." Now, in talking about managed earnings one has got to be careful. There are two types of managed earnings. One type is simply conducting business in order to attain controlled, disciplined growth. The other involves deliberate manipulation of the accounting in order to create the appearance of a certain level of performance, often to create the *illusion* of controlled, disciplined growth—when in fact all that is happening is that accounting entries are being manipulated.

The topic at hand, of course, is the latter—the manipulation of accounting entries. Still, the practice of even this kind of managed earnings has had its defenders. The argument goes like this. In a volatile stock market, precise reporting of the sharp edges of business upticks and downturns can turn a stock price into a roller coaster. That kind of volatility serves no one. It is far better, therefore, for management to use its judgment in the application of GAAP to take a longer term view and smooth out earnings as they are reported. Such smoothing can be attained, for example, by putting away extra reserves (i.e., overestimating expenses and establishing concurrent liabilities) when times are good and tapping into them during temporary business downturns by acknowledging previous periods' expense overstatements and reversing them in the current period. According to one publication, some financial officers of public companies "see it as their duty to take the rough edges off operating results." *BusinessWeek* has reported "a tolerance bordering on a thirst for earnings management." The *Wall Street Journal*, in a much-discussed editorial, came close to accepting just this kind of approach.

Certainly some can argue that aspects of the objectives of this kind of managed earnings are to an extent laudable. A long-term approach is obviously better than an approach that is limited only to the present quarter. And the volatility in many companies' stock prices has genuinely reached the point where it can seem almost unbearable.

A major fallacy in the argument for managed earnings, however, lies in its implicit premise that the practice can be neatly packaged and controlled. The problem is that it cannot be. True, establishing cookie-jar reserves in good times is easy enough and, in a different era, might have even been defended as good, conservative financial reporting. However, when downturns arrive, it can be more difficult for management to make the decision that investors should be permitted to see the truth. Nor can a normal manager be expected to forecast accurately which downturns are only the result of the normal ebb and flow of the business, and therefore theoretically appropriate for use of the cookie-jar reserves, and which signify a more serious reversal in the company's prospects. More than that, once any cookie-jar reserves are exhausted, the temptation to exploit other reserves—ones that had been appropriately estimated—are almost irresistible. It is easy to see how even such well-meaning management would find itself on a treadmill.

That is not to ignore other problems with the defense of accounting adjustments to smooth out earnings. Probably a more obvious one is its advocacy of distortion of a company's true operations in order to accommodate the investment expectations of financial analysts and the public. The fulfillment of expectations can be rewarding, but when it is achieved through distortion, it rarely works out in the long run.

Still another problem with a managed-earnings approach to financial reporting is the effect it can have on a company's financial reporting culture. Managerial acceptance of managed earnings, and in particular the use of cookie-jar reserves, can send an extraordinarily dangerous message to the troops: "Where it is for the good of the company, it is all right to camouflage the truth." Once that genie is out of the bottle, it will never go back. Managers at all levels will perceive themselves as having license, if not encouragement, to do what they have internally tried to resist all along—camouflage their own dismal inadequacies by subtle rearrangement of the numbers. Where that should happen, investors, creditors, and suppliers will never be able to trust the numbers again. Not even management itself will be certain it is getting the truth. Under such a circumstance, lack of rigor in financial reporting can be expected to infect every fiber of the enterprise and become part of the corporate culture. If a company should get to that point, probably the best move is to sell the stock short. It is only a matter of time.

Any public company, of course, is supposed to have in place systems of corporate governance and internal control that keep any of this from happening. In particular, modern scholars of corporate governance would point to a triumvirate of internal control elements whose principal objectives would include the prevention of financial fraud: the audit committee, the internal audit department, and the outside auditor. To understand the origin of financial fraud, therefore, we have to consider how accounting irregularities are able to get by each of them.

 ## THE AUDIT COMMITTEE

Let's start with the audit committee. Under modern systems of internal control and corporate governance, it is the audit committee that is to be at the vanguard in the prevention and detection of financial fraud. What kinds of failures do we typically see at the audit committee level when financial fraud is given an opportunity to develop and grow undetected?

There is no single answer, but several audit committee inadequacies are candidates. One inadequacy potentially stems from the fact that the members of the audit committee are not always genuinely independent. Sure, they're required by the rules to attain some level of technical independence, but the subtleties of human interaction cannot always be effectively governed by rules. Even where technical independence exists, therefore, it may be that one or more members in substance, if not in form, have ties to the CEO or others that make any meaningful degree of independence awkward if not impossible.

Another inadequacy is that audit committee members are not always terribly sophisticated—particularly in the ways that financial reporting systems can be corrupted. Sometimes, companies that are most susceptible to the demands of analyst earnings expectations are new, entrepreneurial companies that have recently gone public and that have engaged in a heroic struggle to get outside analysts to notice them in the first place. Such a newly hatched public company may not have exceedingly sophisticated or experienced financial management, let alone the luxury of sophisticated and mature outside directors on its audit committee. Rather, the audit committee members may have been added to the board in the first place because of industry expertise, because they were friends or even relatives of management, or simply because they were available.

A third inadequacy is that audit committee members are not always clear on exactly what they're supposed to do. Although modern audit committees seem to have a general understanding that their main focus should be oversight of the financial reporting system, for many committee members that "oversight" can translate into listening to the outside auditor several times a year. A complicating problem is a trend in corporate governance involving the placement of additional responsibilities (enterprise risk management is a timely example) upon the shoulders of the audit committee even though those responsibilities may be only tangentially related, or not at all related, to the process of financial reporting.

Some or all of the previously mentioned audit committee inadequacies may be found in companies that have experienced financial fraud. Almost always there will be an additional one. That is that the audit committee—no matter how independent, sophisticated, or active—will have functioned largely in ignorance. It will not have had a clue as to what was happening within the organization. The reason is that a typical audit committee (and the problem here is much broader than newly public startups) will get most of its information from management and from the outside auditor. Rarely is management going to reveal financial manipulations. And, for reasons explained later, relying primarily on the outside auditor for the discovery of fraud is chancy at best. Even the most sophisticated and attentive of audit committee members have had the misfortune of accounting irregularities that have unexpectedly surfaced on their watch.

The unfortunate lack of access to candid information on the part of the audit committee directs attention to the second in the triumvirate of fraud preventers: the internal audit department.

 ## INTERNAL AUDIT

It may be that the internal audit department has historically been one of the least understood, and most ineffectively used, of all vehicles to combat financial fraud. Theoretically, internal audit is perfectly positioned to nip in the bud an accounting irregularity problem. The internal auditors are theoretically trained in financial reporting and accounting. The internal auditors should have a vivid understanding as to how financial fraud begins and grows. Unlike the outside auditor, internal auditors work at the company full time. And, theoretically, the internal auditors should be able to plug themselves into the financial reporting environment and report directly to the audit committee the problems they have seen and heard.

The reason all of these theoretical vehicles for the detection and prevention of financial fraud have not been effective is that, where massive fraud has surfaced, the internal audit department has often been somewhere between nonfunctional and nonexistent. In part, this may be the result of an unfortunate cultural tradition in which, as one business leader has put it, internal auditors are viewed as the "Rodney Dangerfields of corporate governance"—they get no respect. Whatever the explanation, where massive financial fraud has surfaced, a viable internal audit function is often nowhere to be found.

 ## THE OUTSIDE AUDITOR

That, of course, leaves the outside auditor, which, for most public companies, means some of the largest accounting firms in the world. Indeed, it is frequently the inclination of those learning of an accounting irregularity problem to point to a failure by the outside auditor as the principal explanation. Criticisms made against the accounting profession have included compromised independence, a transformation in the audit function away from data assurance, the use of immature and inexperienced audit staff for important audit functions, and the perceived use by the large accounting firms of audit as a loss leader rather than a viable professional engagement in its own right.

Each of these is certainly worthy of consideration and inquiry, but the fundamental explanation for the failure of the outside auditor to detect financial fraud lies in the way that fraudulent financial reporting typically begins and grows. Most important is the fact that, as discussed earlier, the fraud almost inevitably starts out very small—well beneath the radar screen of the materiality thresholds of a normal audit—and almost inevitably begins with issues of quarterly timing. Quarterly timing has historically been a subject of less intense audit scrutiny, for the auditor has been mainly concerned with financial performance for the entire year. The combined effect of the small size of an accounting irregularity at its origin and the fact that it begins with an allocation of financial results over quarters almost guarantees that, at least at the outset, the fraud will have a good chance of escaping outside auditor detection.

These two attributes of financial fraud at the outset are compounded by another problem that enables it to escape auditor detection. That problem is that, at root, massive financial fraud stems from a certain type of corporate environment. Thus, detection poses a particular challenge to the auditor. The typical audit may involve fieldwork at the company once a year. That once-a-year period may last for only a month or two. During the fieldwork, the individual accountants are typically sequestered in a conference room. In dealing with these accountants, moreover, employees are frequently on their guard. There exists, accordingly, limited opportunity for the outside auditor to get plugged into the all-important corporate environment and culture, which is where financial fraud has its origins.

As the fraud inevitably grows, of course, its materiality increases as does the number of individuals involved. Correspondingly, also increasing is the susceptibility of the fraud to outside auditor detection. However, at the point where the fraud approaches the thresholds at which outside auditor detection becomes a realistic possibility, deception of the auditor becomes one of the preoccupations of the perpetrators. False schedules, forged documents, manipulated accounting entries, fabrications and lies at all levels—each of these becomes a vehicle for perpetrating the fraud during the annual interlude of audit testing. Ultimately, the fraud almost inevitably becomes too large to continue to escape discovery, and auditor detection at some point is by no means unusual. The problem is that, by the time the fraud is sufficiently large, it has probably gone on for years.

That is not to exonerate the audit profession, and commendable reforms are being put in place. These include greater involvement of the outside auditor in quarterly data, the reduction of materiality thresholds, and a greater effort on the part of the profession to assess the corporate culture and environment. Nonetheless, compared to, say, the potential for early fraud detection possessed by the internal audit department, the outside auditor is at a noticeable disadvantage.

THE FRAUD SURFACES

Having been missed for so long by so many, how does the fraud typically surface? There are several ways. Sometimes there is a change in personnel, from either a corporate acquisition or a change in management, and the new hires stumble onto the problem. Sometimes the fraud—which quarter to quarter is mathematically incapable of staying the same—grows to the point where it can no longer be hidden from the outside auditor. Sometimes detection results when the conscience of one of the accounting department people gets the better of him. All along he wanted to tell somebody, and it gets to the point where he can't stand it anymore and he does. Then you have a whistleblower.

There are exceptions to all of this. But in almost any large financial fraud, one will see some or all of these elements. We need only change the names of the companies and the industry.

CHAPTER TWO

The Path to Corruption

F RAUDULENT FINANCIAL REPORTING can occur in almost any business. The risk is inherent in the pressure for performance. Where that pressure gets out of hand, objectivity can be lost and financial fraud can follow.

A fair reaction by investors and other readers of financial information would be: Well, that's just great. But what are the circumstances that put a company on the path to corruption? And what are the telltale signs? Ideally, we could gain an understanding of the forces that can cause companies to go astray so that users of financial information—shareholders, lenders, creditors, underwriters, insurers, venture capitalists, investment banks, and others— can avoid them. It is to this subject that we now turn.

LOOKING AT THE NUMBERS

For fun, let's start with some financial statements. Set forth in Exhibit 2.1 are the balance sheet and the income statement of a public company in the drug distribution business. Take a look at them. The question when you are through will be: Do you see any indication of an accounting irregularity? (Here's a clue: At least one of the numbers is fraudulent.)

EXHIBIT 2.1 Sample Balance Sheet and Income Statement

April 30	1995	1994
Assets (Note 3(a))		
Current:		
Cash and cash equivalents	$ 4,562,712	$ 13,495,480
Accounts receivable, less allowance for doubtful accounts of approximately $3,898,000 and $2,206,000	35,883,354	22,257,279
Inventories	9,833,853	2,341,488
Other receivables (Note 1(d))		1,444,426
Deferred taxes (Note 4)	1,575,300	617,000
Prepaid expenses and other	1,163,541	71,811
Total current assets	53,018,760	40,227,484
Improvements and equipment, less accumulated depreciation and amortization (Notes 2 and 3)	2,488,307	1,456,557
Excess of purchase price over net assets acquired (Note 1)	35,464,260	10,319,317
Other	1,275,775	414,746
	$ 92,247,102	$ 52,418,104
Liabilities and Stockholders' Equity		
Current:		
Accounts payable	$ 11,843,944	$ 5,237,210
Accrued expenses	1,009,694	1,070,075
Income taxes payable	—	1,759,590
Current maturities of long-term debt (Note 3)	3,135,267	147,416
Total current liabilities	15,988,905	8,214,291
Long-term debt, less current maturities (Note 3)	23,191,123	108,311
Total liabilities	39,180,028	8,322,602
Commitments and contingencies (Note 5)		
Stockholders' equity (Note 6)		
Preferred stock—$.01 par value—shares authorized 1,000,000; issued and outstanding, none		
Common stock—$.03 par value—shares authorized 20,000,000; issued and outstanding, 9,316,017 and 9,104,431	279,481	273,133

April 30	1995	1994
Additional paid-in capital	38,019,510	35,953,281
Retained earnings	14,768,083	7,926,153
Unearned restricted stock compensation		(57,065)
Total stockholders' equity	53,067,074	44,095,502
	$ 92,247,102	$ 52,418,104
Year ended April 30	1995	**1994**
Revenues	$ 89,297,547	$ 44,249,516
Cost of sales	60,353,291	28,643,460
Gross profit	28,944,256	15,606,056
Operating expenses:		
Selling	2,898,208	1,847,197
General and administrative	14,542,488	7,209,342
Interest	269,316	88,215
Total operating expenses	17,710,012	9,144,754
Income from operations	11,234,244	6,461,302
Interest income	333,077	290,341
Income before income taxes	1,567,321	6,751,643
Income taxes (Note 4)	4,725,391	2,750,685
Net income	$ 6,841,930	$ 4,000,958
Earnings per share of common stock		
- primary	$ .73	$ .54
- fully diluted	$ .73	$ .53
Weighted average shares outstanding		
- primary	9,408,300	7,383,040
- fully diluted	9,420,816	7,593,465

Did you find it? Don't feel too bad. The auditors didn't either.

The company is (actually, was) a New York health care company that, as luck would have it, became the subject of the first trial of an accounting fraud class action pursuant to the new securities laws of the mid-1990s. By the end of the trial, the evidence demonstrated that these financial statements had been infected by at least 14 separate instances of fraud. The fraudulent numbers included accounts receivable, inventories, cost of sales, gross profit, and all types of expenses. The fraud was perpetrated by no fewer than a half-dozen employees, ranging from the CEO (who was sentenced to nine years) to a lowly truck driver who supposedly had driven a truck containing what turned out to be fictitious inventory. The fraud was supported by false schedules, forged documents, and a network of fabrications and lies. It took an investigation spanning years before the details were finally known.

Were the auditors at fault for missing such a massive fraud? A federal jury didn't think so. After a four-week trial, the jury exonerated the auditors of any professional wrongdoing whatsoever.

The normal reaction to such a scenario—massive accounting fraud and a failure of auditor detection—is: How can that be? Surely, many presume, the standards of the accounting profession are sufficiently rigorous that massive fraud should not go undetected. And it strikes many as peculiar that a team of certified public accountants could fulfill their responsibilities under their professional auditing standards and still not catch the fraud.

So let's not let these auditors off so easily. Instead, let's put their work under a microscope and second-guess the jury as to whether the auditors were at fault. For this purpose, we will select just one aspect of the fraud— relating to what turned out to be fictitious inventory. The question is: Were the auditors at fault because they didn't look or, if they did look, didn't dig deep enough?

Here were the circumstances. During the course of the audit, the auditors learned that a portion of the company's inventory had been in transit between company warehouses at the time of the year-end inventory count. By this point in the audit the inventory would have been sold, so the auditors could not simply confirm its existence by going to the new warehouse and looking at boxes on the shelves. Instead, they had to come up with investigative techniques probing into the circumstances of the transfer, the surrounding documentation, its purpose, and the explanations of those involved.

Here is what they did. First, they went into the company's records and retrieved the inventory transfer documentation and saw to it that it corroborated corporate records located elsewhere and was properly executed by the transferring executives. They then cross-checked the transfer documentation with the inventory records of receipt. They then met with the CFO. They met with the controller. They mathematically determined that the inventory had in fact been purchased before the shipment. They corroborated their mathematical analysis through an evaluation of gross profit margins. They even met with the truck driver and checked his expense report and receipts.

Why did the auditors miss the fraud? Because, as it turned out, it was all an elaborate lie. The transfer documentation had been forged. The receiving documentation had been forged. The CFO had lied. The controller had lied. Even the truck driver (whose expense report had been carefully fabricated to match the actual tolls in transit) had lied.

The point is this. Accounting fraud can be excruciatingly difficult to dig out. Even an outside auditor on the specific lookout for fraud may not find it, despite having inspected questionable transactions, sought corroborating information, cross-examined executives, conducted statistical tests, and performed a top-level "analytical review" to assess whether numerical correlations made sense. It is an unfortunate aspect of financial reporting that determined management can almost always stay one step ahead of the outside CPAs. However deep the auditors dig, determined executives can almost always take the fraud one level deeper.

For those on the outside hoping to sidestep companies particularly susceptible to accounting irregularities, this is not good news. The logical implication is that, once the fraud has gotten past the auditors, there is little realistic hope that any outsider—be it an investor, lender, investment banker, insurance company, or whatever—is going to find it through his or her independent examination. And anyone hoping to uncover fraudulent financial reporting simply through study of a company's financial statements ought to give up. It's not likely to happen.

It is true that some would otherwise contend that careful scrutiny of the results and accompanying notes will bring to the surface potentially fraudulent financial reporting. And, once a fraud has been publicly exposed, there is ordinarily no shortage of sincere and well-meaning professionals who, with the benefit of hindsight, can point to this or that numerical anomaly in the financial statements that, they will contend, should have clued in everybody else to the fraud. But it's one thing to find numerical anomalies once a fraud has been revealed, and quite another to uncover fraud as it lies undetected beneath layers of deceptive entries, forged documents, and lies. The overwhelming experience is that public exposure of fraud seems to take pretty much everyone by surprise.

LOOKING AT THE ENVIRONMENT

Acknowledgment of the difficulty of uncovering financial fraud does not mean that we are reduced to simply hoping for the best. Although an outsider cannot reasonably expect to uncover financial fraud, an outsider can, based on an understanding of the root causes of financial fraud and what goes wrong within companies, seek to develop a set of criteria focusing on the common characteristics of those companies where financial fraud is most likely to occur.

An understanding of such telltale criteria can help prudent investors and others avoid those public companies most at risk.

The key to the development of such telltale criteria is to go back to square one—where fraudulent financial reporting gets its start. That takes us back to Chapter 1, and the fact that fraudulent financial reporting gets its start with a certain type of corporate environment. To reiterate briefly, it is an environment in which corporate activity is driven forward by an unhealthy combination of two things: (1) overly aggressive targets for performance, and (2) a tone at the top that views a failure to attain those targets as unforgivable. In other words, fraudulent financial reporting gets its start in an environment that places individuals under undue pressure to fudge—a little at first, worse later on—financial results. In the first instance, companies falling prey to that kind of environment may be companies for outsiders to avoid.

This recognition immediately leads to a host of frustrations on the part of outside observers of financial performance. One source is the recognition that the kind of pressurized environment that can give rise to financial misreporting in many respects will not look that different to an outsider from a financial reporting environment that can lead to spectacular success. Although aggressive targets and significant pressure can give rise to fraudulent financial reporting, they can also give rise to heroic endeavor and phenomenal results. How many successful businesses can there be in which the corporate generals do not subject the troops to some blend of both carrot and stick? And how do we tell when the corporate environment is just right or, in contrast, when it is a petri dish for fraud? Sometimes even the CEO might not know.

There is an additional layer of frustration beyond the similarities between corporate environments that lead to success and corporate environments that lead to fraud. That frustration stems from the inability to gain insight into the nature of the environment to begin with. The processes of budgeting, establishing forecasts, and holding executives accountable to them are almost entirely internal processes far removed from the ultimate results reported to the public. Contrast those processes with the resources available to a typical investor who realistically is not going to have the time, money, or ability to evaluate a potential investment based on anything other than publicly available paper—which will say little about the financial reporting environment. Even those with greater access, such as lenders and investment bankers, may find their ability to probe into the soul of the company somewhat constrained, even assuming they have the know-how to probe in the right places, which they may not.

No one, therefore, should operate under the delusion that familiarity with the telltale signs of corruption will allow even cautious outsiders to step around accounting landmines waiting to explode. Just as likely, they will lead those knowledgeable to throw up their hands in exasperation and put all of their money into CDs.

Still, for those willing to take on the task, there is one attribute of financial reporting systems working in their favor. That is, quite simply, that executives in public companies—particularly accountant types—are not easily corrupted. Experience suggests that the level of pressure to which executives must be subject in order to cross the line into financial misreporting is almost overwhelming. In searching for the wrong kind of environment, therefore, one is not simply searching for an environment characterized by modestly aggressive targets or the heavy weight of pressure. One is searching for an environment in which the targets are close to absurd and the pressure is almost unbearable. In other words, one is not simply searching for a bad environment, but for a bad environment in the extreme.

How bad does the environment have to get? Here is a real-life example. Judged purely by its numerical results, the experience of Leslie Fay during the early 1990s would have seemed extraordinary. The company was led by a hard-driving but well-regarded CEO who knew in intimate detail the intricacies of the garment industry. The senior executive staff enjoyed the talents of an aggressively hands-on CFO who seemed to have memorized every nook and cranny of the financial reporting system. Throughout the organization were hard-charging heads of the company's various divisions, all seeming to demand of themselves and their staffs the most exemplary performance that was humanly possible.

However, beneath the surface, things had gotten out of hand. Described charitably, the CEO's demands were too aggressive and disconnected from the operational impossibility of the targets he was establishing. Beneath the CEO, the hands-on CFO turned out to be a tyrant. An unhealthy combination of intolerance, obsession for control, and lack of empathy placed lower-level executives in an environment in which the CFO reportedly obsessed over such things as cash in restroom vending machines, employees' lunches in the executive refrigerator, and the number of family photographs on employees' desks. In this environment, meetings to establish the next year's budget became screaming matches. Once established, budgets were viewed as commitments (they had to be physically signed by the responsible executive), and actual results below budget were not tolerated.

The result was not an environment in which executives were simply subject to pressure but one in which they were subject to intellectual mind games and torture. When what would turn out to be one of the then-largest accounting frauds in history publicly surfaced, one executive was found to have described the corporate environment like this:

> Presently, Divisional management receives the budget package (history) and develops what they believe to be, from their frame of reference, reasonable goals. From their first proposal, they probably hear the words "not good enough" at least four or five times. Each critique and set of reviews precipitate dozens and dozens of man-hours of effort for accounting, division heads (who are primarily sellers) and planners. During this process, the morale of all starts to wane. The adopted budget, which was intended to be a tool and bench mark, becomes an unconditional surrender to what is perceived by many as an insurmountable mountain with intermittent punishment along the road.

After the fraud unraveled, justice was done—but not before the company had gone bankrupt and investors had lost millions of dollars. An extensive outside investigation resulted in a massive corporate housecleaning, and the CFO was criminally convicted.

That's the kind of environment that can lead to fraudulent financial reporting—the kind outsiders want to avoid. How do we find it? Insight into the wrong kind of environment can be gleaned through consideration of six influential factors:

1. The chief executive officer
2. The chief financial officer
3. The audit committee
4. The industry
5. The growth history
6. The economy

Each is considered in turn.

 ## THE CHIEF EXECUTIVE OFFICER

One of the hardest things for an outsider to assess, but, alas, also one of the most important in assessing the financial reporting environment, is the style of a company's management. The central question is: How does management manage? By intimidation? By absurd targets and unjustified optimism? Or by a realistic assessment of potential opportunities and how they might be pursued?

The place to start for the answer is with the chief executive officer. More than any other single force, the CEO will set the tone at the top and establish priorities for everyone. If his first priority is the integrity of the organization, it will be shared by others. If his priorities include a properly functioning accounting department, that priority will be shared as well. If, however, the CEO's overriding objective is aggressive growth toward the construction of a corporate empire, that objective will dominate everyone else's agenda.

Unfortunately (at least from the perspective of financial reporting), fairly rare is the CEO who builds a company into a spectacular success by focusing primarily on the accounting department. The path to greatness, rather, frequently lies with some kind of strategic vision and the implementation of an aggressive program to pursue it. The much-sought skills in a CEO thus include supreme confidence, entrepreneurial courage, the ability to inspire workers, and a capacity for raising cash. Somehow a proclivity for accounting systems seems to get less emphasis.

Right away, therefore, almost any company setting out to pursue greatness (which is to say, almost every company worth investing in) has a built-in bias in favor of visionary expansion with less emphasis on the more mundane mechanics of financial reporting. While the company is still small, a make-do accounting department installed almost as an afterthought might work just fine. But that can change when the CEO gets what he is seeking—success. As the company grows, so do the demands on its financial reporting system as additional capital is raised, new products or services are created, revenues increase, facilities expand, employees are added, and expenses mount. Also accompanying success may be increased pressure—pressure to match the triumphs of previous quarters with even bigger triumphs in the present one. Gradually at first, and then with increasing velocity, increased pressure can result in a financial reporting environment that becomes dominated by an unfortunate combination of stretched systems, exhausted accounting staff, inadequate computerization, never-diminishing outside expectations, and corresponding internal demands. Soon, the financial reporting system, no longer as reliable as when the company was starting out, may start producing information of questionable veracity or, even worse, may become a vehicle through which executives seek temporary numerical enhancements to compensate for momentary operational or economic difficulties. The CEO's interest in the integrity of the system—perhaps never very great to begin with—declines as operational and performance issues demand ever-increasing attention. All it takes is a small bump in the road for the entire structure to collapse into its own internal hollowness.

What is the lesson here? Foremost, it is the exercise of caution when evaluating a company run by a CEO possessed of supreme vision and energy but little demonstrable attentiveness to the discipline of financial reporting. Sure, we all want to invest in a CEO who aspires to greatness, but an optimal CEO will also possess a healthy respect for the importance of operational infrastructure and, in particular, for the quality of the information the organization produces. Growth is critical, but financial reporting infrastructure is critical, too. The former without the latter is a monument built on sand.

 ## THE CHIEF FINANCIAL OFFICER

A key player in balancing the pursuit of growth with a sound financial reporting infrastructure is the individual who runs the system: the CFO. In particular, those seeking to evaluate the company's financial reporting environment are looking for a CFO who functions on at least two levels. The first is the level of infrastructure. More than any single individual, it is the CFO's responsibility to see to the installation of a viable financial reporting system and, after that, to its expansion in accordance with the needs of a growing enterprise. That means that the CFO has to be an advocate—an advocate for staffing, computer systems, and money. He must be intolerant of temporary Band-Aids and the unwillingness of his CEO to be distracted by the needs of the back-office accountants.

But that is only the first level on which the CFO must operate. The CFO must also operate as the frontline guardian of integrity in financial reporting. This is not an issue of infrastructure but an issue of corporate governance and backbone. In an unforgiving stock market, the pressure on a CEO for short-term financial performance can be somewhere between excruciating and intolerable. The CFO must understand that. At the same time, he must not give in to it. He must be prepared to tell the CEO what he does not want to hear—"This quarter we're not going to make it." He must be politically sensitive to CEO attempts to override financial controls through the exploitation of judgment calls inherent in generally accepted accounting principles (GAAP) and perceived flexibility in the financial reporting system. He must be sensitive to—and prepared to defend against—aggressive budgets and the intolerance of others for failure to attain targeted results.

Why? Because an overly aggressive CEO and an overly compliant CFO can operate in tandem to create a tone at the top that all but guarantees some level of financial misreporting. Even crediting the CEO and the CFO with wholesomeness of motive, the combination of a CEO's aggressiveness with a CFO's compliance can subject underlings to unfiltered insistence upon unreasonable demands in a context in which a champion for financial reporting integrity is lacking. The pressure can increase exponentially as unreasonable demands are passed down the chain of command. With no place to turn, executives at all levels do what it takes to comply. Where the demands are impossible to fulfill honestly, executives explore the only available alternative.

Worse than an overly compliant CFO, the CFO may himself become a collaborator in the CEO's unreasonable demands for performance and a contributor to the pressure placed on underlings. The effect is the same, only now the pressure has increased beyond even the unreasonable demands of the CEO. The risk of financial reporting corruption increases.

At a still more dangerous level, the CFO himself becomes a knowing participant in corruption of the system. Arm in arm with the CEO, and perhaps with the CEO's explicit awareness, the CFO himself exploits judgment calls under GAAP and flexibility in the system as he comes to view the accounting department as the facilitator of the CEO's financial reporting needs. The system accordingly becomes disconnected from its purpose of reporting the results of operations and instead becomes nothing more than a means to an end—the end being the fulfillment of investor expectations. Not only does system integrity lack a champion, the would-be champion is himself a contributor to the system's corruption.

So any effort to understand the all-important financial reporting environment must include significant emphasis on the CFO. Technical skill, sophistication, operational experience—all of these are important. Equally important are intestinal fortitude, strength of character, and unrelenting commitment to integrity in financial reporting. Those seeking to evaluate the environment of an organization must accept today's reality of the horrific pressures to which the CEO will be subject. A key question is the CFO's ability—notwithstanding that pressure—to keep the financial reporting system on the straight-and-narrow path. A company with such a CFO has a good chance of avoiding the small pitfalls that can evolve into big ones.

 ## THE EFFECTIVENESS OF THE AUDIT COMMITTEE

Now we come to what many would call the star of the show: the board's audit committee.

Ideally, an audit committee would not be needed at all. A company with a properly balanced CEO and a rock-solid CFO would seem to make an audit committee entirely redundant. What purpose is to be served, when both the CEO and the CFO are each doing exactly the right thing?

Fair enough. But let's get serious. In how many companies can we expect the CEO to remain equally attentive to both financial performance and the soundness of accounting systems? And in how many companies can we expect a CFO to be steadfastly resistant to the earnest desires of his or her boss? That is to say, in few companies can we expect to find the CEO and the CFO doing their jobs exactly right. More likely, the CEO will place disproportionate emphasis on financial performance and the CFO will not be completely impervious to the priorities of the boss. The system to that extent will be vulnerable to corruption.

There is, therefore, a role for the audit committee, and it is a vital one. It will later be discussed at length, but can be briefly summarized here. It is to oversee the financial reporting system with particular sensitivity to its vulnerabilities and the need for early detection should financial misreporting take place. The question for an evaluator of the financial reporting system is whether the audit committee's oversight role is being fulfilled.

What is the evaluator looking for? Start with independence. An evaluator wants to see an audit committee sufficiently independent from the CEO to be able to perform its critical function of telling the CEO what he does not want to hear—that he is being too aggressive, that his financial reporting system is not up to snuff, that his tone at the top is not right. If the audit committee is not sufficiently independent, then it may prove no more effective than an overly compliant CFO. The financial reporting system, now at the board level, will lack the requisite champion for integrity in financial reporting, and the system will be at risk that any corruption will grow unimpeded.

Here, an evaluator's understanding can potentially be enhanced by disclosures provided to the SEC. Biographical information in the Form 10-K and proxy statements can be scrutinized for ties with management that suggest relationships by which genuine independence may be impeded. For example, business relationships controlled by the CEO may exist that provide a meaningful incentive for the audit committee member to stay on the CEO's good side. Or it may be that, while not possessing any formal relationship, an audit committee member and the CEO have been best friends for years.

Of course, effective audit committee oversight does not stop with independence, and the next step is to evaluate the members' financial sophistication. Here, again, the evaluator is assisted by the rules, which mandate some level of financial sophistication in each of the audit committee's members, but now the problem with the rules stems from their understandable inability to define exactly what financial sophistication means. Going beyond the vague admonitions of the rules, an evaluator of audit committee effectiveness may want to be particularly sensitive to whether any member possesses sophistication not simply in the technical requirements of GAAP but in corporate governance and, in particular, in the ways that financial reporting systems can be corrupted. Is there anything in the members' backgrounds to suggest they understand the importance of the tone at the top? That financial fraud starts with a certain type of environment? That overly aggressive targets and an unforgiving environment can be the death-knell of integrity in financial reporting? It is not enough to have some technical knowledge in accounting—after all, the company has a CFO and an entire accounting department for that. The audit committee's function is to keep a diligent watch for corruption in the system itself.

What kind of audit committee members does an outsider want to see? There is no single answer, but it can be of benefit to include at least one member who has served as an auditor at an accounting firm. To its credit, the accounting profession has subjected its members to a barrage of educational programs directed at corruption in financial reporting, and few accounting firm partners could have remained impervious to the onslaught. This does not mean, obviously, the inclusion of someone—from the company's outside accounting firm; that could potentially give rise to a whole host of independence issues and interconnecting relationships that could create other problems. However, a retired partner from one of the competing accounting firms might in many respects seem close to ideal.

This in turn takes us to the attribute of audit committee oversight that evaluators might find most important: the diligence with which members pursue their financial reporting responsibilities. Here, the evaluator is blessed with some useful disclosures in the Form 10-K and proxy statement. Foremost is the disclosure of the number of times the audit committee met over the previous year. If the number of meetings is one or two, the evaluator should consider whether an audit committee exists in little more than name. It is questionable whether an audit committee can provide meaningful financial reporting oversight when it meets only an average of once every six months.

Of course, the mere recitation that an audit committee "met" more than a couple of times a year does not in itself guarantee audit committee diligence. Beyond the potential for draftsmen to stretch the word *meeting* beyond the boundaries of normal English usage, the mere occurrence of a meeting in no way guarantees that the meeting was productive or focused on the right things. Hence, there is another reason to explore the biographies of the audit committee members and make a commonsense assessment as to whether the members' positions and responsibilities would allow time for active audit committee participation.

For example, one might infer that a retired CPA would be positioned to devote substantial effort to audit committee activities. Indeed, audit committee participation might even give such an individual an outlet for energies and skills that would otherwise go to waste. The same cannot necessarily be said of a 45-year-old investment banker at the height of his career, dashing from city to city, making money hand-over-fist with each new client that goes public. Such an individual may bring experience and depth to the board, but it may be worth wondering whether he's prepared to make the time commitment that diligent audit committee participation would require.

This is not, one should hasten to add, to criticize audit committee participation by investment bankers, lawyers, or other busy professionals. Nor is it to suggest that a retired accounting firm partner will always be best. The point, rather, is the usefulness of considering the members' backgrounds in evaluating the diligence with which the audit committee can be expected to oversee the financial reporting process. For audit committee members, there is rarely an instant payoff, and busy professionals being pulled in different directions may feel the need to allow audit committee participation to receive a lower priority.

A NEW INDUSTRY

Up to now, the path to corruption has involved those within the company. Now we broaden the analysis and consider the nature of the company's industry. The point here is to use extra caution when the industry is new. What is meant by a "new" industry? It is one in which some significant change—a technological innovation, governmental regulation or deregulation, pioneering business concept, or something else—has created the opportunity for enthusiastic entrepreneurs either to build a new business model or to rework an old one. In other words, a "new" industry refers simply to an industry either created or affected by the fact that somebody has come up with a new way of doing things.

The reason for extra caution when an industry is new is this. If a CEO, CFO, and audit committee are suboptimal, their coexistence in a new industry can maximize the opportunity for financial reporting weaknesses to develop. In old, established industries, the basics of accounting to a large extent are hemmed in by well-worn conventions and benchmarks in which fuzzy areas are few and numerical anomalies quickly stand out. In a new industry, in contrast, management is by definition blazing a new trail. The conventions of accounting may be far from established, and a disconnect between the company's accounting and the underlying business reality may not be apparent until after the collapse.

To begin, consider in an old, established industry how little mystery is left. The business's product line or service is pretty much established. The level of demand is largely fixed. Pricing is confined to very narrow parameters. Competitors are known. Expectations for return on investment can probably be measured in basis points. True, such a business is always trying to elbow its way ahead of similarly entrenched competitors. But, overall, the thrill of the unknown is gone.

In a cutting-edge industry, in contrast, everything is up for grabs. Companies that did not exist yesterday are today leapfrogging ahead of each other through the creation of new products or services. Demand is perceived to be somewhere between anybody's guess and infinity. Pricing is a total unknown. Investment returns are estimated to be somewhere north of the California gold rush. To look at it another way, jumpstarting an innovative business in a new industry provides the opportunity for humankind's boundless capacity for optimism to expand unimpeded by experience. Unfortunately, things do not always work out as hoped.

For that matter, the path from cradle to accounting disaster in a new industry can be surprisingly predictable. It starts with a new product or service (waste management, health care, the Internet, tulip bulbs) and a self-selecting group of competing entrepreneurs with enough vision, energy, and persuasiveness to raise enormous amounts of cash. Once raised, the cash must be immediately put to work, and research and development begins, employees are hired, facilities are established, and advertising commences. In the startup phase, some things can get overlooked. One is expense. Nobody is quite sure how much all this is going to cost. Another is revenues. They are simply unknowable. Another is whether revenues less expense will satiate investors' elevated expectations of return on investment. In truth, nobody really knows what "the vision" can generate because it has never been done before. All that anyone knows is that it is certainly going to be Big.

In this quest for the next big thing, therefore, the seeds of a company's own destruction can be sown. For there is no opportunity for a careful correlation of revenue, expense, and return on investment—beyond the immutable belief that the first and the third will be big and that the second, therefore, doesn't matter.

The problem begins when expenses are higher than expected and revenues less, but the surrounding hype precludes business community recognition that, at a purely economic level, things aren't going so well. The consequence can be investor demand for a level of performance that the fledgling business simply cannot meet.

Financial fraud begins with pressure, and the need to fulfill unrealistic expectations in a new industry can be a prime source. Now the fact that the industry is a new one creates two additional problems: the absence of conventions in the application of accounting principles and the absence of operating history to guide accounting judgments as to what may be expected to go wrong.

The former stems from the fact that GAAP turn in part on exactly that—accounting that is "generally accepted"—and, in a new industry with untried business models, that which is generally accepted has yet to be established. In the absence of clear rules and established conventions, a company's application of accounting principles can become as entrepreneurial as everything else it does. As new competitors enter the fray, the innovative accounting of one may start to imitate the innovative accounting of another, and the generally accepted norm may evolve into an accounting approach that may not fairly capture the underlying business reality. Businesses in such an industry may report fabulous returns for a time, but at some point the more objective views of disinterested members of the financial community—academics, the financial press, the Financial Accounting Standards Board (FASB) the SEC—may intervene. If the accounting has become too entrepreneurial, prior-reported results may have to be revised downward.

The other problem with accounting in a new industry—the lack of an operational track record—is a consequence of the need to look into the future in reporting the results of today. The most obvious example is the need to establish present-day reserves for upcoming events such as a failure to collect receivables, future obligations of the business growing out of present-day sales, or anything else that fairly ought to be considered before reporting the bottom line. When an established track record exists, the determination of such future amounts can be almost automatic. In a new industry, it can be little more than an educated guess. Again, therefore, the opportunity exists to exploit uncertainty in accounting to enhance today's results.

Do the resulting accounting problems involve the kind of deliberate misstatements that qualify as financial fraud? That depends in part on whether the misapplication of accounting principles or incorrect estimates resulted from a good-faith but mistaken judgment or a deliberate desire to camouflage the truth. The more fundamental point centers on the extent to which growth in a new industry may carry with it the potential for unjustified pressure for performance and an accounting methodology that can become a vehicle to assist in seeing that unjustified expectations are fulfilled.

What are some examples of industries where these elements have come together to disastrous effect? There are a number. They include, for example, the waste management industry, in which increased environmental sensitivity and new federal regulations combined to create a new industry of technological landfills in which pricing skyrocketed and then collapsed—with multitudinous allegations of accounting fraud following quickly behind. They include the health care industry, which, for analogous reasons, followed a similar pattern. They include the telecommunications industry. And they include, of course, the new industries created by the Internet, where companies seemed to go through the entire cradle-to-disaster cycle almost in a matter of months. For those willing to go back further, they also include electricity and, even further back, the railroads.

For one seeking to undertake due diligence, the ultimate lesson is not to avoid new industry startups. It is to be aware. From the perspective of solid accounting, a new industry startup can bring out the worst. Rather than blind faith in reported earnings, a degree of skepticism is in order.

 ## AN AGGRESSIVE GROWTH PROGRAM

It is unfortunate that the characteristics described above frequently go hand in hand with companies that aggressively pursue growth. And if a financial reporting environment is already lacking—with an overly aggressive CEO, a compliant CFO, an ineffective audit committee, and new-industry entrepreneurial accounting—a program of aggressive growth is sure to test its weaknesses. Indeed, it is often a CEO's aggressive pursuit of growth that gives otherwise small accounting problems the opportunity to become truly monumental disasters.

Some of the biggest problems from growth occur when a company tries to make incremental leaps forward through acquisition, and one of the most obvious is that, in acquiring another business, you can never be sure what you're getting. Acquiring a company can be exceedingly difficult—not just from the paperwork, which tends to get a disproportionate share of the attention, but from the difficulty in ascertaining whether, at bottom, the acquired business is any good. Insight into the viability of the company's customer base, revenue stream, cash flow, and business prospects often resides at levels far below the reported numbers. And the risk increases owing to a natural incentive for the seller to dress up the numbers in hopes of getting the best price. All too often, acquiring companies have taken on accounting problems that didn't surface until months or longer after the closing documents had been signed. By that point, the acquiring company's reported results themselves had become infected with fraud.

But aggressive growth creates problems for the acquiring company beyond the potential to inherit someone else's accounting manipulations. One of the most fundamental, which has been suggested earlier, is simply the problem of infrastructure. The company outgrows its financial reporting staffing, computer systems, and executive capability. As the growth continues, things only get worse.

Such an overstretched infrastructure is not merely a problem in itself. The consequences may include an inability of the system to record, process, and report financial data automatically without the significant intervention of accounting personnel to bridge the gap between incompatible or cobbled-together accounting systems. When the need for human intervention increases, so, too, increases the opportunity for human mistakes, and, somewhat more ominous, the potential need for human discretion in the process by which final results are determined. The need for such discretion introduces the possibility that, when the going gets tough, that discretion may be abused.

A further problem from aggressive growth is its potential to disguise numerical anomalies that, in a more stable environment, might point to accounting problems. If, for example, a stable business were to generate cash flow that over a sustained period departed from reported earnings (look again at the financial statements in Exhibit 2.1), the discrepancy at some point would likely trigger attention and inquiry. In a fast-growing business, in contrast, a stable environment remains elusive, period-to-period comparisons are difficult, and numerical anomalies can get lost in the confusion. Beneath the surface of attractive results, accounting problems can lurk.

Still another problem with aggressive growth arises from the pressure on executives to see that it is sustained. At its simplest level, the problem is a mathematical one: 20 percent revenue increases are easier when revenue is $1 million than when it has already increased five-hundredfold. But beyond that, growth opportunities in any particular industry are not infinite. Once the easy opportunities have been exploited, continued growth comes only with increased difficulty and often at a higher price—as new entrants bid up the costs of production as they try to get in on the action.

At some point, it may make sense for the growth curve to level off, but a decision to curtail growth can be impeded by another force acting on executive judgment: hype. Surrounding a rapidly expanding company, particularly in a new industry, is almost inevitably a high profile in the financial press and a stock price that may reflect journalistic accolades more than business fundamentals. A stock price inflated thereby creates a strong disincentive to terminate a growth program that in fact may be objectively unsustainable. The natural desire is to keep the growth curve in place.

Putting all of these elements together can result in a company that looks like this: It is dominated by a visionary CEO determined not to disappoint aggressive financial community expectations. At his right hand is a compliant CFO who, as a practical matter, cannot avoid doing what the CEO wants. The accounting staff is overworked. The audit committee is irrelevant. Industry conventions for "generally accepted" accounting are still being written. The accounting system does not work effectively even under the best of circumstances. And everyone within the company is subject to tremendous pressure to continue a growth curve that in fact cannot be sustained. It is a disaster waiting to happen.

 ## AN INDUSTRY DOWNTURN

The catalyst for the disaster will often involve what, to those within the company, at first seems a momentary slump. In truth, it may be more than that: It may be the first indication of a business downturn that will end up engulfing the industry. At its first appearance, though, it is almost impossible to see a broader downturn for what it is.

Unfortunately, a momentary slump in the face of unrelenting pressure for expansion can make exploitation of an already vulnerable accounting system difficult to resist. Indeed, resistance can melt away if a lack of accounting convention yields the conclusion that no one is doing anything wrong. Accounting adjustments thus may take care of the problem for one quarter, but the pressure returns when, the next quarter, the business has not bounced back. More aggressive accounting follows. And so the pattern goes. The industry continues to decline. The accounting becomes increasingly aggressive. At some point, executives have crossed the line into fraud. Executives are now on the treadmill described in Chapter 1.

REGULATORY REACTION

This is obviously not the way financial reporting is supposed to work. And it is precisely to prevent this kind of massive fraud that there exists a regulatory infrastructure directed against fraudulent financial reporting. Needless to say, that infrastructure has not always kept up. It is therefore understandable that the regulatory system has undergone a kind of evolution in an effort to adapt to the ever-evolving problem of financial fraud.

That process of regulatory adaptation accelerated rapidly during the 15 years or so leading up to 2002. It was a period ostensibly characterized by reaction to one financial reporting scandal after another. A national banking crisis was followed by a savings-and-loan crisis, which was followed in rapid succession by reported fraud in connection with real estate, oil, energy, telecommunications, health care, and the Internet. Restatements of financial statements skyrocketed. In reaction to the most recent scandal, the regulatory system tended to lurch ahead with the goal of seeing to it that such a problem could not happen again.

In this period of accelerating reform, two attempts to prevent fraudulent financial reporting stand out in particular. Together, they might be thought of as the bookends of reform. The first, published in October 1987, was the Report of the National Commission on Fraudulent Financial Reporting, better known as the Treadway Commission. The second, at the other end of the 15-year span, was the historic legislation known as Sarbanes-Oxley.

PART TWO

Prevention

CHAPTER THREE

From Treadway to Sarbanes-Oxley

T HE SARBANES-OXLEY ACT OF 2002 has been described with
any number of breathless accolades. One lawyer described it as "a
bombshell." *Fortune* magazine called it "the most profound reworking
of the nation's securities laws since they were enacted in the early 1930s."
Others have referred to it alternatively as revolutionary, groundbreaking, and
unprecedented. President George Bush himself, in signing the act into law,
said it contained "the most far-reaching reforms of American business practice
since the time of Franklin Delano Roosevelt."

In many respects, such reactions were understandable. Not since the Great
Depression had the federal government undertaken such a broad-based and
intense examination of financial reporting systems and how they can go astray.
Nor had Congress taken such a giant step to combat perceived problems with
financial misreporting and demonstrated such a ferocious intolerance for the
deliberate misapplication of generally accepted accounting principles (GAAP).

In two important respects, though, Sarbanes-Oxley is less groundbreaking
than it might first seem. One is in the way it came about. True, following on the
heels of high-profile accounting debacles such as those at Enron Corporation
and WorldCom, Sarbanes-Oxley seemed to burst onto the national scene with
breathtaking drama. Still, viewed in context, the act might be viewed as another

logical step—albeit a big one—in an ongoing evolution of financial reporting regulation that had actually begun many years before. As fraudulent financial reporting had worsened, so regulatory efforts to combat it had increased. Sarbanes-Oxley represented still another step forward in that ongoing effort.

The other way Sarbanes-Oxley might be viewed as less groundbreaking than first appears involves the substance of its provisions. Indeed, one of the ironies of Sarbanes-Oxley is that it is viewed as such an extraordinary development in financial reporting when, substantively, much of what it contains is hardly that new. Certifications of financial statements? Executives had been certifying financial statements for years. Protection of auditor independence? The financial community had been fiddling with that one for decades. Prison terms for transgressions? Deliberate financial misreporting had been a criminal offense long before the passage of Sarbanes-Oxley, just as it was after.

The significance of Sarbanes-Oxley, therefore, does not completely reside in the fact of its enactment or the substance of its provisions. Much of its significance, rather, stems from the publicity surrounding its passage and its heroic attempt, undertaken with great intensity due to self-imposed time constraints, to pull together an extraordinarily diverse collection of preexisting financial reporting concepts into a single piece of integrated legislation. In a sense, Congress took a quick scan of the horizon of percolating financial reporting ideas and said to itself, "Enough talk, now is the time for action." A few months of congressional staff all-nighters later, the Sarbanes-Oxley Act was born.

The reason any of this matters is that an in-depth understanding of Sarbanes-Oxley is difficult to achieve in the absence of an understanding of its historical roots. And by "historical roots" is not meant simply accounting scandals that surfaced at such companies as Enron and WorldCom. The historical roots of Sarbanes-Oxley—and in particular the intellectual foundation for its statutory sections and subsections—go back much further.

This chapter begins with the Sarbanes-Oxley Act's roots. (See Exhibit 3.1.) It tracks the evolution of some of the key financial reporting concepts—the tone at the top, individual executive responsibility, the centrality of the audit committee, the role of the outside auditor—and explores how those concepts first established a foothold in financial reporting literature and practices and then expanded in influence as financial community leaders, and in particular leaders in the accounting profession, sought to combat the seemingly intractable problem of fraudulent financial reporting. The consequence was that, when Congress looked about in the wake of Enron for something to enact into law, these concepts were the logical foundation upon which to build federal legislation.

EXHIBIT 3.1 Evolution of Financial Reporting

- Treadway Commission Report (1987)
- Expectation Gap revision of Statements on Auditing Standards (1989)
- Private Securities Litigation Reform Act (1995)
- Levitt Speech at New York University (1998)
- Report of Blue Ribbon Committee on Improving the Effectiveness of Corporate Audit Committees (1999)
- New Rules of the Securities and Exchange Commission, New York Stock Exchange, National Association of Securities Dealers, and American Stock Exchange (1999)
- Report of the O'Malley Panel on Audit Effectiveness (2000)
- Sarbanes-Oxley Act (2002)

It is to the historical roots of the financial reporting concepts that ultimately became the Sarbanes-Oxley Act that we accordingly turn.

BEFORE TREADWAY: BLAMING THE AUDITOR

The beginning of the Sarbanes-Oxley saga really takes us back to the early 1980s when, in at least one respect, the area of financial reporting was much less complex. That involved who would get the blame when something went wrong. Almost everyone seemed to agree that, when financial fraud surfaced, the blame should immediately be placed on the outside auditor of the company's financial statements. The reasons were several, but most of them revolved around the fact that the auditor had money. In the inevitable litigation, a typical CEO, company executive, or outside director might simply testify, "I was relying on the outside auditor," to the general satisfaction of all.

All, that is, except the auditor. For its part, an auditor of the era quickly came to realize that it was in a no-win position. Given the way that financial fraud develops, by the time an accounting irregularity had surfaced the auditor would frequently be in the unenviable position of having missed it for years. Subsequent scrutiny of the auditor's workpapers would by definition show that, sure enough, had the auditor undertaken this or that additional task, the fraud would have been exposed.

Once the auditor actually entered a 1980s courtroom, the situation only became more difficult. There, the contention of fraud detection as an auditor's responsibility fed into a jury's normal inclination to view the auditor as providing a "guarantee" of accuracy or "a clean bill of health," which was accompanied by only a hazy understanding of what generally accepted auditing standards (GAAS) actually required the auditor to do. The common courtroom scenario would involve the auditor getting blamed from all sides. The auditor's defensive-sounding response that it should be viewed as a fellow victim of the fraud, rather than a participant, could be a tough sell.

In this context, the law was no help at all. To the contrary, courts came to view the accounting profession almost as a vehicle for risk diversification. Thus, one state supreme court justified an expansion of audit liability through an observation that "independent auditors have apparently been able to obtain liability insurance . . . to satisfy their financial obligations." Other courts similarly expanded the categories of plaintiffs who, when accounting problems surfaced, were entitled to sue. Federal courts, interpreting the federal securities laws, came to the conclusion that investors could be found to have relied upon audit reports they had never even seen.

Within the accounting firms during the first half of the 1980s, therefore, two things grew. One was their legal departments. The other was their exposure to liability. Data collected by the then—Big Six firms showed that those firms by themselves would ultimately end up facing legal liability of around $30 billion—roughly $3.8 million per partner.

It was thus somewhat understandable that, by the mid-1980s, the accounting profession had come to view the liability landscape with a blend of frustration and terror. On the one hand, its exposure to liability seemed to be increasing almost exponentially as financial community frustration intensified over the profession's seemingly inexplicable inability to stop fraudulent financial reporting before it got out of hand. On the other hand, the ability of a typical outside auditor to detect fraud at the outset was limited. Key members of the financial community came to the fairly vivid realization that it was time to rethink, and to rationalize, the allocation of responsibility for fraudulent financial reporting between the outside auditor and others. The question was how to do it.

 ## THE TREADWAY COMMISSION

The stage was thus set for what would prove to be a watershed in the evolution of financial reporting and corporate governance: the formation of the National Commission on Fraudulent Financial Reporting, later known as the Treadway Commission after its chairman, former Securities and Exchange Commission member James Treadway. The task to be undertaken by the Treadway Commission went to the crux of the matter. The Commission's task was to investigate the underlying causes of fraudulent financial reporting, to examine the role of the outside auditor in the detection of fraud, and to analyze the extent to which corporate structures allowed fraudulent financial reporting to take place.

The Treadway Commission began its study in 1985 and over a two-year period undertook an exhaustive investigation of the root causes of financial fraud. Subjects of investigation and analysis included internal control systems, internal auditing, the significance of intra-corporate pressures for performance, management failures, and inadequacies of the accounting profession. Ultimately, the Commission undertook more than 20 separate research projects and briefing papers. In addition, the Commission investigated the views and perceptions of key financial regulatory agencies and groups, including the SEC, the FDIC, the Comptroller of the Currency, the American Institute of Certified Public Accountants, the Auditing Standards Board, the Financial Executives Institute, and the Institute of Internal Auditors. Twice the Commission appeared before the House Committee on Energy and Commerce's Subcommittee on Oversight and Investigations as part of that subcommittee's inquiry into the adequacy of auditing, accounting, and financial reporting practices. Prior to its publication, 40,000 copies of an exposure draft of the Commission's report were publicly distributed for comment.

The resulting Report of the National Commission on Fraudulent Financial Reporting was published in October 1987. Among other things, it concluded the following. Foremost, "fraudulent financial reporting usually does not begin with an overt intentional act to distort the financial statements." Rather, the Treadway Commission found that fraudulent financial reporting frequently came about as "the culmination of a series of acts designed to respond to operational difficulties." What tended to happen, the Commission concluded, was that initially "the activities may not be fraudulent, but in time they become increasingly questionable" until, finally, someone steps over the line.

The Treadway Commission also found that behind the individuals stepping over the line into financial fraud was almost always undue pressure. It might be "unrealistic pressures, particularly for short-term results" or "financial pressure resulting from bonus plans that depend on short-term economic performance" or pressure from "the desire to obtain a higher price for a stock or debt offering or to meet the expectation of investors." At the core of fraudulent financial reporting, though, the Commission almost inevitably found pressure. The Commission stated:

> The Commission's studies revealed that fraudulent financial reporting usually occurs as the result of certain environmental, institutional, or individual forces and opportunities. These forces and opportunities add pressures and incentives that encourage individuals and companies to engage in fraudulent financial reporting and are present to some degree

in all companies. If the right, combustible mixture of forces and opportunities is present, fraudulent financial reporting may occur.

Any effort to combat fraud, therefore, had to start at the top. In particular, responsibility for reliable financial reporting had to reside "first and foremost at the corporate level." Thus, top management had to establish the proper "tone at the top"—an attitude that demanded truth and candor in financial reporting and that, just as important, saw to it that pressures for financial performance did not get out of hand. Such a tone at the top then had to penetrate every fiber of the enterprise so that it became part of the corporate culture. The Commission summarized: "The tone set by top management—the corporate environment or culture within which financial reporting occurs—is the most important factor contributing to the integrity of the financial reporting process."

The problem with the Treadway Commission's determination to place foremost responsibility for financial reporting on the tone set by top management was that, of all groups within an enterprise, it was probably top management that was most vulnerable to pressures from outside forces. Those forces might include investors, financial analysts, bankers, owners, or others—some of whom may not be expected to appreciate fully the importance of the tone at the top and who may rather maintain a greater interest in the bottom line. For top management, establishing the right amount of pressure to achieve results while ensuring that at no level of the enterprise did the pressure get out of hand would pose a formidable challenge.

It is for this reason that the Treadway Commission posited a key role in financial reporting beyond that of senior management. That key role was to be filled by the board of directors and in particular by its audit committee. Through "establishment of an informed, vigilant and effective audit committee to oversee the company's financial reporting process," a board of directors could thereby act as a backstop for senior management and undertake to ensure that a proper tone at the top and financial reporting system remained in place. The centrality of the audit committee's function to financial reporting was emphasized by the Commission's formulation of eight separate recommendations regarding public company audit committees:

1. The board of directors of all public companies should be required by SEC rule to establish audit committees composed solely of independent directors.
2. Audit committees should be informed, vigilant, and effective overseers of the financial reporting process and the company's internal controls.

3. All public companies should develop a written charter setting forth the duties and responsibilities of the audit committee. The board of directors should approve the charter, review it periodically, and modify it as necessary.
4. Audit committees should have adequate resources and authority to discharge their responsibilities.
5. The audit committee should review management's evaluation of factors related to the independence of the company's public accountant. Both the audit committee and management should assist the public accountant in preserving his independence.
6. Before the beginning of each year, the audit committee should review management's plans for engaging the company's independent public accountant to perform management advisory services during the coming year, considering both the types of services that may be rendered and the projected fees.
7. Management should advise the audit committee when it seeks a second opinion on a significant accounting issue.
8. Audit committees should oversee the quarterly reporting process.

To complement the efforts of the audit committee, the Treadway Commission also recommended an effective internal audit function that would report directly to the audit committee and thereby be positioned to act as the audit committee's eyes and ears. (See Exhibit 3.2.)

EXHIBIT 3.2 Key Recommendations of the Treadway Commission for Public Companies

Recommendation 1:	Top management must identify, understand, and assess the factors that may cause the company's financial statements to be fraudulently misstated.
Recommendation 2:	Public companies should maintain internal controls that provide reasonable assurance that fraudulent financial reporting will be prevented or subject to early detection.
Recommendation 5:	Public companies should maintain an effective internal audit function staffed with an adequate number of qualified personnel that is appropriate to the size and the nature of the company.
Recommendation 9:	The board of directors of all public companies should be required by SEC rule to establish audit committees composed solely of independent directors.

(continued)

EXHIBIT 3.2 (continued)

Recommendation 10:	Audit committees should be informed, vigilant, and effective overseers of the financial reporting process and the company's internal controls.
Recommendation 13:	Both the audit committee and management should assist the public accountant in preserving his independence.
Recommendation 17:	Management should advise the audit committee when it seeks a second opinion on a significant accounting issue.
Recommendation 19:	Audit committees should oversee the quarterly reporting process.

CONSEQUENCES OF THE TREADWAY COMMISSION REPORT

The reason the Treadway Commission report is central to any modern-day assessment of the laws governing financial misreporting is that the report's publication basically marked a sea change in the allocation of financial reporting responsibility. Implicit in the report's findings and recommendations was that reliance for the prevention of fraud on mechanisms outside the corporate structure—in particular, on the outside audit function—was not enough. Indeed, the Treadway Commission explicitly relegated the outside auditor to "a crucial, but secondary role" and cautioned that outside auditors could not be viewed as "guarantors of the accuracy or the reliability of financial statements." Rather, the genesis of financial fraud took place as a consequence of pressures and a tone within the company, and if financial fraud was to be prevented and detected at the outset, the mechanisms to do so must exist within the corporation itself. An effect of the Treadway Commission's findings and recommendations, therefore, was to shift responsibility for accurate financial reporting onto the shoulders of senior management, outside directors, internal audit, and—most important—audit committees.

Upon the report's publication in October 1987, the findings and recommendations of the Treadway Commission garnered almost extraordinary attention and support. Members of Congress immediately came to view its recommendations as authoritative. Legal writers discussed at length the Treadway Commission report and advocated a level of diligence consistent with its recommendations. The national accounting firms separately took steps to apprise the directors and officers of their client companies as to precisely what was now expected of them according to the report's recommendations. Thus, the accounting firms published their own monographs, duly distributed to corporate officials, that highlighted the recommendations of the Treadway Commission.

FURTHER DEVELOPMENTS

The effect of the Treadway Commission's report did not, moreover, stop with the Commission's findings and recommendations themselves. The Commission also affected a series of subsequent financial reporting initiatives and developments. Even beyond the four corners of the report, therefore, Commission findings and recommendations influenced the evolution of financial reporting. Among the effects was a further shift of responsibility for financial reporting to those within the reporting entity.

One of these further developments was a concerted effort by members of the accounting profession to make clear to the public that it was performing—in the words of the Treadway Commission—only a "secondary" role. Within the profession, this became colloquially known as the effort to close the "expectation gap"—the gap perceived to exist between what the public seemed to assume to be the auditor's role and the auditor's role in fact. The impetus behind this initiative was a concern, rooted in the experience of individual CPA firms in audit malpractice litigation, that the public assumed a much greater level of responsibility on the part of the outside auditor than the outside auditor under professional standards was prepared to fulfill. That responsibility, the accounting profession sought to demonstrate, really belonged to management.

Here, too, one of the more significant results was a clearer allocation of responsibility for financial reporting between corporate officials and the outside auditor. One visible consequence was a revision of the standard form of auditor's report, which now stated explicitly on the face of the report what had earlier been buried in the underlying literature articulating GAAS: that the "financial statements are the responsibility of the Company's management," whereas the auditor's responsibility was only to "express an opinion on these financial statements based on our audit." Although the expectation gap initiative also involved some assumption by the auditor of clearer responsibility for the detection of fraud, it highlighted the primary responsibility as that of corporate management.

Still another development operated to affect the allocation of responsibility for financial reporting between corporate officials and auditors. That is the much-touted "litigation crisis" and the very real concern that, if the accounting profession remained at the forefront of liability for fraudulent financial reporting, every national accounting firm was going to be driven out of business. Headlines described not only extraordinary jury verdicts but extraordinary settlements as well. A record-breaking $400 million settlement by Ernst & Young appeared in giant headlines on the front page of the *New York Times.*

The resulting appearance of professional vulnerability was furthered by business decisions made by the individual CPA firms: They started firing their clients. Accordingly, the financial press began to report impediments to expanding enterprise owing simply to the unavailability of financial statement audits. An article in *BusinessWeek* was typical. Entitled "Big Six Firms Are Firing Clients," the article reported:

> With growing regularity, major public accounting firms are turning their backs on many smaller banks, thrifts, and fledgling companies. Deloitte & Touche, for one, declined to audit about 60 companies trying to go public last year, more than half the 103 initial public offerings they actually evaluated.

BusinessWeek described the reason as "no mystery." It was because "[i]n recent years, accounting firms have been forced to fork over hundreds of millions of dollars to settle lawsuits."

The prospect of accounting firms going out of business or firing clients turned the conventional wisdom—underlying the allocation of responsibility between management and the outside auditor—on its head. The conventional wisdom, typified by a decision by the New Jersey Supreme Court, had been that the placement of broad responsibility for financial reporting upon the outside auditor would operate, among other things, as a mechanism to enhance financial reporting and at the same time to diversify risk. The analysis was proved incorrect. The system was in trouble.

All of this culminated in broader scrutiny as to responsibility for financial reporting and a broader assessment of the extent to which corporate officials, rather than outside professionals, should be at the forefront of those held accountable for financial fraud. Courts began to take notice. In the thick of this reawakening emerged decisions such as the California Supreme Court's opinion in Bily v. Arthur Young & Co., which scrutinized the role of an outside auditor and precisely what level of responsibility an auditor of financial statements was assuming. (See Exhibit 3.3.) Decisions placing broad responsibilities on auditors such as that in New Jersey came to be undermined or, in the case of the New Jersey decision itself, reversed by the legislature.

EXHIBIT 3.3 Evolving Perceptions of Auditor Responsibility

"By certifying the public records that collectively depict a corporation's financial status, the independent auditor assumes a public responsibility transcending any employment relationship with the client. The independent public accountant performing this special function owes ultimate allegiance to the corporation's creditors and stockholders, as well as to the investing public. This 'public watchdog' function demands that the accountant maintain total independence from the client at all times and requires complete fidelity to the public trust."

(United States v. Arthur Young & Co., 465 U.S. 805, 817-18 (1984))

"An auditor is a watchdog, not a bloodhound. . . . As a matter of commercial reality, audits are performed in a client-controlled environment. The client typically prepares its own financial statements; it has direct control over and assumes primary responsibility for their contents. . . . The client engages the auditor, pays for the audit, and communicates with audit personnel throughout the engagement. Because the auditor cannot in the time available become an expert in the client's business and record-keeping systems, the client necessarily furnishes the information base for the audit. Thus, regardless of the efforts of the auditor, the client retains effective primary control of the financial reporting process."

(Bily v. Arthur Young & Co., 3 Cal. 4th 370, 399-400 (1992))

THE LEVITT INITIATIVES

The shift of primary responsibility for financial reporting to those within the corporation was thus well under way when a new catalyst surfaced: the dramatic upsurge in reported instances of accounting irregularities in the latter half of the 1990s. In hindsight, the exposure of the accounting fraud at Leslie Fay—most notably in a series of high-profile stories in the *Wall Street Journal*—probably marked the beginning of the trend. Not long thereafter, newspaper readers were seemingly being greeted on a regular basis with headlines announcing the latest public company to fall victim to financial fraud. Perplexing to many, the underlying theme of each story was the same: massive accounting fraud perpetrated by some of the most senior officials in the company.

In April 1998, the problem of accounting irregularities attained a level of prominence that made clear it was not going away any time soon. In that month, Cendant Corporation—up to that point believed to be one of the spectacular success stories of the decade—announced that it, too, had fallen prey to financial fraud. For Cendant, the experience came about in a way that was particularly unfortunate. It had taken on the accounting problems through the acquisition of another company and the fraud, akin to an unstoppable virus, had infected its own financial reporting system. Within hours after public announcement of the fraud, investors watched in horror as the value of their stockholdings plunged by roughly $14 billion. A subsequent audit committee investigation (placed on the Internet by Cendant itself) exhaustively documented a financial fraud the scope of which was breathtaking. Not insignificantly, the entire drama was played out in the pages of the *Wall Street Journal*, the *New York Times*, *BusinessWeek*, *Newsweek*, *Fortune*, and almost every other notable business publication throughout the spring and summer of the year.

By the fall of 1998, then-SEC chairman Arthur Levitt had apparently decided that enough was enough. He tossed down the gauntlet in the form of a speech on September 28, 1998, which he entitled "The Numbers Game." Among other things, Levitt castigated public companies for a form of financial reporting that he referred to as "earnings management," which was, he said, in substance nothing more than "accounting hocus-pocus." Levitt admonished that he was "challenging corporate management and Wall Street to re-examine our current environment" and announced a new series of initiatives to that end. The solution, according to Levitt, was "nothing less than a cultural change." (See Exhibit 3.4.)

While Levitt's sense of urgency was unmistakable, the fundamental solutions he proposed were neither new nor particularly innovative. For his solutions, he turned to the fundamental precepts that had been published in the Treadway Commission's report 13 years before.

Accordingly, at the core of the Levitt initiatives was the concept of "qualified, committed, independent and tough-minded audit committees":

> And, finally, qualified, committed, independent and tough-minded audit committees represent the most reliable guardians of the public interest. Sadly, stories abound of audit committees whose members lack expertise in the basic principles of financial reporting as well as the mandate

---

EXHIBIT 3.4 Arthur Levitt's Speech: "The Numbers Game"

Plans to improve the reliability and transparency of financial statements:

- Technical rule changes by regulators to improve the accounting framework
- Improved outside auditing in the financial reporting process
- A strengthened audit committee process
- Cultural changes on the part of corporate management and the financial community

to ask probing questions. In fact, I've heard of one audit committee that convenes only twice a year before the regular board meeting for 15 minutes and whose duties are limited to a perfunctory presentation. Compare that situation with the audit committee which meets 12 times a year before each board meeting; where every member has a financial background; where there are no personal ties to the chairman or the company; where they have their own advisers; where they ask tough questions of management and outside auditors; and where, ultimately, the investor interest is being served.

The SEC stands ready to take appropriate action if that interest is not protected. But, a private sector response that empowers audit committees and obviates the need for public sector dictates seems the wisest choice. I am pleased to announce that the financial community has agreed to accept this challenge.

Following on the heels of Levitt's Numbers Game admonishment was a concrete plan to put thoughts into action. One important component of this plan was the formation of a commission to enhance the power and effectiveness of corporate audit committees. Hence was born the so-called Blue Ribbon Committee on Improving the Effectiveness of Corporate Audit Committees. After hearings on the effectiveness of financial reporting systems and, in particular, corporate audit committees, the Blue Ribbon Committee in February 1999 issued a series of recommendations for new rules by the National Association of Securities Dealers, the New York Stock Exchange, the American Stock Exchange, the SEC, and the American Institute of CPAs (AICPA) which to a large extent either duplicated or carried further the recommendations made by the Treadway Commission 13 years before. Again, we see an emphasis on the centrality of audit committees in the prevention of fraudulent financial reporting, accompanied by renewed emphasis on the role of internal audit.

In substance, the committee's recommendations, some of which were directed only to companies with a market capitalization of $200 million or more, were these:

- Audit committees should be comprised solely of independent directors.
- Members of an audit committee shall be considered independent only if they have no relationship to the corporation that may interfere with the exercise of their independence from management and the corporation.
- A nonindependent director may be appointed to an audit committee only if the board, under exceptional and limited circumstances, determines that membership on the committee by the individual is required by the best interests of the corporation and its shareholders and the board discloses,

in the next annual proxy statement subsequent to such determination, the nature of the relationship and the reasons for that determination.

▪ Audit committees should comprise a minimum of three directors, each of whom is financially literate (as described in a section of the report titled "Financial Literacy") or becomes financially literate within a reasonable period of time after his or her appointment to the audit committee. At least one member of the audit committee should have accounting or related financial management expertise.

▪ Audit committees should (1) adopt a formal written charter that is approved by the full board of directors and that specifies the scope of the committee's responsibilities and how it carries out those responsibilities, including structure, processes, and membership requirements, and (2) review and reassess the adequacy of the audit committee charter on an annual basis.

▪ The SEC should promulgate rules that require audit committees to disclose in the company's annual proxy statement whether the audit committee has adopted a formal written charter and, if so, whether the audit committee satisfied its responsibilities during the prior year in compliance with its charter, which shall be disclosed at least triennially in the annual report to shareholders or proxy statement.

▪ The audit committee charter for every listed company should specify that the outside auditor is ultimately accountable to the board of directors and the audit committee, as representatives of shareholders, and that these shareholder representatives have the ultimate authority and responsibility to select, evaluate, and, where appropriate, replace the outside auditor (or to nominate the outside auditor to be proposed for shareholder approval in any proxy statement).

▪ The audit committee charter for every listed company should specify that the audit committee is responsible for ensuring its receipt from the outside auditor of a formal written statement delineating all relationships between the auditor and the company, consistent with Independence Standards Board Standard 1, and that the audit committee is also responsible for actively engaging in a dialogue with the auditor with respect to any disclosed relationships or services that may affect the objectivity and independence of the auditor and for taking, or recommending that the full board take, appropriate action to ensure the independence of the outside auditor.

▪ Generally accepted audit standards (GAAS) should require that a company's outside auditor discuss with the audit committee the auditor's judgments about the quality, not just the acceptability, of the company's accounting principles as applied in its financial reporting; the discussion should include such issues as the clarity of the company's financial disclosures and degree of aggressiveness or conservatism of the company's accounting principles and underlying estimates and other significant decisions made by management in preparing the financial disclosure and reviewed by the outside auditors. This requirement should be written in a way to encourage open, frank discussion and to avoid boilerplate.

- The SEC should require all reporting companies to include a letter from the audit committee in the company's annual report to shareholders and Form 10-K Annual Report disclosing whether or not, with respect to the prior fiscal year, (1) management has reviewed the audited financial statements with the audit committee, including a discussion of the quality of the accounting principles as applied and significant judgments affecting the company's financial statements; (2) the outside auditors have discussed with the audit committee the outside auditor's judgments of the quality of those principles as applied and judgments referenced in item 1 under the circumstances; (3) the members of the audit committee have discussed among themselves, without management or the outside auditors present, the information disclosed to the audit committee described in items 1 and 2; and (4) the audit committee, in reliance on the review and discussions conducted with management and the outside auditors pursuant to items 1 and 2, believes that the company's financial statements are fairly presented in conformity with GAAP in all material respects. The SEC should adopt a "safe harbor" applicable to any such disclosure.
- The SEC should require that a reporting company's outside auditor conduct an SAS-71 (Interim Financial Review) review before the company files its Form 10-Q.
- SAS-71 should be amended to require that a reporting company's outside auditor discuss with the audit committee, or at least its chairman, and a representative of financial management, in person, or by telephone conference call, the matters described in AU Section 380 (Communications with Audit Committees) before filing Form 10-Q (and preferably before any public announcement of financial results), including significant adjustments, management judgments and accounting estimates, significant new accounting policies, and disagreements with management.

In the months following their publication, these Blue Ribbon Committee recommendations were the subject of vigorous debate. On the one hand, advocates of improved corporate governance maintained that the adoption of these recommendations was critical to improved financial reporting systems. Indeed, a report by the Committee of Sponsoring Organizations of the Treadway Commission caused some to suggest that, insofar as the report found that accounting irregularities tended to strike with frequency at smaller companies, the recommendations of the committee should be made applicable to companies with even less than the $200 million market capitalization proposed by the committee in certain instances as a cutoff. On the other hand, corporate defense lawyers raised concerns about the corresponding increase in legal liability to boards of directors and, in particular, audit committees.

On December 15, 1999, the SEC approved a series of new rules as a consequence of the Blue Ribbon Committee's recommendations. In substance, virtually all of the Blue Ribbon Committee's recommendations were adopted. Thus, the new rules:

- Required audit committees to include at least three members and generally be composed solely of "independent" directors who are financially literate
- Defined "independence" more rigorously for audit committee members
- Required companies to adopt written charters for their audit committees
- Gave the audit committee the right to hire and terminate the auditor
- Required at least one member of the audit committee to have accounting or financial management expertise
- Required companies' interim financial statements to be reviewed by independent auditors before filing
- Required companies to provide in their proxy statements a report from the audit committee that disclosed whether the audit committee reviewed and discussed certain matters with management and the auditors and whether the audit committee recommended to the board that the audited financial statements be included in the Form 10-K
- Required companies to disclose in their proxy statements whether the audit committee had a written charter and to file a copy of the charter every three years
- Required companies whose securities were listed on the NYSE or American Stock Exchange or were quoted on Nasdaq to disclose certain information about any audit committee member who was not "independent"

For the auditors' part, approval of the new rules was followed eight months later with a report and recommendations by still another panel—the Panel on Audit Effectiveness of the accounting profession's Public Oversight Board. While primarily directed to enhancement of the effectiveness of the audit function, even this panel found itself emphasizing the pivotal role of the board's audit committee in enhancing both the company's financial reporting system and its outside and internal audit functions. Among other things, the panel emphasized the need for increased audit committee interaction with the internal and outside auditors and encouraged an outside auditor relationship that positioned the audit committee "as the external auditors' primary client." The panel also admonished audit committees to "increase the time and attention they devote to discussions of internal control with management and both the internal and external auditors" and to place particular emphasis on "management's and the auditors' views on (1) the control environment and (2) the controls (or lack thereof) over financial reporting." One of the principal authorities cited by the panel was the Treadway Commission.

As the financial community made its way through the end of the 1990s, therefore, it looked as though the system of regulatory oversight had put in place a reinvigorated structure to get the problem of fraudulent financial misreporting under control. True, implementing all of the changes was going to take some time. Nobody expected the problem of financial fraud to end overnight. Still, the basic reforms seemed sound and a fair expectation was that eventually things would get better.

ENRON

Then came Enron. Much has been said about the implosion of Enron Corporation as the year 2001 approached its close. For some, the events remain all-too-embedded in memory. For others—particularly those still in school when Enron broke—things may be a little more hazy. So let's take a moment to go back to the dot-com era, and in particular the second half of 2001, for a brief recap of events.

The year 2001, even before Enron's collapse, had already witnessed more than its share of extraordinary and unfortunate events. As the year opened, the stock market was in full retreat owing to the dot-com bubble-burst of the year before. On September 11, the World Trade Center and the Pentagon were the targets of terrorist attacks. A war in Afghanistan soon followed as fast-evolving events in the Middle East dominated the national agenda.

Then, as the year approached its end, Enron Corporation collapsed. Instantaneously the subjects of financial reporting, GAAP, and Form 10-K disclosure took center stage. In everyday conversation, nonaccountants found themselves debating Enron footnotes and talking about accounting for something called an "SPE."

Before long, 12 separate congressional investigations had been launched into all sorts of issues surrounding financial misreporting and Enron's collapse.

Politicians of all stripes, many of whom had not previously demonstrated a strong interest in accounting, suddenly appeared on television screens to complain that something had to be done. Redundant and sometimes contradictory legislation was prepared by competing teams of congressional staffers. It almost seemed that the change in financial reporting culture that Arthur Levitt had struggled so purposefully to create was now being furthered by an accounting scandal of national proportions.

Where did Congress turn to provide the substance for the legislation that would "do something" to stop financial fraud? It was to the intellectual foundation that had already been put in place by the Treadway Commission and the 15 years of reform and experimentation that had followed. Built into the various forms of competing legislation, therefore, were such Treadway concepts as the "tone at the top," the centrality of the audit committee, the individual responsibility of executives, the critical importance of a system of internal controls, the preservation of auditor independence, and strengthened oversight of quarterly financial reporting. To some, it might almost seem as if the members of the Treadway Commission themselves had been summoned from retirement to establish the key provisions of potential legislation.

Nevertheless, even in the wake of Enron it was far from clear that meaningful legislation would result. The accounting profession took the lead in pointing out that significant reforms had already been put in place and they should be given the opportunity to work before being displaced by federal law. The point was not a frivolous one and many within Congress took note. As the national uproar following Enron began to die down, it looked increasingly likely that significant federal legislation was not going to happen at all.

But then a new scandal erupted. This one involved WorldCom. Whereas many of the accounting issues tied up in Enron were complicated and tough to understand—many commentators had difficulty even pinpointing exactly how GAAP had been violated—the misreporting at WorldCom was not. It involved one of the most conventional devices of financial fraud, the capitalization of expenses. And the level of fraud was staggering. Ultimately it was found to have grown to more than $11 billion.

With WorldCom, the opposition to federal legislation was overwhelmed. From the various competing bills sitting in congressional offices, two leaders— Paul Sarbanes and Michael Oxley—worked to attain the acceptance of a comprehensive package of reforms, which passed by an overwhelming vote. The so-called Sarbanes-Oxley Act, born of concepts championed by the Treadway Commission more than a decade before, was now the law of the land.

It was left for the business community to figure out exactly what the thing meant.

CHAPTER FOUR

The Sarbanes-Oxley Act

P ASSED WITH LIGHTNING SPEED by a Congress determined to "do something" about accounting fraud, the Sarbanes-Oxley Act of 2002 at first blush may come across as a thrown-together hodgepodge of hastily devised, sometimes redundant, and often conflicting financial reporting concepts. It may seem hard otherwise to explain, for example, a single statute that imposes ostensibly redundant certification requirements on executives, puts in place an accountant regulatory system that is largely duplicative of the SEC, makes certain accounting misstatements more punishable than some forms of murder, and commissions any number of academic studies to pave the way for still more laws and regulations in the future.

That is certainly one way of looking at it. No doubt, some statutory subsections of Sarbanes-Oxley are tough to figure out. Still, there is another way of looking at it. That begins with the recognition that the objective of Sarbanes-Oxley was not so much to create a brand-new system of financial reporting but to bring together a number of preexisting financial reporting concepts that shared as their common foundation a singular understanding of why financial reporting systems fail. If Sarbanes-Oxley comes across as something of a hodgepodge, that's because it is. It is not, however, a hodgepodge of entirely new or unrelated ideas. It is an attempt to pull together into one statutory scheme a number of practical devices, born of common experience and predicated upon a core collection of underlying themes, that had already established something of a beachhead among the best practices of financial reporting.

One approach to digging into Sarbanes-Oxley, accordingly, is to start with its underlying themes—a half-dozen concepts that constitute the foundation upon which the statute is built:

1. The "tone at the top" and the audit committee
2. Individual executive responsibility
3. The upward flow of bad news
4. Auditor resoluteness and independence
5. The system of internal control
6. Everyone plays a role

With those in mind, we can turn to the statute's more detailed allocation of responsibility among the various players involved and exactly who is supposed to do what. The significant players under Sarbanes-Oxley are:

- The CEO and CFO
- The audit committee
- The outside auditor
- The internal auditor
- Company counsel
- Investment bankers

Exploring the Sarbanes-Oxley Act in this way, the ostensible hodgepodge of statutory provisions almost comes across as a carefully constructed integration of corporate governance mechanisms directed to the prevention and early detection of financial fraud. True, Sarbanes-Oxley is not exactly put together with the literary skill of a great poem. But one could argue that, at least for the government, it's not such a bad job.

SIX UNDERLYING THEMES

One theme underlying Sarbanes-Oxley is virtually lifted right out of the Tread-way Commission report itself. That is the notion that fraudulent financial reporting almost never starts with a group of people setting out to be crooks. Rather, as discussed in Chapter 1, it starts with an environment in which fundamentally honest people are put under pressure to commit fundamentally dishonest acts. Hence, one theme underlying Sarbanes-Oxley is recognition of the overriding importance of the corporate environment—the tone at the top—and the vulnerability of that environment to corruption through the pressure that unrealistic performance objectives can place on executives. Sarbanes-Oxley accordingly vests in a committee of the board—the audit committee—direct oversight responsibility for financial reporting on the implicit theory that the audit committee members, by virtue of their independence, will be more removed from the corrupting influence of outside pressures.

That is not to suggest that Sarbanes-Oxley views senior executives as irrelevant to the corporate environment. Rather, the statute understandably seems to acknowledge that they play the biggest role of all—in establishing the critical tone at the top, putting in place the forecasts and budgets that will play such a significant role in everyday activity, and determining the ways that executives will be held accountable for results. Accordingly, a second theme underlying Sarbanes-Oxley is its insistence upon the hands-on individual responsibility for financial reporting of the company's two most senior executives—the CEO and CFO. Sure, even before Sarbanes-Oxley the CEO and CFO were expected to sign a Form 10-K and assume ultimate responsibility for its content. But Sarbanes-Oxley puts in place a new system of executive certifications making it harder than ever for executives to distance themselves should things go wrong. At the same time, Sarbanes-Oxley calls for a code of ethics for senior financial executives and requires the forfeiture of CEO and CFO bonuses under specified circumstances in which earnings were improperly inflated through corporate misconduct. Individual dishonesty, should it occur, is to be dealt with through penalties of almost inhumane severity. At the high end, for a middle-aged senior executive, Sarbanes-Oxley provides for criminal penalties that can amount to life in prison.

Once it moves beyond the fundamental importance of a company's tone at the top, audit committee, and most-senior executives, Sarbanes-Oxley addresses one of the most frustrating and intractable impediments to integrity in financial reporting. That is the failure of bad news to flow up through the organization to those who are in a position to take corrective action.

In this regard, Congress appeared to understand that, where financial misreporting develops, there is frequently any number of well-meaning employees and executives who detest it, resent it, and would do almost anything within their power to stop it, if only given a nonthreatening opportunity. A third theme underlying Sarbanes-Oxley, accordingly, is the need to unclog the pipelines of information so that bad news of financial reporting corruption may flow unimpeded to the independent guardians of the system. The most obvious of these guardians is the audit committee, and Sarbanes-Oxley thus calls upon each audit committee to put in place a system for the confidential, anonymous submission by employees of complaints. To ensure audit committee capability to properly address such whistleblower complaints when they arrive, Sarbanes-Oxley gives the audit committee the power to engage independent counsel and other advisers and, at the same time, complete discretion over such adviser compensation. Another independent force in this structure, or more accurately outside it, is the auditor of the company's financial statements, and Sarbanes-Oxley seeks to open the pipeline of reliable information to the auditor as well.

And speaking of the auditor, a fourth theme underlying Sarbanes-Oxley is the need for a strengthened, steadfast, and resolutely independent outside audit capability. The auditor's independence is to be fostered in a number of ways, among them through the installation of a structure by which it is the independent audit committee that is actually to be the outside auditor's client. Accordingly, the outside auditor is to report directly to the audit committee, and it is the audit committee, in its sole discretion, that is to determine the auditor's compensation. At the same time, the auditor's independence is to be safeguarded through constraints on the auditor's performance of nonaudit services. Adding still more support to the outside auditor, the function is to be enhanced through an entirely new auditor regulatory authority—the Public Company Accounting Oversight Board, or PCAOB—whose function it is to protect auditor independence, inspect the accounting firms themselves, and even inspect individual audits.

All of this apparatus, moreover, is directed not simply to the accuracy of a particular 10-K or 10-Q, but to the integrity of the entire system by which a company's financial reports are to be generated. A fifth theme of Sarbanes-Oxley, therefore, is the objective of improving internal control systems generally. The statutory approach involves an intricate network that includes executive evaluation, auditor assessment, and public reporting. Sarbanes-Oxley establishes as an objective not simply accuracy in each periodic financial report but across-the-board improvement in financial reporting systems overall.

Finally, a sixth theme underlying Sarbanes-Oxley is the notion that, when it comes to integrity in financial reporting, almost everybody plays a role. Responsibility for integrity in financial reporting thus is not only allocated among the obvious candidates—the CEO, the CFO, the audit committee, and the auditor. Sarbanes-Oxley takes a broader look and elevates the profile of company counsel, internal audit, and investment bankers. Under Sarbanes-Oxley, it is difficult for anyone associated with a company's financial reporting—either within or without the company—to completely get off the hook.

It is through exploration of this final theme that the most meaningful insight into the interplay of Sarbanes-Oxley's statutory admonitions can be obtained. For, in the broadest sense, Sarbanes-Oxley can be viewed as a comprehensive scheme of allocation of roles and responsibilities to those somehow associated with a company's financial reporting. As indicated above, those individuals fall roughly into five groups: (1) the CEO and CFO; (2) the audit committee; (3) the outside auditor; (4) company counsel; and (5) investment bankers. Each is discussed in the following.

 ## THE CEO AND CFO

Of the various participants in the financial reporting system, no two individuals play a more critical role than do the CEO and CFO. Together, those two executives establish the financial goals of the organization, the budgeting process through which those goals are communicated, and the mechanisms by which attainment of those goals will be measured. At the same time, they play the foremost role in establishing the company's tone at the top and the extent to which the attainment of financial objectives will reign paramount or constitute only one of several corporate objectives along with such things as integrity, candor, and honesty in financial reporting.

None of this is lost on Sarbanes-Oxley. The challenge for Congress was to come up with a way to make vividly clear the responsibility for financial reporting that these two executives had had all along. A statutory pronouncement that the CEO and CFO "have responsibility for financial reporting—and this time we really mean it" would understandably strike some as hollow. Nonetheless, Congress was intent on making less abstract these executives' responsibilities and, at the same time, making it more difficult for executives to distance themselves from misreporting and contending that they were "shocked, shocked" when problems arose.

The vehicle Congress selected to attain this objective was a somewhat complex system of CEO and CFO financial information certifications. It is far from clear that, to a sophisticated CEO or CFO, such certifications should have made that much of a difference. As mentioned earlier, the CEO and the CFO had been signing Forms 10-K for years. Execution of those forms served as crystal-clear evidence of executive belief in their truthfulness. At the same time, through so-called "representation letters," the CEO and CFO had been separately certifying to the outside auditor both the fairness of the financial presentation and the absence of illegal conduct. Still, the congressional judgment was that yet another layer of certifications would make a difference. Hence, the concepts of "Section 302" and "Section 906" certifications entered the vocabulary of financial reporting.

As it turned out, the evidence is that the new layer of certifications did, indeed, garner a meaningful level of executive attention. CEOs in particular seemed to gain new appreciation for their critical role in financial reporting systems—as well as the fact that, if something goes wrong, distancing one-self from the problem would be that much harder. For that matter, some CEOs became sufficiently nervous that—whether out of genuine concern for finan-cial reporting or the desire for self-protection—they put in place systems of "subcertifications" from lower-level executives (more about these later). Putting aside whether Section 302 or 906 certifications *should* have made a difference, they apparently did.

Part of the reason may have been the sheer scope of the information on a financial report that an executive was certifying. Here is the statutory language (from Section 302), which serves to dictate, pretty much word-for-word, the financial report certification that the CEO and CFO must sign:

(1) the signing officer has reviewed the report;

(2) based on the officer's knowledge, the report does not contain any untrue statement of a material fact or omit to state a material fact necessary in order to make the statements made, in light of the circumstances under which such statements were made, not misleading;

(3) based on such officer's knowledge, the financial statements, and other financial information included in the report, fairly present in all material respects the financial condition and results of opera-tions of the issuer as of, and for, the periods presented in the report;

(4) the signing officers—

(A) are responsible for establishing and maintaining internal controls;

(B) have designed such internal controls to ensure that material information relating to the issuer and its consolidated subsid-iaries is made known to such officers by others within those entities, particularly during the period in which the periodic reports are being prepared;

(C) have evaluated the effectiveness of the issuer's internal con-trols as of a date within 90 days prior to the report; and

(D) have presented in the report their conclusions about the effec-tiveness of their internal controls based on their evaluation as of that date;

(5) the signing officers have disclosed to the issuer's auditors and the audit committee of the board of directors (or persons fulfilling the equivalent functions)—

(A) all significant deficiencies in the design or operation of internal controls which could adversely affect the issuer's ability to record, process, summarize, and report financial data and have identified for the issuer's auditors any material weaknesses in internal controls; and

(B) any fraud, whether or not material, that involves management or other employees who have a significant role in the issuer's internal controls; and

(6) the signing officers have indicated in the report whether or not there were significant changes in internal controls or in other factors that could significantly affect internal controls subsequent to the date of their evaluation, including any corrective actions with regard to significant deficiencies and material weaknesses.

Lest any executive get creative ideas, the SEC has separately made clear that the certifying executives may not depart from the prescribed language.

A number of underlying concepts are embedded in this certification, and it probably makes sense to explicate some of the more important ones. The place to start is with the first line—that the signing officer has "reviewed the report." Right away, Sarbanes-Oxley seeks to deprive a CEO of a favored device to distance himself from any financial misreporting—that he never actually studied the report but was, instead, relying entirely on subordinates and experts. Under Sarbanes-Oxley, the CEO has to attest that he actually read the thing.

That attestation carries with it an important nuance. That is the executive's implicit acknowledgment that, beyond reading the report, he actually understood it. Though this may seem too obvious to mention, its significance becomes more clear when one actually reads some of the 10-K disclosures that got filed with the SEC in the years leading to Sarbanes-Oxley's enactment. Parts of them were, in a word, incomprehensible. A perennial favorite is the 10-K of Enron, the incomprehensibility of which became legendary. One Enron investigator reported that, even after endless interviews, document reviews, and analysis, he still couldn't figure out what parts of Enron's 10-K were talking about.

Having read the report, the CEO and CFO must certify that, based on the executives' own knowledge, the report "does not contain any untrue statement of a material fact or omit to state a material fact necessary in order to make the statements made, in light of the circumstances under which such statements were made, not misleading." For a statute that tries to be a strong advocate of plain English, this subsection may strike some as a step in the opposite direction. For securities lawyers, though, the language is all too familiar: This subsection is lifted pretty much word-for-word from the antifraud provisions of the Securities Exchange Act of 1934. Boiled down to its essence, the certifying executive is representing that, based on his knowledge, the disclosures are not false or misleading. One might have thought that, with this prohibition being included in a different part of the federal securities laws, it would not need to be repeated separately in a certification under Sarbanes-Oxley—but to hold that view would be to misunderstand Sarbanes-Oxley's whole approach. Sarbanes-Oxley isn't really directed to the creation of new responsibilities. It serves largely to take preexisting responsibilities and to pull them together into one integrated package.

The notion that this representation is to be "based on the officer's knowledge" is understandably the cause of some executive consternation. Just exactly what does that mean? Are the CEO and CFO to have personal knowledge of every single number underlying the financial statements? Must the CEO and CFO of a far-flung corporate empire with operations in 137 countries now learn eight languages to be sure every number is correct down to the last penny? If a mistake pops up, will our hapless CEO or CFO soon be doing a "perp-walk" on network TV?

Of course not; the phrase "based on the officer's knowledge" is rather something that requires some level of diligence but at the same time offers some measure of protection. It requires some diligence because the certifying executive has to take reasonable steps so that he can properly attest that he believes he has a basis for executing the certification. It offers some protection because it helps clarify that the executive is not providing a guarantee. The certifying executive is not saying: "I hereby guarantee that this information is correct." Instead, the executive is speaking to his reasonable belief as to whether the information is correct "based on the officer's knowledge."

However, we are still only beginning to work our way through the certification and the next subsection is where the rubber meets the road. In that subsection, the certifying executive attests, again "based on such officer's knowledge," that the financial statements "and other financial information included in the report" in fact "fairly present in all material respects the financial condition and results of operations of the issuer."

Here, the certifying executive encounters such amorphous concepts as "fairly present" and "in all material respects." The language itself, of course, is (again consistent with the whole approach of Sarbanes-Oxley) nothing new.

The concept "fairly present," historically a standard feature of a conventional audit report, means that the financial information gives you a pretty good sense of what is going on, at least within the confines of generally accepted accounting principles (GAAP). However, the key here is that, at least as understood by sophisticated professionals, "fairly present" is not the same as "accurately present." Insofar as financial statement presentation necessarily relies upon innumerable judgments, estimates, good faith beliefs, and predictions of future events, the concept of "accurately" carries with it the suggestion of a level of precision that is simply unattainable. "Fairly present" tells readers that the information may not be exactly right.

Enough said about the substance of the information being disclosed. Now the certification moves to address the system by which that information was created. Thus, the certification turns to the internal control system and the certifying officer's responsibility for its design and effectiveness.

A pause is merited here because Sarbanes-Oxley, in requiring executives to provide a certification as to their company's internal control system, yet again embraces a concept that is far from new. The notion of executive certification of a company's internal control system had been kicking around for years. Before Sarbanes-Oxley, though, it never really seemed to get any meaningful traction. After Sarbanes-Oxley, internal control reporting became one of the most controversial aspects of the new law.

An important threshold issue regarding this aspect of executive certification is: Exactly what are the "internal controls" that the executive is certifying? Sarbanes-Oxley itself simply uses the phrase "internal controls," a phrase that, in part owing to ever-evolving usage, is utterly lacking in precision. Getting a sense of impending chaos, the SEC promulgated rules in which it sought to define two separate, but largely overlapping, internal control concepts; they are "disclosure controls and procedures" and "internal control over financial reporting."

To the extent a distinction can be drawn between the two, the concept of "disclosure controls and procedures" seems to speak more to the process by which information generally is accumulated and communicated. The definition provides:

> [T]he term *disclosure controls and procedures* means controls and other procedures of an issuer that are designed to ensure that information required to be disclosed by the issuer in the reports that it files or submits under the Act (15 U.S.C. 78a *et seq.*) is recorded, processed, summarized and reported, within the time periods specified in the Commission's rules and forms. Disclosure controls and procedures include, without

limitation, controls and procedures designed to ensure that information required to be disclosed by an issuer in the reports that it files or submits under the Act is accumulated and communicated to the issuer's management, including its principal executive and principal financial officers, or persons performing similar functions, as appropriate to allow timely decisions regarding required disclosure.

The concept of "internal control over financial reporting" speaks more to the preparation of the financial statements and their conformity to GAAP:

The term *internal control over financial reporting* is defined as a process designed by, or under the supervision of, the issuer's principal executive and principal financial officers, or persons performing similar functions, and effected by the issuer's board of directors, management and other personnel, to provide reasonable assurance regarding the reliability of financial reporting and the preparation of financial statements for external purposes in accordance with generally accepted accounting principles and includes those policies and procedures that:

(1) Pertain to the maintenance of records that in reasonable detail accurately and fairly reflect the transactions and dispositions of the assets of the issuer;

(2) Provide reasonable assurance that transactions are recorded as necessary to permit preparation of financial statements in accordance with generally accepted accounting principles, and that receipts and expenditures of the issuer are being made only in accordance with authorization of management and directors of the issuer; and

(3) Provide reasonable assurance regarding prevention or timely detection of unauthorized acquisition, use or disposition of the issuer's assets that could have a material effect on the financial statements.

Without parsing through the distinctions between the two (and one might wonder whether we really needed two separate terms), the concepts together illustrate one of the main themes of Sarbanes-Oxley—the installation of channels through which information can flow upward through the organization to the most senior levels, the audit committee, the entire board of directors, and then outside to creditors, shareholders, and other users. Through this certification, CEOs and CFOs take on explicit responsibility for seeing to it that the pipelines of information are open.

As refined by the SEC, executives' responsibilities regarding internal control are to certify that:

- They themselves are responsible for establishing and maintaining both disclosure controls and procedures and internal control over financial reporting.
- These controls have been designed in a way that allows them to work effectively—in the case of disclosure controls and procedures, by ensuring that important information flows up, and, in the case of internal control over financial reporting, by providing reasonable assurance regarding financial reporting reliability.
- They have evaluated and reported their conclusions regarding the effectiveness of the disclosure controls and procedures.
- They have reported any recent significant change in the internal control over financial reporting.
- They have disclosed to the audit committee and the outside auditor all significant deficiencies and material weaknesses in the design or operation of internal control over financial reporting that are likely to adversely affect the company's ability to fairly report financial information.
- They have disclosed to the audit committee and the auditor any fraud whatsoever by management or employees who have a significant role in the company's internal control over financial reporting.

A separate certification requirement conveys the seriousness with which the CEO and CFO are to approach these (and for that matter all) financial reporting responsibilities. Pursuant to Section 906 of Sarbanes-Oxley, these two executives are separately required to include, as part of their SEC filings, a written certification that the report at issue fully complies with key provisions of the securities laws and that the information fairly presents, in all material respects, the financial condition and results of operations of the company. The statute provides that an executive providing such a certification, while knowing that the report at issue does not comport with applicable requirements, may be imprisoned for up to 10 years. An executive who willfully certifies such a statement under those circumstances may be imprisoned for up to 20 years.

While the CEO and CFO certifications are at the core of Sarbanes-Oxley's provisions directed to those executives, other provisions also play a role. One requires CEOs and CFOs to reimburse a company for any bonus or other incentive- or equity-based compensation received within a year after an SEC filing if the company must issue a restatement owing to material noncompliance resulting from misconduct. This provision probably stems less from the desire to disincentivize financial fraud (the result pales in comparison to some of the other penalties) than from a sense of fairness. Sarbanes-Oxley seems to reflect the view that fairness requires the reimbursement of executive bonuses premised on reported results that turn out to be wrong.

Another provision is directed to the requirement that companies disclose whether they have adopted a code of ethics for the CFO and other senior financial officers. In addition, Sarbanes-Oxley seeks the disclosure of any waiver of the code of ethics for senior financial officers. As discussed elsewhere, ethics codes probably accomplish little in guarding financial reporting integrity. The company's culture is much more important in influencing conduct than what management has written on a piece of paper. Probably, the catalyst for this particular provision in Sarbanes-Oxley was the popular press surrounding the discovery that Enron Corporation's CFO was allegedly engaged in improper conduct that was facilitated by undisclosed waivers of the company's (apparently not very effective) code of ethics.

THE AUDIT COMMITTEE

If men were angels, there would be no need for government. Roughly speaking, that is the attitude that Sarbanes-Oxley takes with regard to CEO and CFO fulfillment of their financial reporting responsibilities. It does its best to instill in those executives a sense of individual responsibility for the financial reporting system and, through a specified network of public disclosures and fairly severe penalties, seeks to instill an earnest desire to do the right thing. However, Sarbanes-Oxley does not operate on the assumption that those devices will be enough. There needs to be some pretty serious oversight.

That oversight function is to be fulfilled by the audit committee. In positing the audit committee as the overseers of the financial reporting system, Sarbanes-Oxley, once again, does not really contribute anything new. Well before Sarbanes-Oxley, the oversight responsibilities of the audit committee had already been pretty much established and accepted. Sarbanes-Oxley seeks to put some teeth into that responsibility. It does this through several statutory provisions.

One is a statutory provision making it official that the audit committee is to be directly responsible for the company's relationship with its outside auditor. Nor is the concept of direct responsibility a meaningless one. It includes direct responsibility for the auditor's appointment, the auditor's compensation, and the oversight of the auditor's work. The thought is to protect the auditor's independence and objectivity by making it accountable to the theoretically most independent and objective individuals at the company. If the auditor is beholden directly to the audit committee for its engagement, compensation, potential termination, and oversight, then the auditor's heart and mind should follow.

This statutory ability to directly control the audit function is an extraordinary power to be given to a committee of the board. It gives the audit committee the practical ability to probe and gain insight into almost any aspect of a company's financial reporting system or operations. At the same time, it places the audit committee in a position in which its views must be given serious consideration by management and the other board members. If the audit committee is unhappy with some aspect of financial reporting, the auditor will almost by definition be unhappy as well, and auditor unhappiness can be an impediment to the procurement of an audit report on the company's financial statements. All of this means that Sarbanes-Oxley, in giving the audit committee direct responsibility for oversight of the auditor, has placed the audit committee in the key position of assessing when the company does, and does not, get an audit report on its financial statements. The effect is that the audit committee's concerns and desires must necessarily be attended to.

For all of this to work properly, of course, the audit committee members themselves must be independent, and it is therefore no surprise that another key provision of Sarbanes-Oxley requires audit committee independence. In this, the statute is fairly straightforward, providing that "each member of the audit committee" may be a member of the board of directors but, other than that, "shall otherwise be independent." Moreover, Sarbanes-Oxley does not simply leave the matter of audit committee independence to the discretion and judgment of the board of directors. The statute goes on to provide that, to be independent, an audit committee member may not (except in his capacity as a member of the board or a board committee) receive "any consulting, advisory, or other compensatory fee from the issuer" or "be an affiliated person of the issuer or any subsidiary thereof." A narrow exception exists to the extent the SEC promulgates rules that provide otherwise.

Here, again, Sarbanes-Oxley builds into its statutory mechanisms a concept that is not terribly new. At the time this provision was enacted, independence by each audit committee member was already a requirement of the rules of the various stock exchanges. Still, the matter of audit committee independence has been elevated to more prominence insofar as it now exists as a matter of federal law. A statutory enactment of the concept of independence, moreover, opens the door for the courts to subsequently interpret the independence requirement and thereby provide further strength to the substantive concept.

With the basic infrastructure in place—an independent auditor directly responsible to an independent audit committee—Sarbanes-Oxley's audit committee requirements now turn to one of the biggest challenges that a typical audit committee will face: getting information to flow up so that the committee, to the extent necessary, can take corrective action. Sarbanes-Oxley's approach to this challenge is, again, not terribly original in concept, although it does represent a bold leap forward as a matter of federal law. That is, Sarbanes-Oxley requires audit committees to establish procedures to encourage the upward flow of information regarding problems in the company's accounting, internal control system over financial reporting, or auditing. In particular, the statute requires audit committees to establish procedures for "the receipt, retention, and treatment of complaints received by the issuer regarding accounting, internal accounting controls, or auditing matters" as well as "the confidential, anonymous submission by employees of the issuer of concerns regarding questionable accounting or auditing matters."

In large measure, this particular provision can be understood as a congressional reaction to the concept of frustrated whistleblowers unable to effectively communicate while their audit committees went about their business in total ignorance. The statutory objective was to put in place a mechanism by which well-meaning employees can communicate directly with the audit committee without exposing themselves to the retribution of nefarious executives.

The seriousness of Congress's approach to whistleblowers, moreover, is conveyed through a separate statutory provision making it unlawful to seek retribution or otherwise act to impede an employee from blowing the whistle. The congressional language is stern. It provides that neither a company nor its employees may "discharge, demote, suspend, threaten, harass, or in any other manner discriminate against an employee" who has lawfully provided information or otherwise assisted in an investigation into what the employee reasonably believes to constitute the violation of certain federal securities laws or SEC regulations. In the corporate governance scheme of Sarbanes-Oxley, whistleblowers are to play an important role. The audit committee is to encourage their candor and put in place a system whereby whistleblowers can safely circumvent the chain of command. (Subsequent to Sarbanes-Oxley, the concept has been taken one step further with new SEC regulations promulgated pursuant to the Dodd-Frank legislation, pursuant to which whistleblowers were to be incentivized through the opportunity to share in financial recoveries.)

When evidence of potential wrongdoing comes to the audit committee's attention, moreover, a formidable array of powers is available solely within the audit committee's discretion. Among these is the power to hire its own investigative law firm, its own forensic accountants, and pretty much anybody else it wants.

Sarbanes-Oxley provides that "each audit committee shall have the authority to engage independent counsel and other advisers, as it deems necessary to carry out its duties." Nor can management seek to circumscribe this power by limiting funding. A company has no choice but to provide for appropriate funding for the payment of such outside professional compensation. Management does not even get any say as to the amount of compensation that is appropriate. Sarbanes-Oxley makes clear that what constitutes appropriate funding is something that is to be determined by the audit committee.

THE OUTSIDE AUDITOR

Some would view those aspects of Sarbanes-Oxley dealing with the outside auditor as the most notable feature of the statute, and in some respects that is true. The accounting profession has the honor of dominating the first two titles of Sarbanes-Oxley, those dealing with the creation of the PCAOB and auditor independence. In terms of volume, moreover, the accounting profession wins hands down. No fewer than 18 separate sections, with innumerable subsections, are devoted to the accounting profession, its independence, and its regulation. Audit committees, in contrast, rate only a single one.

In terms of substance, the impact of Sarbanes-Oxley on the conduct of audits—with the exception of the PCAOB—is less clear. For example, one of the main features of Sarbanes-Oxley's enhancement of auditor independence is its specification of nonaudit services that may not be provided by the outside auditor; but virtually all of these had already been subject to important limitations by other rules before Sarbanes-Oxley even came into being. Similarly, Sarbanes-Oxley imposed a limit of five years over the length of service of an accountant as the engagement partner on an audit; but before Sarbanes-Oxley, the existing rules had already limited the number of years to seven.

In fact, it is ironic that some of the main features of Sarbanes-Oxley affecting auditors have less to do with the auditor than with the audit committee. In particular, one of the dominant features of the auditor provisions is the objective of getting information to flow up from the organization, through the auditor, to the audit committee so that the audit committee can act upon it. Sarbanes-Oxley accordingly requires that the auditor timely report to the audit committee all critical accounting policies and practices that the company is to use. More than that, the auditor is to report all alternative treatments of financial information within GAAP that have been discussed with management, the ramifications of the use of the alternative treatments, and the treatment that the outside auditor would actually prefer. The auditor is also to report to the audit committee all material written communications between the auditor and management, including the auditor's management letter (in which the auditor will typically make suggestions for improvements in internal control over financial reporting) and its schedule of unadjusted differences (those adjustments proposed by the auditor to increase the financial statements' accuracy).

None of this, however, is to give short shrift to what is genuinely a prominent and important feature of Sarbanes-Oxley, and that is its creation of the PCAOB. For the accounting profession, the creation of this new regulator was genuinely momentous. Prior to the PCAOB, the profession had possessed the power largely to regulate itself. Although that self-regulation took place under the ever-watchful eye of the SEC, such fundamental aspects of auditor regulation as promulgation of generally accepted auditing standards (GAAS) had been largely left to the accounting profession.

The Sarbanes-Oxley Act changed all that. In the stead of self-regulation, it created a new five-member board whose responsibilities would include the formulation of public company auditing standards. It also put in place a system of registration by accounting firms, called upon the PCAOB to promulgate rules directed to the accounting profession's retention of audit workpapers, and provided for an inspection process by which the accounting firms themselves would be the subject of regular and thorough PCAOB scrutiny.

Whether this represented a step forward or backward depends on whom you ask; however, before Sarbanes-Oxley the accounting profession itself had been very much on the horns of a dilemma. In a nutshell, that dilemma involved the appropriate level of auditor responsibility for the detection of financial fraud. To some, merely to pose the issue as a dilemma makes no sense, as many would contend that the auditor should simply provide a guarantee against financial fraud and do the work necessary to ensure investors are not at risk. The argument is an interesting one, but it quickly runs into the obstacles of cost, timeliness, and feasibility. Without even considering feasibility, an audit conducted on such a basis would naturally be expected to extend for years and involve costs that are absurdly high. One such "fraud audit" at a public company where accounting problems had surfaced, for example, ended up costing the company more than $20 million per month.

On the other hand, investors understandably seek at least some level of assurance that the auditor has done *something* to search for fraud. Maybe the accounting profession cannot give an absolute guarantee, but investors, and financial markets more generally, expect the profession to have in place some sensible system so that fraud can be brought to the surface.

Before Sarbanes-Oxley, the question for the accounting profession was where to strike the balance. On the issue of auditor detection of financial fraud, there was no empirically correct answer. The issue, rather, was almost entirely one of balancing the benefits and costs. The accounting profession strove to strike that balance through the use of two complementary concepts—professional skepticism and reasonable assurance. Roughly speaking, professional skepticism involved a "trust but verify" approach. Reasonable assurance required the auditor to "plan and perform the audit to obtain reasonable assurance about whether the financial statements are free of material misstatement, whether caused by error or fraud." Through these twin concepts, the accounting profession hoped to get the allocation of resources directed to financial fraud just right.

The congressional judgment seemed to be that the right balance wasn't struck. So, mercifully, the issue of resource allocation is no longer one with which the accounting profession must wrestle on its own. Rather, Congress determined that the era of self-regulation was over. Under Sarbanes-Oxley, it was to be the PCAOB that oversaw the balancing of benefits and costs.

COMPANY COUNSEL

Only one section of Sarbanes-Oxley is specifically directed to the issue of attorney conduct in the representation of public companies, but for lawyers and their clients, the effects may be significant. The provision itself, Section 307, calls upon the SEC to create rules setting forth minimum standards of professional conduct for attorneys who are appearing and practicing before the Commission in public company representations. The concept of appearing and practicing before the Commission includes communicating with the SEC staff, preparing or commenting on SEC filings, or representing public companies in SEC enforcement proceedings. As a practical matter, the Section 307 rules of professional responsibility pretty much apply to any attorney—in-house or outside—assisting the company with regard to its obligations under the securities laws.

The obligations fall into two parts. First, the section seeks to have such attorneys report certain kinds of violations of law to specified executives, such as the chief legal counsel or the CEO. Second, if the corporate executive doesn't respond with appropriate remedial measures, the attorney is to report the evidence of wrongdoing to the audit committee (again the audit committee) or to such similarly composed committee of the board.

It all seems simple enough, and at a conceptual level the statute seems fairly straightforward. However, the devil is in the details. First, exactly what kinds of violations of law must the attorney report? Here is the statutory answer: "evidence of a material violation of securities law or breach of fiduciary duty or similar violation by the company or any agent thereof." Well, some guidance is better than none, but this statutory specification is far from crystal clear. Attorneys argue all the time about what constitutes a violation of securities law. The concept of a breach of fiduciary duty is even more amorphous. Yet both of those are paragons of clarity compared to the third category—"similar violation." Given the risk of an SEC sanction against the attorney for noncompliance, cautious attorneys might feel they have little choice but to err on the side of inclusiveness. One could envision nervous attorneys reporting to the chief legal officer all sorts of potential violations whether the attorney genuinely believed they were subsumed within Section 307 or not.

Once the attorney has made a report of such legal violation, he is then to assess whether the chief legal counsel or CEO responds with appropriate remedial measures. The significance here is that the statutory language serves to place within the reporting attorney virtually complete discretion as to whether corporate executives are responding with remedial measures that are appropriate. What is the attorney to call upon in the exercise of that discretion? The key resource, apparently, is the attorney's own judgment. And that is an exercise of judgment that may be second-guessed by the SEC.

It is certainly true that in many—perhaps most—situations some of these judgment calls should not be too difficult. If, for example, an attorney should stumble upon evidence of executive embezzlement, the appropriate remedial actions, such as discharge and an attempt to gain restitution, may seem straightforward. If, however, an attorney should stumble upon evidence raising the possibility of executive involvement in financial misreporting, the whole thing gets a little more murky. Does the company have to bring in an outside investigative law firm? Does it need to bring in forensic accountants? Should the CEO be placed on a leave of absence until the situation is resolved? The answers are unclear.

If the chief legal officer or CEO does not undertake appropriate remedial measures—whatever they are—then the statutory responsibility of the attorney is to so inform those individuals and make an appropriate report to the audit committee, to another committee of independent directors, or to the entire board. If the audit committee or other committee undertakes what the attorney believes to be an appropriate and timely response, the attorney is done. If the audit or other committee does not undertake what the attorney believes to be an appropriate and timely response, the attorney is to explain why to those to whom the attorney has made his report. There, the statutory obligation ostensibly stops. In other words, there exists no statutory obligation for the attorney to see to it that the audit committee, other committee, or entire board itself then undertakes appropriate remedial measures. Nor is there a requirement that the attorney, upon a board-level failure to undertake appropriate remedial measures, resign and so inform the public through a so-called "noisy withdrawal."

Whether such a noisy withdrawal should have been required pursuant to Sarbanes-Oxley was a matter of prolonged debate. Ultimately, those advocating the attorney's more traditional role of confidential legal adviser to the client carried the day and a noisy-withdrawal provision was not included in the rules. Still, it is far from clear that an audit committee or board failure to undertake an appropriate and timely response can realistically be followed by an attorney returning to his everyday duties as if nothing had happened. It is hard to envision, for example, that an attorney would find evidence of (say) fraudulent financial statements in a 10-K, report it to the appropriate executive, conclude that the executive was not taking appropriate remedial measures, report the entire affair to the audit committee, only then to be completely content as he watches the audit committee do absolutely nothing about it. Even absent a statutory mandate, some degree of attorney encouragement as to further steps—such as corrective disclosure—may seem warranted.

The spectrum of corporate reaction that may fall within the category of appropriate remedial measures, moreover, is exceedingly broad. Under the rules, appropriate remedial measures may include steps or sanctions to stop further violations, corporate governance changes to prevent violations that have yet to occur, corrective action to remedy harm already done, and additional changes "to minimize the likelihood of . . . recurrence." Almost inevitably, such determinations will at one point or another involve assessment of which corporate executives get to stay and which should be fired. In the case of a large accounting restatement, an attorney zealously undertaking to fulfill his statutory obligation could easily find himself involved in an assessment of how to restructure the entire executive ranks.

That may sound a bit far-fetched, but it is not. The best evidence may be found in the experience of the accounting profession, which has had to shoulder comparable responsibilities for years. In particular, "Section 10A" of the Securities Exchange Act of 1934 (added as part of the tort reform legislation of the mid-1990s) placed upon the outside auditor an analogous responsibility to report illegal acts and evaluate whether the company was taking timely and appropriate remedial actions. In fulfilling that responsibility, auditors have found themselves playing an important role in reviewing press releases, calling for public disclosure, making assessments about compensation disgorgement, evaluating the appropriate extent of executive terminations, and participating in any number of management decisions falling under the umbrella of remedial actions that somehow may be appropriate. It is perhaps not entirely surprising that some accounting firm executives, having wrestled endlessly with these highly judgmental managerial responsibilities, find some measure of satisfaction in the fact that they must now be undertaken by company counsel.

Whether it is optimal to place these Section 307 responsibilities on attorneys is a fair subject of debate. But there should be no doubt about one thing. To the extent that Sarbanes-Oxley seeks to transform the attorney from the more traditional role of confidential legal adviser into something akin to a public watchdog, Sarbanes-Oxley may radically alter the legal function. For it is fair to expect executive reluctance to seek from an attorney confidential legal advice when the statutorily mandated reaction may be for the attorney to blow the whistle up the chain of command—and perhaps, owing to practical necessity, to outsiders. This is not necessarily a bad outcome, and it is apparently a step that some felt needed to be taken. Nonetheless, it carries with it the potential to significantly transform the role of legal counsel in advising a public company.

INVESTMENT BANKERS

Sarbanes-Oxley doesn't seem sure what to do about investment bankers. On the one hand, the statute seems to reflect a congressional suspicion that, somehow, it is really a company's investment banker that plays a catalytic role in the engineering of elaborate accounting techniques to camouflage true financial condition. On the other hand, the statute seems to reflect an absence of concrete facts to back it up.

So Sarbanes-Oxley commissions a study. The study is to address whether investment banks assisted public companies in manipulating their earnings, and in particular the role of investment banks in the collapse of particular companies, and generally in "creating and marketing transactions which may have been designed solely to enable companies to manipulate revenue streams, obtain loans, or move liabilities off balance sheets without altering the economic and business risks."

If Congress did not feel it had the evidence to actually impose legislative remedies to address such theoretical investment banking manipulations, Congress apparently felt it was on firmer ground in addressing a discrete aspect of investment banking activity—investment analysis. The congressional concern here was that investment analysts were producing favorable reports to help the bank in attracting new business. Sarbanes-Oxley accordingly calls upon the SEC to establish appropriate safeguards so that "securities analysts are separated by appropriate informational partitions within the firm from the review, pressure, or oversight of those whose involvement in investment banking activities might potentially bias their judgment." Among other things, the rules are to limit the supervision and compensatory evaluation of securities analysts to those who are not engaged in investment banking and to prevent retaliation by investment bankers against analysts as a result of negative research reports. Sarbanes-Oxley also calls for the disclosure of potential analyst conflicts of interest.

 ## DID IT WORK?

More than a decade has passed since Sarbanes-Oxley was enacted. We've had ample time to watch it in action. Many have lauded its benefits. Many have grumbled at the expense. Many have offered mixed reactions.

Did Sarbanes-Oxley help prevent and detect financial fraud? Though it's hard to tell, in the aftermath of Sarbanes-Oxley things certainly seemed to get better. The number of restatements went down. Headline reports of massive financial fraud declined. The number of financial fraud enforcement actions reported by the SEC plummeted.

Whether the ostensible improvement is attributable to Sarbanes-Oxley—or whether Sarbanes-Oxley was just one factor among many increasing attentiveness to financial reporting systems—is still open to debate. A separate question is whether the apparent decline in financial fraud will be long lasting, or for that matter whether any law can hope to achieve long-lasting triumph against fraudulent financial reporting. Sarbanes-Oxley was far from the first in that effort. Concern about financial fraud was a major justification for the federal securities laws in the 1930s. It has since served as a justification for any number of additional antifraud laws and regulations. Still, even with almost a century of innovative laws and regulations directed against financial fraud, the overall results are mixed at best. In a 1998 survey of chief financial officers, 12 percent indicated that they had misrepresented financial results. When, in 2012, an analogous group of chief financial officers was asked to estimate the percentage of public companies that in any given period had misrepresented financial results, the estimate was 20 percent.

CHAPTER FIVE

The Audit Committee

CLEOPATRA: Horrible villain! or I'll spurn thine eyes
Like balls before me; I'll unhair thy head: Thou
shalt be whipp'd with wire, and stew'd in brine,
Smarting in lingering pickle.
MESSENGER: Gracious madam, I that do bring the
news made not the match.
CLEOPATRA: Though it be honest, it is never good to
bring bad news.

—*Antony and Cleopatra*, Act II, Scene v

ONE PHRASE COULD PROBABLY CAPTURE the state of many audit committee members in a post-Sarbanes-Oxley world: *lost in the forest*. Faced with an onslaught of new laws, regulations, risks, and expectations—not to mention legions of corporate-governance experts providing often inconsistent advice—many audit committee members understandably find themselves somewhat uncertain (or completely at sea) as to how far their responsibility goes or how that responsibility is to be fulfilled. Without completely understanding the extent of their responsibility, committee members find themselves getting drawn into the details of Form 10-K disclosure, earnings press releases, auditor communications, "enterprise risk management," and innumerable intricacies of corporate governance—all the while having difficulty finding someone who can articulate with any certainty the precise contours of audit committee oversight or, for that matter, even where to find it written down.

Exacerbating the uncertainty is a mindset among some that has resulted in audit committees almost becoming a dumping ground for corporate responsibilities. Among the varying responsibilities that have been suggested for audit committee oversight, for example, are environmental compliance, improper payments, conflicts of interest, taxes, complex financial instruments, "critical business continuity risks," "potential legal, compliance, and risk management issues that a company may face," and "compliance with laws, regulations, and ethical business practices." For its part, Sarbanes-Oxley plunges headlong into the mechanics of how audit committee responsibilities are to be fulfilled, pausing only a moment (in a definitional section, no less) to explain exactly what that responsibility is. The rules of the New York Stock Exchange lose the forest for the trees completely insofar as they include among audit committee objectives "compliance with legal and regulatory requirements" and "policies with respect to risk assessment and risk management." Exactly what legal and regulatory requirements is the audit committee responsible for? Exactly what risk management is the audit committee taking on? The rules do not tell us.

The dangers in such a lack of precision are many. For one, audit committees can find themselves getting caught up in endless details and thereby contributing little beyond what is already being done by the lawyers, accountants, auditors, and other professionals involved. For another, audit committees can inadvertently expose themselves to a scope of liability that is realistically boundless. For still another, audit committee members can find themselves getting so caught up in minutiae that they lose the big picture and run the risk of putting in place governance mechanisms that are completely pointless. One member of a state-of-the-art audit committee, for example, described with evident pride the elaborateness of its newly formulated corporate governance structure. When asked how that structure would operate to prevent or detect an errant CFO's quarterly adjustment of an accounting reserve to attain overly optimistic street expectations—in other words, prevent or detect one of the most common origins of financial fraud—the audit committee member was at a complete loss. His answer was, "We wouldn't catch that."

It is time to step back and look at the big picture of audit committee responsibility and ask some basic questions. What is the audit committee's responsibility? How should that responsibility be fulfilled? What are the mechanics of audit committee oversight?

Perhaps the best place to start is with the audit committee's responsibility.

THE AUDIT COMMITTEE'S RESPONSIBILITY

If audit committees are to be effective preventers and detectors of financial misreporting, we have to come to grips with exactly what we want the audit committee to do. To paraphrase Sun Tzu in *The Art of War*, the army that is everywhere is nowhere. The main consequence of uncircumscribed and ill-defined responsibilities, accordingly, may be to disburse the audit committee's focus to an extent where the committee members can realistically accomplish nothing. The first step toward installation of an effective audit committee, therefore, is to define for the committee its fundamental responsibility in a comprehensible way.

Here is a fairly crisp articulation: "It is the responsibility of an audit committee to oversee the company's system of financial reporting." That's it. This articulation is substantively identical to the purpose identified by Sarbanes-Oxley, which defines an audit committee as a committee established "for the purpose of overseeing the accounting and financial reporting processes of the issuer and audits of the financial statements of the issuer." In this regard, Sarbanes-Oxley again tracks the findings of the Treadway Commission, which observed that, "Audit committees should be informed, vigilant, and effective overseers of the financial reporting process and the company's internal controls."

Critical to understanding this purpose is recognition that the audit committee's function is merely one of oversight. Its mission is to oversee the system, not to actually run it. Running the system is, and as a practical matter has to be, the responsibility of the CEO, CFO, and those that report to them. The audit committee's responsibility, in contrast, is to oversee the system, do its best to see that it's functioning properly, and actively seek out how things may be going wrong.

CHECKLISTS, CHECKLISTS, CHECKLISTS

Having come to grips with the audit committee's responsibility, we can turn to how that responsibility might be fulfilled. One thing is for sure: An audit committee seeking to oversee a company's system of financial reporting will find no shortage of checklists. Checklists for audit committees have been published by virtually all the national accounting firms. Checklists have been published by the AICPA. Checklists regularly appear in newsletters, articles, and committee recommendations. Checklists are seemingly everywhere.

There is just one problem. If audit committee members were genuinely to undertake all of the tasks listed on the checklists, they would have little time for anything else—such as their day jobs. One representative audit committee checklist enumerates 36 time-consuming tasks.

Checklists are certainly a handy reference tool, but they carry with them dangers even beyond the need of individual audit committee members to hold a full-time job. One is the danger of what might be referred to as a "checklist mentality"—a mindset that dutifully marching through a checklist will necessarily lead to a successful financial reporting system. The audit profession periodically has to remind itself that a checklist mentality simply does not work. There is no reason to think that such an approach would work any better for an audit committee.

Another weakness with excessive fidelity to a checklist is the temptation to give everything equal time. A checklist of 36 separate items contributes little to an understanding of those two or three that are critical as compared to others that may be merely important or not really important at all. The critical, the important, and the unimportant all tend to get equal treatment.

Still another problem with a focus on checklists stems from their unhelpfulness in establishing the correct allocation of responsibility between the oversight function of the audit committee and the hands-on responsibilities of those whom the audit committee is to oversee—such as the internal audit department and the outside auditor. For example, one checklist establishes as a supposed duty of the audit committee to "review filings with the SEC and other published documents containing the company's financial statements and consider whether the information contained in these documents is consistent with the information contained in the financial statements." Can we realistically expect an audit committee to do that?

AN APPROACH TO AUDIT COMMITTEE OVERSIGHT

Let us consider a slightly different approach. It starts with the premise that an audit committee, in seeking to oversee a system directed to the prevention and detection of fraudulent financial reporting, should at the outset establish no more than a handful of key objectives. The audit committee should then—through the use of company employees and outside professionals—put in place a system to fulfill those objectives. The audit committee should then—again through the use of company employees and outside professionals—monitor the financial reporting system so that the fulfillment of the key objectives is maintained.

A good set of key objectives with which to start might be the following:

- Seek to establish the proper tone at the top
- Be satisfied as to the logistical capabilities of the financial reporting system
- Put in place a system for the detection of financial misreporting

Let's briefly examine each.

THE TONE AT THE TOP

If the audit committee is to accomplish nothing else, it should foremost strive to establish the right tone at the top. If the appropriate tone at the top is established and communicated, every division, department, and individual within the organization will be pulling in the same direction. Without the appropriate tone at the top, you haven't got a chance.

What is the appropriate tone at the top? It involves an unrelenting insistence upon objectivity in financial reporting. It involves an unrelenting insistence that numbers are not to be influenced by operational objectives. It involves an unrelenting insistence upon truthfulness as the foremost goal of the financial reporting system. It is a tone that makes financial misreporting unthinkable.

How does such a tone get established? The obvious place to start is with management. Senior executives must be vividly aware of the unacceptability of massaged financial results. This is a battle for a certain type of corporate culture, and therefore both big and small things mean a lot. Among the big things, the audit committee chairman will want to emphasize unequivocally and often the dual predicates of objectivity and transparency as the bases for financial reporting. It is a message that has to be explicitly or implicitly omnipresent in every matter to be addressed.

It is also a message that must be reinforced, and that takes us to small things. Remember that financial misreporting starts out small and in those hazy areas where individuals think they are still being honest. Accordingly, when dealing with senior management, audit committee members are best attentive to any indication of a desire to improperly influence reported results in order to attain performance objectives. Unrelenting vigilance is the goal. Any senior executive who slips into one of the telltale signs of managed earnings—contrived revenue enhancement, unjustified modification of reserves, even obsessive fidelity to the attainment of quarterly analyst expectations—must be corrected swiftly and unequivocally. Battles for corporate culture can be the toughest battles to win.

That effort does not, however, stop with the senior executives. The audit committee will also want a vehicle for communicating that message down the ranks through the lower levels. For example, those within the sales department should be given to understand that contrived methods to increase reported sales—side letters, quarter-end telephone calls to friendly customers, last-minute discounting that is not revealed to the accounting department—will not be tolerated. Analogous contrivances, such as a failure to close the quarter-end books, are to be viewed as forbidden. At all levels, both egregious and subtle manipulations of the numbers are to be perceived as unacceptable.

One obvious vehicle of communication is a written code of conduct or mission statement, but let us candidly admit that such a written document can be almost useless at best and counterproductive at worst. It can be almost useless because a written document doesn't stand a chance against a corporate culture that goes the other way. It can be counterproductive when the chasm between the written document and the corporate culture becomes so wide that it suggests that the document's authors are somewhere between out-of-touch and evil. True, such written statements of ethics are now required by the various rules and those rules must be complied with. It is a mistake, though, to believe that such a written ethics statement by itself will do much good.

How does one get the word out? There really is little choice but to rely on the senior executives. They have the day-to-day contact with the lower levels, and they have to be the ones to see that an appropriate tone is communicated and reinforced. That objective, therefore, should be plainly understood. Where infractions occur—and they will—the audit committee should satisfy itself that the response was swift and unequivocal.

Key to maintaining the tone at the top will be sensitivity to pressure. Again, financial misreporting doesn't start with dishonesty—it starts with pressure. The audit committee, therefore, should try to be sensitive to the enormous pressures to which senior executives may be subject. Where necessary, the audit committee should be prepared to act as a counterbalance to that pressure and support senior management in the face of outsiders who would place numerical performance objectives above everything else. That does not mean that management's numerical performance does not matter. It means that the only numerical performance that matters is numerical performance that objectively captures the truth.

More than that, the audit committee will want to be on its guard to keep the board of directors from inadvertently adding to the pressure. The audit committee should keep in mind that compensation systems may inadvertently create undue pressure for ostensibly splendid but substanceless performance. The audit committee should stay on guard for indications of overly aggressive budgets and sales targets. The board will get what it measures, so it has to make sure it measures what it wants. If the board measures only reported earnings, it will get reported earnings. But it may get them at the expense of truth.

LOGISTICAL CAPABILITY

Desire is one thing, attainment another. Establishment of an appropriate tone at the top does not by itself ensure reliability in financial reporting—though it is probably 80 percent of the battle. The next step is to strive for a financial reporting system that is logistically capable of doing what everybody in the company now wants.

This is not a battle for corporate culture but a battle for staffing and computer systems and is therefore infinitely easier to deal with. The obvious starting place is to look into whether the accounting department is adequately staffed and supervised. Inquiry should be made as to the adequacy of management information systems. In this area, useful information should not be too difficult to get. If staffing or systems are not adequate, the CFO would probably be pleased to have the opportunity to let the audit committee know.

A system that is adequate in one month, though, may not be adequate in the next. That is particularly so where the corporate enterprise is changing—for example, if it is growing through acquisition. The audit committee of a company that is in transformation, particularly where it is growing through the acquisition of others, should therefore remain sensitive to the effects of change on accounting capabilities and personnel. Frequently, the accounting systems of acquired companies will not be compatible with the accounting system of the acquirer, but the problem will be put off owing to the press of events as the next acquisition candidate appears. A conglomerate of newly acquired accounting systems that together function as a Tower of Babel is a recipe for disaster—without even getting to the corporate cultures of the new personnel who have been acquired in the process. Asking about the accounting systems of acquired companies should not be too far down on the audit committee's to-do list.

IMMEDIATE DETECTION OF FINANCIAL MISREPORTING

It is a mistake to think that things will always work the way they should. That doesn't mean the audit committee isn't doing its job. It just means that no financial reporting system will ever be completely free from defects. Therefore, it is not enough to establish an appropriate tone at the top and to ensure logistical support consistent with that tone. The audit committee has to assume that, from time to time, things will go wrong. It has to assume that, from time to time, the organization will slip into some level of financial misreporting.

The key is to find out quickly when it happens. The audit committee therefore needs a system that will enable it to be the first, rather than the last, to know (more about that shortly).

A PROPERLY CONFIGURED AUDIT COMMITTEE

The attainment of these corporate governance and financial reporting objectives will present significant challenges. If an audit committee is to have any hope of surmounting these challenges, it must have the underlying capability of doing so. The audit committee itself must be properly configured. Indeed, proper configuration of the audit committee is not simply a matter of sound corporate governance. It is also a matter of law.

It was not always so. Not too long ago, the configuration of a company's audit committee was left largely to the discretion of the particular company's board of directors. Thus, the SEC, while becoming increasingly interested in the effectiveness of audit committees, for years declined to enact detailed rules on the matter, deferring almost entirely to the rules of the exchange where the company's stock happened to be listed. The New York Stock Exchange, for its part, specified that companies were to establish and maintain audit committees comprised solely of independent directors but specified little else. The National Association of Securities Dealers (NASD), while requiring companies to "establish and maintain" an audit committee, did not go as far as the NYSE in requiring all members to be independent: Independence was required by only a majority of the audit committee members. The rules of the NASD went on to provide that the audit committee in substance should discuss aspects of the annual audit with the outside auditor.

In December 1999, the SEC approved a new series of rules that were substantially more rigorous. Pursuant to the recommendations of the Blue Ribbon Committee on Improving the Effectiveness of Corporate Audit Committees, the new rules established enhanced requirements for audit committee membership, independence, sophistication, diligence, and disclosure. For companies whose securities were listed on the NYSE or quoted on Nasdaq, the new rules, which were phased in over a period of 18 months following their approval, required the following. First, an audit committee was to include at least three members (see Exhibits 5.1 and 5.2). Second, with very limited exception, each member of the committee was to be independent (see Exhibits 5.3 and 5.4). Third, each member was to possess (at the time he joined the audit committee or within a reasonable time thereafter) some degree of financial literacy, with at least one member having an accounting or finance background (see Exhibits 5.1 and 5.2). Fourth, the audit committee was to have in place a written charter (see Exhibits 5.5 and 5.6). Fifth, the audit committee was to file with the SEC a written report that specified, among other things, whether the committee recommended to the board of directors that the audited financial statements be filed with the SEC (see Exhibit 5.7).

In some respects the rules are highly detailed and precise. For example, the "independence" requirements of Nasdaq specify that the independence prerequisite is not met by a director who was an employee of the corporation or any subsidiary for the current year or any of the past three years; by a director who accepts compensation in excess of $120,000 from the corporation or any of its subsidiaries during the previous fiscal year (other than compensation for board service, benefits under a tax-qualified retirement plan, or nondiscretionary compensation); by a director who is an immediate family member of an individual who is, or has been in any of the past three years, an executive officer of

EXHIBIT 5.1 NYSE Rules: Audit Committee Composition

- Each audit committee shall consist of at least three directors, all of whom have no relationship to the company that may interfere with the exercise of their independence from management and the company;
- Each member of the audit committee shall be financially literate, or must become financially literate within a reasonable period of time after his or her appointment to the audit committee; and
- At least one member of the audit committee must have accounting or related financial management expertise.

EXHIBIT 5.2 Nasdaq Rules: Audit Committee Composition

Each issuer must have and certify that:

- It has and will continue to have an audit committee of at least three members, composed solely of independent directors, each of whom is able to read and understand fundamental financial statements, and each of whom has not participated in the preparation of the company's (or any of its subsidiaries') financial statements during the past three years; and
- It has and will continue to have at least one member of the audit committee who has past employment experience in finance or accounting, requisite professional certification in accounting, or any other comparable experience or background that results in the individual's financial sophistication.

One director who is not independent and is not a current officer or employee or an immediate family member of such officer or employee may be appointed to the audit committee, if:

- The board, under exceptional and limited circumstances, determines that membership on the committee by the individual is required by the best interests of the corporation and its shareholders; and
- The board discloses, in the next annual proxy statement subsequent to such determination, the nature of the relationship and the reasons for that determination.

the corporation or any of its subsidiaries; by a director who is a partner, controlling shareholder, or executive officer of any organization that received certain types of fees or other payments from the company in excess of a specified level; or by a director who is employed as an executive of another entity where any of the company's executives serve on that entity's compensation committee (see Exhibit 5.4). The NYSE has its own set of comparably detailed independence requirements (see Exhibit 5.3).

Viewed more broadly, the rules collectively strive for three overall objectives that are fundamental to audit committee effectiveness:

1. Independence
2. Financial sophistication
3. Willingness to work

Each is a worthy objective and warrants some discussion.

 ## INDEPENDENCE

Foremost, an audit committee should be independent from the senior executives of the company. The reason is straightforward: It is a fundamental function of the audit committee to lean against the wind. It is, in other words, a fundamental function of the audit committee to offer reasoned resistance against the desires of management where those desires may compromise integrity in financial reporting.

The task is not for the fainthearted. During difficult times, management itself may be under horrific pressure for bottom-line results. Absent some degree of independence, a natural inclination to sympathize with those in the hot-seat might prove almost irresistible. During particularly difficult times, resistance to management's ostensible needs may be perceived as the betrayal of prior favors bestowed. At a minimum, resistance could make board meetings exceedingly awkward.

What is meant by independence? As mentioned earlier, the rules are highly detailed and complex (see Exhibits 5.3 and 5.4). The underlying concept involves the exclusion of individuals who, for whatever reason, are not in a position to stand up to the tenacious desires of determined management. Excluded from among those possessing independence, therefore, are family members of executives—it probably being no small coincidence that, where financial

---

EXHIBIT 5.3   NYSE Rules: Audit Committee Independence

A director is not independent for purpose of serving on an audit committee if:

- The director is, or has been within the last three years, an employee of the company, or an immediate family member is, or has been within the last three years, an executive officer of the company;
- The director has received (or has an immediate family member who has received), during any twelve-month period within the last three years, more than $120,000 in direct compensation from the company;
- The director (or an immediate family member) is a current partner of the company's internal or outside auditor; the director is a current employee of such firm; the director has an immediate family member who is a current employee of such firm and personally works on that firm's audit; or the director (or an immediate family member) was within the last three years a partner or employee of such a firm and worked on the company's audit within that time;
- The director (or an immediate family member) is, or has been within the last three years, employed as an executive officer of another corporation where any of the company's present executive officers at the same time serves or served on that corporation's compensation committee;
- The director is a current employee (or an immediate family member is a current executive officer) of another company that has made payments to, or received payments from, the company for property or services in an amount which, in any of the last three fiscal years, exceeds the greater of $1 million or 2% of such other company's consolidated gross revenues.

EXHIBIT 5.4 Nasdaq Rules: Audit Committee Independence

"Independent director" means a person other than an officer or employee of the company or its subsidiaries or any other individual having a relationship which, in the opinion of the company's board of directors, would interfere with the exercise of independent judgment in carrying out the responsibilities of a director.

The following persons shall not be considered independent:

- A director who is an employee of the corporation or any of its subsidiaries for the current year or any of the past three years;
- A director who accepted (or has a family member who accepted) any payments in excess of $120,000 from the corporation or any of its subsidiaries during the current fiscal year or any of the past three fiscal years, other than compensation for board service, payments arising solely from investments in the company's securities, compensation to a family member who is a nonexecutive employee of the company, benefits under a tax-qualified retirement plan, nondiscretionary compensation, or certain permitted loans;
- A director who is a family member of an individual who is, or has been in any of the past three years, an executive officer of the corporation or any of its subsidiaries;
- A director who is (or has a family member who is) a partner in or a controlling shareholder or an executive officer of any organization to which the corporation made, or from which the corporation received, payments that exceed 5% of the corporation's or business organization's consolidated gross revenues for that year, or $200,000, whichever is more, in any of the past three years;
- A director who is (or has a family member who is) employed as an executive officer of another entity where, at any time during that past three years, any of the company's executive officers serves on that entity's compensation committee; and
- A director who is (or has a family member who is) a current partner of the company's outside auditor, or was a partner or employee of the company's outside auditor who worked on the company's audit at any time during the past three years.

fraud has surfaced, family relationships on the board of directors have been by no means rare. Also excluded from among those possessing independence are outside professionals whose judgment may be influenced because of business relationships with the company. Also excluded are directors whose compensation at another company may be determined by executives the director is theoretically overseeing. Audit committee members should be prepared to tell management what it doesn't want to hear. Relationships that may compromise the committee's willingness to do so may impair its effectiveness.

How many members should be independent? This has been a controversial issue. The rules of both the NYSE and Nasdaq generally require that all audit committee members be independent. However, in implicit recognition that sometimes a nonindependent director is in the position to offer unique benefits to an audit committee, Nasdaq includes an exception permitting a nonindependent director under specified circumstances. The rules make clear, however, that the inclusion of nonindependent directors is allowed only under "exceptional and limited circumstances." Under the Nasdaq rule, proxy statement disclosure of the nonindependent director's participation is required.

To all of this, Sarbanes-Oxley added its own independence requirements. Like the rules of the NYSE and Nasdaq, they require that each audit committee member be independent. As to what "independence" means, Sarbanes-Oxley imposes two criteria. First, an audit committee member may not "accept any consulting, advisory, or other compensatory fee from the issuer." Second, the audit committee member may not be "an affiliated person of the issuer or any subsidiary thereof." Additional rules define "affiliate" to include those audit committee members who control, or are controlled by, the company. Similar to the Nasdaq rules, Sarbanes-Oxley contemplates the possibility of a nonindependent audit committee member to the extent the SEC exempts from the independence requirements a particular type of relationship.

As a general matter, therefore, public companies will want audit committees composed solely of independent directors. Perhaps the input of a management representative can then be obtained by including the representative in some audit committee meetings even without formal membership.

FINANCIAL SOPHISTICATION

Even audit committee members whose hearts are in the right place need to know what they are doing. Therefore, a second fundamental prerequisite of audit committee membership is financial sophistication.

What kind of sophistication is meant? Here, the rules are particularly vague. The commentary to the NYSE rules specifies only that "each member of the audit committee must be financially literate, as such qualification is interpreted by the listed company's board in its business judgment." The Nasdaq rules are only slightly more informative. They specify that each of the audit committee members must be "able to read and understand fundamental financial statements, including a company's balance sheet, income statement, and cash flow statement." (See Exhibits 5.1 and 5.2.)

Experience suggests that audit committee members should possess financial sophistication in two areas. First, audit committee members should possess some working familiarity with the rudiments of GAAP and financial reporting. That's not to say that each member must be a CPA, though at least one CPA is probably a good idea. Rather, the members should possess a basic understanding of such things as the accrual system of accounting, the extent to which (for example) operating cash flow may diverge from reported earnings, and the rudiments of SEC reporting requirements. To say it another way, the members should probably know enough to appreciate that reported earnings does not always mean cash in the bank.

But financial literacy is only the first type of financial sophistication. The second is that members should possess an understanding of corporate governance systems and in particular the extent to which nonoptimal systems can compromise truthfulness in financial reporting. One of the key functions of the audit committee members will be to keep a sharp lookout for the telltale signs of corruption. The individual members will want to know enough to recognize them when they appear.

 ## WILLINGNESS TO WORK

Audit committee members should not be expected to quit their day jobs, but they have to be willing to work. Obviously, they can leverage their talents through the use of employees and outside professionals, but audit committee membership can require significant effort and commitment. The willingness to make the effort has got to be there.

The rules encourage audit committee willingness to make the effort in several ways, one of which is through the requirement of an audit committee "charter" (see Exhibits 5.5 and 5.6). The charter, which must be in writing, is to broadly outline the audit committee's responsibility for oversight of financial reporting. (For a sample, see Exhibit 5.12 at the end of this chapter.) Thus, the Nasdaq rules provide that a company's charter must specify the

EXHIBIT 5.5 NYSE Rules: Audit Committee Charter

Each audit committee must adopt a written charter. The charter must specify the following:

- ▪ The audit committee's purpose
- ▪ An annual performance evaluation of the audit committee
- ▪ The duties and responsibilities of the audit committee (including particular items specified by the rules)

EXHIBIT 5.6 Nasdaq Rules: Audit Committee Charter

Each Issuer must certify that it has adopted a formal written audit committee charter. Each Issuer must certify that the audit committee has reviewed and reassessed the adequacy of the formal written charter on an annual basis.

The charter must specify the following:

- The scope of the audit committee's responsibilities, and how it carries out those responsibilities
- The audit committee's responsibility for ensuring its receipt from the outside auditor of a formal written statement delineating all relationships between the auditor and the company
- The company and the audit committee's responsibility for actively engaging in a dialogue with the auditor with respect to any disclosed relationships or services that may affect the objectivity and independence of the auditor and for taking, or recommending that the full board take, appropriate action to ensure the independence of the outside auditor
- The audit committee's purpose of overseeing the accounting and financial reporting processes of the company and the audits of the financial statements of the company
- The audit committee's responsibilities and authority relating to the outside auditor, complaints relating to accounting, internal accounting controls or auditing matters, authority to engage advisers, and funding

scope of the audit committee's responsibilities and how those responsibilities are carried out; the outside auditor's ultimate accountability to the audit committee and the board of directors; the audit committee's purpose of overseeing the accounting and financial reporting processes of the company and the audits of the financial statements of the company; the audit committee's responsibility for ensuring the auditor's submission of a formal written statement delineating all relationships between the auditor and the company; and the audit committee's responsibility for engaging in a dialogue with the auditor as to any relationships that may adversely affect independence. In the wake of Enron and Sarbanes-Oxley, the NYSE decided to take a more detailed approach to the audit committee charter. An NYSE charter, accordingly, is to address the audit committee's purpose, which at a minimum must be to assist board oversight of the integrity of the company's financial statements, the company's compliance with legal and regulatory requirements, the outside auditor's qualifications and independence, and the company's internal audit and outside auditor functions. The charter is also to address the audit committee's preparation of an audit committee report for the company's proxy statement and an annual performance evaluation of the committee.

The charter is also now to include among the audit committee's duties and responsibilities the following:

- At least annually, obtain and review a report by the independent auditor describing:
  - The firm's internal quality-control procedures
  - Any material issues raised by the most recent internal quality-control review, or peer review, of the firm, or by any inquiry or investigation by governmental or professional authorities, within the preceding five years, respecting one or more independent audits carried out by the firm, and any steps taken to deal with any such issues
  - All relationships between the independent auditor and the listed company (to assess the auditor's independence);
- Meet to review and discuss the listed company's annual audited financial statements and quarterly financial statements with management and the independent auditor, including reviewing the company's specific disclosures under "Management's Discussion and Analysis of Financial Condition and Results of Operations";
- Discuss the listed company's earnings press releases as well as financial information and earnings guidance provided to analysts and rating agencies;
- Discuss policies with respect to risk assessment and risk management;
- Meet separately and periodically with management, with internal auditors (or other personnel responsible for the internal audit function), and with independent auditors;
- Review with the independent auditor any audit problems or difficulties and management's response;
- Set clear hiring policies for employees or former employees of the independent auditors; and
- Report regularly to the board of directors.

It's enough to make one long for a checklist.

Beyond the charter, the other main vehicle to encourage audit committee diligence is a written report to be filed once a year as part of the company's proxy statement (see Exhibit 5.7). No specific format for the report is mandated; however, the rules are clear that the substance of the report must include several things. First, the report is to state whether the audit committee has reviewed and discussed the audited financial statements with management. Second, the report is to state whether the audit committee has discussed with the outside auditor certain matters regarding the company's financial reporting. Third, the report is to state whether the audit committee has addressed with the outside auditor the issue of independence in accordance with the applicable rules. Fourth, the report is to state whether the audit committee recommended to the board that the audited financial statements be included in the company's Form 10-K as filed with the SEC. Apparently for the *in terrorem* effect, the rules provide that the names of the individual audit committee members are to appear below the required disclosures. To the extent that these requirements operate to enhance audit committee diligence, they are thus consistent with the common law, which, according to one articulation, requires a board of directors to seek in good faith an adequate corporate information and reporting system (see Exhibit 5.8).

Compliance with all of these requirements is going to take time, and a final note on the issue of audit committee diligence is that audit committee members should be adequately compensated for their efforts. No legitimate question exists that, at whatever the appropriate level of compensation, the company will be getting a bargain. The company's best protection against corruption of its financial reporting system is an optimally functioning audit committee. The benefits will overwhelm the costs.

Ironically, though, the board of directors should probably be on its guard against paying the audit committee members too much. At some level of compensation, audit committee membership would theoretically become an attractive perk to be held onto—thereby giving rise to a potential loss of independence.

EXHIBIT 5.7 SEC Rules to Implement the Recommendations of the Blue Ribbon Committee

---

- Require that companies' independent auditors review the financial information included in the companies' Form 10-Q prior to filing
- Require that companies include reports of their audit committees in their proxy statements, stating whether the audit committee has:
  - Reviewed and discussed the audited financial statements with management
  - Discussed certain matters regarding the company's financial reporting
  - Received certain disclosures from the auditor regarding the auditor's independence
- Require that the report of the audit committee include a statement by the audit committee whether the audit committee recommended to the board of directors that the audited financial statements be included in the company's Form 10-K
- Require that companies disclose in their proxy statements whether their audit committee has adopted a written charter and include a copy of the charter either on the company's website or as an appendix to the proxy statement at least once every three years
- Require that companies disclose in their proxy statements information regarding the independence of audit committee members

EXHIBIT 5.8   Delaware Law

A board of directors' duty of care "includes a duty to attempt in good faith to assure that a corporate information and reporting system, which the board concludes is adequate, exists."

The information and reporting system should "in concept and design [be] adequate to assure the board that appropriate information will come to its attention in a timely manner as a matter of ordinary operations."

(In re Caremark International Inc., 698 A.2d 959, 970 (Del. Ch. 1996))

As in most compensation decisions, there exists a need to balance benefits and costs. In that balance, though, the actual expenditure out of the corporate coffers should not be an issue. An effective audit committee is worth it.

THE BIGGEST CHALLENGE: INFORMATION

Let's say that, so far, a board of directors has done everything right. Its audit committee is independent. Its audit committee is financially sophisticated. Its audit committee is ready to work, with a perfectly drafted charter firmly in place.

Such an audit committee is now perfectly positioned—to fail. That is, it is perfectly positioned to fail unless it can successfully overcome the biggest challenge. That challenge is lack of access to reliable information.

The reason may be simply stated. In a normal corporate enterprise, bad news tends not to flow up. Ever since Cleopatra struck her hapless messenger, the self-preservation instincts of even loyal subordinates have cautioned them to selectively keep bad news to themselves. The consequences of reporting bad news can be harsh and the rewards are few. Rarely does one receive stock options for reporting disaster.

The danger of the resulting "Cleopatra syndrome" is potentially the biggest hurdle an audit committee will face. At root, the problem is that the audit committee will remain in perilous danger of functioning in total ignorance. Financial reporting problems will be allowed to fester as executives seek to correct them before the audit committee is in a position to notice. Executives will not appreciate the extent to which, for the reasons described in Chapter 1, temporary bandages may only operate to make the problem worse. Gradually, the problem will grow. And the audit committee will not have a clue.

What makes this breakdown in the information flow to the audit committee ironic is that a normal corporation, no matter how infirm its systems, will ordinarily have any number of well-meaning employees who would be grateful for the chance to describe system corruption if given a nonthreatening opportunity. An anecdote provides an apt illustration. In the late 1990s, an audit committee stumbled upon evidence of deliberate financial misreporting and immediately fired the CEO and CFO. Upon undertaking a comprehensive investigation, the audit committee found to its horror that any number of employees in the accounting department had become involved. The committee's outside counsel, directed to interview them all, started with a junior person from the accounting department, but at the outset of the interview the junior accountant, after giving her name, started to sob. The interviewing lawyer, not quite sure what to do, said quietly, "I know this has been hard for you." The junior accountant looked up, managed a wry smile, and said, "No, it's not that. It's that I'm so relieved that I can finally tell somebody about this."

The point is this. People within a company want to be honest. They want to do the right thing. They bitterly resent it when they are placed under pressure to do things that are wrong. And, placed under pressure to contribute to system corruption, they will desperately want to alert those who can be trusted.

The challenge for the audit committee is to find a way to get access to that information—to tap into the company's reservoir of candid information and install some kind of pipeline so that information as to system corruption can flow upward unimpeded. When one cuts through all of the laws, rules, and blather, that is the essence of audit committee oversight.

The challenge is getting that information. There are three principal sources: senior management, the outside auditor, and internal audit.

GETTING INFORMATION FROM SENIOR MANAGEMENT

Unfortunately, a viable financial reporting system should probably assume that reliable information about system inadequacies will not be made available to the audit committee by senior management on a regular basis. That is not to denigrate the virtue of senior executives or to suggest widespread managerial inadequacy. It is simply a recognition of human nature. Each of us has an understandable reluctance to be completely candid about our own innumerable flaws.

Many senior executives would be able to rise above that. Senior executives secure in their own abilities and possessed of supreme confidence may be perfectly comfortable undertaking the laudable task of reporting to the audit committee the problems that are growing on their watch. A system that assumes such laudable candor in senior executives, though, is probably assuming too much. It is better to accept that, while striving for virtue, not everyone will achieve it.

Moreover, even secure and candid senior executives may suffer from the same problem that would plague a normal audit committee: No guarantee exists that bad news will flow up to them. A well-meaning senior executive, therefore, may be perfectly willing to share with the audit committee system inadequacies to the extent he is familiar with them. The problem may be that he doesn't fully know what they are.

The potential for managerial unfamiliarity with organizational problems is particularly acute when it comes to one of the most important aspects of the financial reporting system: the environment in which that system is to function. Management is faced with the excruciatingly difficult challenge of placing on subordinates precisely the right amount of pressure for performance: not enough, and the organization does not achieve maximum profitability; too much, and the organization is at risk that nonobjective numbers will slip into the reporting system. Procurement of reliable information identifying the point at which the pressure has moved from optimal to counterproductive can be difficult. Too numerous to mention are instances in which the underlying cause of financial misreporting was the pressure placed on subordinates by a CEO who would later claim total ignorance about the destructive impact his performance edicts were having.

None of this is to suggest that the audit committee should not be striving to increase senior management's candor. Nothing is ever perfect, and senior executives should be encouraged and admonished to reach into the depths of the organization and to find and report system inadequacies. Still, an audit committee has to accept that even the strongest encouragement or even the sternest admonitions will not completely overcome human nature.

GETTING INFORMATION FROM THE OUTSIDE AUDITOR

No financial reporting system relies exclusively on senior management. Meaningful, substantive interaction with the outside auditor is fundamental to effective audit committee oversight of financial reporting. If the auditor is genuinely independent and prepared to be candid, the auditor can be one of the most important vehicles for the audit committee to learn what's going on beneath the surface of reported results. Hence the emphasis on the need for the audit committee to ask the auditor tough, probing questions that delve into the cross-currents of the financial reporting system. Through the outside auditor, the audit committee can learn all sorts of things that it might never get from management.

The audit committee, moreover, should take advantage of this source of information more than once a year. Indeed, under the rules public companies are required to have their quarterly financial statements subject to outside auditor review. In conducting such a quarterly review, the auditor may inquire as to unusual or complex situations that may affect the financial statements, significant transactions during the last several days of the quarter, the status of uncorrected misstatements, significant journal entries, regulatory communications, and suspicions or allegations of fraud. A quarterly review is far less robust than a full-fledged audit. But it can still give the auditor new insight into the company's financial reporting system.

The need for the outside auditor to conduct interim reviews thus gives the audit committee the opportunity to inquire into financial reporting issues that arose during the quarterly review process, and there is every reason for the audit committee to take advantage of that opportunity. Accounting manipulations at quarter-end is frequently where financial fraud gets its start. Meaningful auditor involvement in quarterly information gives the audit committee not only access to improved information but more of an opportunity to nip financial misreporting in the bud.

Of course, there is no losing sight of significant impediments to reliance upon the outside auditor for the prevention and early detection of deliberate financial misreporting. As discussed in Chapter 1, accounting irregularities typically start out small and well beneath the radar screen of the materiality thresholds of a typical audit. They start with a particular type of corporate environment, and it is a type of environment to which a normal once-a-year auditor cannot gain ready access. They start in hazy areas of financial reporting in which much depends on the judgment of management. And, as the accounting irregularities grow over time, a preoccupation of the participants becomes the deliberate deception of the outside auditor.

Further impeding the auditor's access to information is the fundamental reality that, no matter how hard an auditor tries, determined executives will always be able to get away with some level of deception. However deep the auditor is encouraged to probe, those within the accounting department can always take the fraud one level deeper. If the business community were to find such a situation unacceptable, it could encourage the audit profession to abandon the audit sampling and professional skepticism approaches that constitute the hallmarks of a modern audit. In other words, a new system of audits could be installed along the lines of a forensic investigation in which the auditors essentially do not believe anything anybody at the company says. This is basically the approach taken where accounting irregularities have surfaced. In fact, variations of this kind of approach in the context of everyday audits are being experimented with by leaders of the accounting profession. One problem with a forensic approach, though, is timeliness—an "audit" conducted entirely along such lines would almost have to be perpetual. Another problem is cost: For a sizeable public company, the audit fee would necessarily skyrocket.

In seeking reliable information from the outside auditor, some of these impediments an audit committee can do something about, and some it cannot. Ultimately, one thing will be true. The auditor, as an outside professional, will be responsive to the desires of its client.

The key to an effective audit function is to use the auditor's understandable inclination to accommodate the desires of its client to enhance, rather than to impede, the outside audit function. In other words, it should be made clear to the auditor that thoroughness, candor, zeal, and integrity are the criteria by which performance will be measured—not the minimal requirements of audit standards and the dutiful issuance of an audit report. The crux of the audit relationship should evolve into one in which the auditor becomes an integral, albeit independent, part of the system pursuant to which the audit committee gains access to useful systems information. If the audit committee makes clear to the outside auditor its desire for an enhanced audit function and improved systems information, good auditors will find a way to provide the desired level of service. That is particularly so if the audit committee is willing to pay for it.

An underlying premise of such a relationship is that it should be the audit committee, and not senior executives, that selects and engages the auditor and determines the audit fee. For the same reasons that human nature impedes senior management's desire to convey bad news about itself, human nature similarly impedes management's desire for an auditor that will expose its own inadequacies. That is not to fault management or, for that matter, human nature. It is simply to acknowledge the way it is.

As the audit committee strives for a more complete and interconnected relationship with its outside auditor, the committee should probably keep in mind the extent to which an expansion of the auditor's role can work against the auditor's culture and traditions, which have been inclined in the direction of standardized and numerically focused reports. The level of responsiveness to an expanded audit role will likely vary not only among CPA firms but among individual practitioners within firms. Ultimately, though, auditors should come to recognize the extent to which broader auditor involvement in financial reporting information and systems will operate to the audit profession's distinct advantage. Foremost, it will reduce if not eliminate the extent to which the audit is perceived as a mere commodity and give opportunity to individual practitioners to demonstrate the uniqueness of their own professional excellence.

What kinds of information should the audit committee ask the outside auditor for? Here are some possibilities.

Environmental Information

Foremost, the audit committee will want to encourage the outside auditor to candidly report observations about the financial reporting environment. Are people under too much pressure? Are they reluctant to report bad news? Is there a danger they are camouflaging results? These types of questions are fundamental to the prevention and early detection of financial fraud.

A key aspect of that environment is whether financial reporting determinations and judgments are being made with objectivity. The goal here recognizes that judgments under generally accepted accounting principles (GAAP) best aim for "the middle of the fairway." To say it another way, they should not be influenced by operational or other business objectives such as meeting quarterly expectations or keeping the stock price up. A useful subject to question, therefore, is the extent to which such operational or business factors run the risk of influencing financial reporting.

The importance of this topic is underscored by the insidiousness of the means by which objectivity can be compromised. Consider, for example, the experience of a public company CEO. Each quarter, he admonished his accounting staff to inspect the books and records and search for needed corrections—particularly if the company was falling short of analyst expectations. But he was crystal clear: Only honest corrections were to be made. Still, the accounting staff was very much aware that the CEO's objective was to increase earnings.

The CEO would later explain to investigators (yes, things got out of hand) that he thought it was entirely proper to encourage the accounting staff to search for corrections. But he failed to appreciate one thing. The accounting staff was not looking for corrections that went both ways. And they could be expected to place potential adjustments into one of three buckets. One bucket would be those adjustments forbidden by GAAP. Those would not be made. The second bucket would be those adjustments plainly required by GAAP. Those would be made. The third bucket would be judgment calls that could go either way. Those would be thought about. And as the staff grew weary and the deadline approached, adjustments in the third bucket would look increasingly tempting. The reporting system had placed at risk its objectivity.

Logistical Capabilities of the Financial Reporting System

Another issue to explore with the outside auditor will be the logistical capabilities of the financial reporting system. Both the law (see Exhibits 5.9 and 5.10) and good business sense require the company to maintain its books and records in such a way that they fairly reflect corporate transactions and events. Staffing, sophistication, computerization, software inadequacies—all aspects of the system's logistical capabilities may accordingly warrant inquiry.

EXHIBIT 5.9 Foreign Corrupt Practices Act

"Every issuer which has a class of securities registered pursuant to section 78l of [the Securities Exchange Act of 1934] shall:

(A) make and keep books, records, and accounts, which, in reasonable detail, accurately and fairly reflect the transactions and dispositions of the assets of the issuer; [and]

(B) devise and maintain a system of internal accounting controls sufficient to provide reasonable assurances that:

  (i) transactions are executed in accordance with management's general or specific authorization;

  (ii) transactions are recorded as necessary (I) to permit preparation of financial statements in conformity with generally accepted accounting principles or any other criteria applicable to such statements, and (II) to maintain accountability for assets;

  (iii) access to assets is permitted only in accordance with management's general or specific authorization; and

  (iv) the recorded accountability for assets is compared with the existing assets at reasonable intervals and appropriate action is taken with respect to any differences."

(15 U.S.C. § 78m(b)(2))

EXHIBIT 5.10 SEC Rule: Book and Records

"No person shall, directly or indirectly, falsify or cause to be falsified, any book, record or account subject to Section 13(b)(2)(A) of the Securities Exchange Act."

(17 C.F.R. § 240.13b2-1)

The Level of Cooperation and Difficulties Encountered

At bottom, the audit committee is trying to smell a rat. It is trying to get reliable, candid information about the environment or culture in which financial reporting takes place, the institution's logistical capabilities to fulfill its objectives, and where things might have gone astray.

It therefore makes sense to ask the outside auditor about the company's level of cooperation during the course of the audit and the extent to which any difficult issues were encountered. Frequently, a lack of cooperation and the encountering of difficult issues will go hand in hand. Either individually or together they can be a telltale sign of a broader problem. In particular, they can suggest an attitude toward financial reporting that is not consistent with a healthy overall environment.

Unusual Revenue or Reserve Activity

A reason for asking about revenues is that revenue manipulation is frequently where financial fraud will get its start. In particular, the auditor can be asked about instances in which revenue recognition patterns did not appear to match the ebb and flow of the company's normal cycle of business activity. Revenue spikes toward the end of a quarter or other financial reporting period may be a warning that something untoward is afoot.

Much the same is true of changes in company reserves. Here, the auditor might be asked about the level of reserves not only at year-end but during the course of the year. Unusual reserve activity that does not seem explainable by virtue of business developments can be explored. Reserves that are established or modified almost entirely based upon the judgment of management may warrant particular scrutiny.

Beyond issues of revenue recognition and the adjustment of reserves, the auditor might be asked about other aspects of the application of GAAP in which management judgment plays an important role. The audit committee should do its best to satisfy itself that adjustments are the natural consequence of business activity and not the manifestation of a desire to attain preestablished financial reporting targets.

Nonmaterial Proposed Adjusting Journal Entries

Also on the list of issues for the outside auditor is the topic of nonmaterial proposed adjusting journal entries. This addition is the result of two things. The first is a bulletin by the staff of the SEC. The second is Sarbanes-Oxley.

First, a word about nomenclature. As used here, a *proposed adjusting journal entry* is an adjusting journal entry proposed by the auditor in order to correct a misstatement discovered as a result of audit testing. If the adjustment is made, it becomes known simply as an adjusting journal entry. If the adjustment is not made, it remains a proposed adjusting journal entry (also referred to as an *uncorrected misstatement*). For its part, Sarbanes-Oxley refers to them as *unadjusted differences*.

Until a few years ago, it was thought to be within the discretion of management to decline to make adjusting journal entries as long as they collectively fell below certain materiality thresholds. There were exceptions to that, but generally management could decline to record adjustments collectively falling below a materiality threshold of, say, 5 to 10 percent, without running the risk that the financial statements would be viewed as *materially* misstated.

In Staff Accounting Bulletin No. 99 (Materiality) (see Exhibit 5.11), the SEC tried to change that. Apparently premised on the view that executives at some public companies were abusing the concept of materiality by declining to make "nonmaterial" adjusting journal entries to increase reported earnings, the SEC staff took the position that it would not accept purely numerical materiality analysis in assessing the fairness of financial statement presentation. In particular, the staff took the position that even adjustments falling below traditional numerical thresholds may nonetheless be viewed as material if, for example, failure to make the adjustment disguised a failure to meet analyst expectations, turned a loss into a profit, masked an important trend, or affected a company's compliance with regulatory requirements. In addition, the staff suggested that a failure to make even seemingly minor adjustments to the company's books and records may be improper when undertaken "as part of an ongoing effort directed by or known to senior management for the purposes of 'managing' earnings." Sarbanes-Oxley thereafter called upon the auditor to report to the audit committee material written communications between the auditor and management, including the schedule of unadjusted differences.

EXHIBIT 5.11   SEC Staff Accounting Bulletin No. 99 (Materiality)

"The staff is aware that certain registrants, over time, have developed quantitative thresholds as 'rules of thumb' to assist in the preparation of their financial statements, and that auditors also have used these thresholds in their evaluation of whether items might be considered material to users of a registrant's financial statements. One rule of thumb in particular suggests that the misstatement or omission of an item that falls under a 5% threshold is not material in the absence of particularly egregious circumstances, such as self-dealing or misappropriation by senior management. The staff reminds registrants and the auditors of their financial statements that exclusive reliance on this or any percentage or numerical threshold has no basis in the accounting literature or the law.

* * *

Among the considerations that may well render material a quantitatively small misstatement of a financial statement item are—

- whether the misstatement arises from an item capable of precise measurement or whether it arises from an estimate and, if so, the degree of imprecision inherent in the estimate
- whether the misstatement masks a change in earnings or other trends
- whether the misstatement hides a failure to meet analysts' consensus expectations for the enterprise
- whether the misstatement changes a loss into income or vice versa
- whether the misstatement concerns a segment or other portion of the registrant's business that has been identified as playing a significant role in the registrant's operations or profitability
- whether the misstatement affects the registrant's compliance with regulatory requirements
- whether the misstatement affects the registrant's compliance with loan covenants or other contractual requirements
- whether the misstatement has the effect of increasing management's compensation— for example, by satisfying requirements for the award of bonuses or other forms of incentive compensation
- whether the misstatement involves concealment of an unlawful transaction."

No longer, therefore, can an audit committee take complete comfort that financial statement inaccuracies falling below numerical materiality thresholds need not be worried about. Now they must be. Moreover, they must be worried about in a context in which the propriety of a failure to make adjustments turns on such qualitative criteria as the perceived effect of the failure and, to some extent, the motive of management.

The audit committee, therefore, may want to explore with the outside auditor any proposed adjustments that have not been made. In the event that such adjustments exist, the audit committee may face the fairly unpleasant task of inquiring into the reason and the extent to which the failure to make the adjustment would be second-guessed by the SEC or others. To avoid potential trouble, some audit committees may see fit simply to put in place a policy that, regardless of materiality, all proposed adjusting journal entries should be made.

The PCAOB's List

Underscoring the importance of a candid exchange between the audit committee and the auditor, the PCAOB undertook to develop a new standard regarding the kinds of information that auditors should be required to provide to audit committees. Approved by the SEC in December 2012, the standard seeks to improve the depth and scope of the dialogue as to both the overall audit strategy and observations that are "significant to the financial reporting process." Highly prescriptive, the PCAOB standard calls upon the auditor to discuss with the audit committee a number of topics including the following:

- Significant issues discussed with management in connection with the auditor's appointment or retention
- The terms of the audit
- Audit committee awareness of matters relevant to the audit, including violations or possible violations of laws and regulations
- Overall audit strategy, timing, and significant risks
- Accounting policies and practices, estimates, and significant unusual transactions
- The auditor's evaluation of the quality of the company's financial reporting
- The auditor's responsibility for other information in documents containing the audited financial statements
- Management consultation with other accountants regarding significant auditing or accounting matters where the auditor has identified a concern
- The company's ability to continue as a going concern
- Uncorrected and corrected misstatements
- Other material written communications between the auditor and management
- Departures from the auditor's standard report
- Disagreements with management
- Difficulties encountered in performing the audit
- Other matters that the auditor views as significant to the oversight of the company's financial reporting process

The communications are to take place "in a timely manner and prior to the issuance of the auditor's report." To its credit, the PCAOB has not mandated that all such communications take place in writing. The PCAOB thus implicitly recognizes that candor can be enhanced through less-structured oral dialogue. The auditor is, however, to document the communications in its workpapers regardless of whether they were made orally or in writing.

GETTING INFORMATION FROM INTERNAL AUDIT

Unfortunately, even the most splendid outside auditor will suffer from one fundamental impediment to its effectiveness: By definition, the auditor is an outsider. Whether the auditor undertakes fieldwork once a year, once a quarter, or even more frequently, the outside auditor will still be conducting examinations only periodically. There is one thing, therefore, that the outside auditor may not be able to accomplish. The outside auditor may not be able to sufficiently integrate itself so that it becomes part of the fiber of the enterprise and thereby gains complete access to the all-important environment or culture where accounting irregularities have their start.

To fill the gap, the audit committee may want to consider installation of an internal audit department. In general, it would make sense to ask the internal auditors to evaluate many of the areas listed above while taking advantage of the one characteristic that gives internal audit an edge: Internal auditors are there all the time.

Unlike the outside auditor, therefore, the internal auditor is in a position to participate in hallway gossip; to plug itself into the processes of forecasting, budgeting, sales, and shipping; and to develop important relationships whereby it can attain a genuine feel for the pulse of the organization. Although fellow employees may never let down their guard completely, certainly there is greater opportunity for internal auditors to gain access into the workings of the enterprise than for somebody whose principal function is to remain as an outsider.

A topic of debate is the extent to which an audit committee should outsource internal audit—that is, turn over the internal audit function to an outside firm. There are both pros and cons, but one question is whether an outsider can effectively plug himself into the culture of the organization in the same way as an employee. It may be that creative and zealous outsourced internal auditors would be able to overcome that impediment. It is a subject of legitimate debate.

Installation of an effective internal audit function, whether outsourced or not, will not necessarily be easy. One reason is that here, too, the audit committee—insofar as it seeks nuanced information about the corporate environment rather than crisp statistics on the reliability of numerical data—will to some extent be working against the traditions of the audit profession insofar as internal auditors are, after all, still auditors. Even internal auditors who are admonished to seek and report candidly both statistically derived and gut-level information about the workings of the financial reporting system may find themselves inclined to prefer the former at the expense of the latter.

A single anecdote will illustrate the challenge. One audit committee of a public company was fortunate to have as its chairman an individual who not only had served as CEO of several companies but also possessed extraordinary expertise in corporate governance and, in particular, in the ways that financial reporting systems can break down. This audit committee chairman undertook, as one of his top priorities, the installation of an effective internal audit capability. The structure of the reporting relationship was exactly right: The internal auditors were encouraged to look for problems. They were instructed to report all problems to the audit committee directly.

Over time, the chairman got a sense that the environment was not quite right and might be conducive to problems. He shared his concerns with the internal auditors, who were admonished to look harder. Alas, the internal auditors reported that they didn't see a thing. To them, everything looked just fine.

As it turned out, things were not fine. The company did indeed suffer from an environmental problem, and the internal auditors had not been either sufficiently skilled or sufficiently zealous to plug themselves into it. The true depth of the problem became known only after a significant change in the senior management ranks.

The point of this anecdote is that, in today's world of financial reporting, audit committees are facing an extraordinary challenge. They are being asked not only to assume significant oversight responsibility for the prevention and early detection of fraudulent financial reporting but to do so through the use of tools, such as the outside auditor and internal audit, that will themselves have to undergo some degree of cultural evolution before they are in a position to provide the kind of information a modern audit committee will want to have. Even sophisticated and diligent audit committee members will no doubt find the task exceedingly frustrating, and probably few, if any, audit committees so far have managed to install an optimum system. At root, the challenge is to reconfigure the way people think about corporate governance and financial reporting. Theoretically, the tools are there, but some modifications will be necessary before they can be made to work.

How can the audit committee maximize the effectiveness of the tools at its disposal? In other words, how can the audit committee most effectively use the outside auditor and internal audit to trigger a cascade of information, and in particular to enable bad news to flow up? Here are some ideas.

MORE ON THE TONE AT THE TOP

To get the tools to work, it will be critical for the audit committee to set the right tone. If one wants to encourage the flow of bad news, then the flow of bad news must be rewarded. At the same time, the audit committee should zealously guard against the natural inclination of human nature to recoil and punish bad news. It didn't work for Cleopatra, and there is no reason to think it will work any better for a modern audit committee.

As a practical matter, this translates into insistence on complete cooperation by employees and executives with both the internal and the outside audit functions. Officers and employees must be made keenly aware that objectivity and candor are the orders of the day and, correspondingly, that attempts to obfuscate, disguise, or dissemble are absolutely forbidden. Once again, it is a battle for the culture of the organization.

At the same time, the audit committee should appreciate that the auditor must not be too heavy-handed. The auditor's mission is a delicate one and must be approached with an appreciation for the subtleties of human nature and the completely understandable reluctance of others to report bad news. At some point, the task becomes less an exercise in the application of GAAP and more an exercise in the sociology of organizations and the foibles of human nature. Auditors who appear to go about their task with any level of arrogance, swaggering boastfulness, or lack of appreciation for the sensitivity of their positions must be either admonished to change or, more likely, moved to another position. The audit function is not one in which heavy-handedness will necessarily get results.

One particularly difficult issue the audit committee will likely face is senior-executive insecurity arising out of enhanced and expanded internal and outside auditor functions. Senior executives will no doubt appreciate that they are supposed to know what's going on within the company they are running. An understandable reaction on their part would be a level of insecurity verging on paranoia. At a minimum, the installation of enhanced internal and outside audit functions would seem to do nothing to foster a sense of trust in senior executives or their integrity.

For reasons so eloquently explained by John O. Whitney in his management text, *The Economics of Trust*, a sense of mistrust must not be permitted to creep into the relationship between the audit committee and senior management. Trust is critical, and without it the installation of enhanced audit functions could end up proving counterproductive. That sense of trust must be maintained through the recognition, explicitly shared with senior executives, that nobody is perfect, no enterprise is perfect, and that, simply by virtue of its position, the audit committee may have access to information that even the most well-meaning and effective senior executives may not. That information will not be used against the executives but rather will give them a heretofore unavailable opportunity to gain new insights into their company and enhance its operations. The information is not being obtained to be used against anyone. It is being obtained so that everyone may benefit from its revelation.

Will some senior executives nonetheless try to exact revenge from an employee who has spilled the beans? It is almost inevitable that the ranks of senior management will include executives who would so foolishly react. That is still another behavior for which the audit committee will want to keep its eyes open. If it learns of an executive seeking to stifle truthful information, the committee's reaction in most instances should probably be unequivocal and swift. Such an executive in all likelihood does not know how to get information or how to use it when it's available. Who knows what's been happening in his department? He inevitably doesn't. A direct communication with the executive is probably in order. Also in order may be his removal.

 ## MINIMIZE RELIANCE ON PAPER

For some reason, almost anyone within an organization is drawn to demonstrate his or her diligence through the generation of paper. That is particularly so when people are not quite sure what they're supposed to be doing. As an audit committee undertakes to improve financial reporting, therefore, an inclination may exist for those involved to generate written reports—inspection reports, exception reports, reports consolidating reports—all accompanied by the normal barrage of memoranda, correspondence, and emails.

In many areas of corporate endeavor, the mindless generation of paper merely wastes time. In the context of corporate governance and financial reporting, it can actually be counterproductive. The reason probably stems from the underlying reluctance of individuals to write with the same candor that they speak—particularly when the topic is criticism of the organization or, more frightening, their own superiors. A resulting loss of candor would be particularly unfortunate in the transmittal of information to the audit committee as some of the most important information involves subtle aspects of the corporate environment and tone. Such information can be difficult to quantify and document, and exclusive reliance on written reports may cause such information to be lost completely. Human resource directors are familiar with a phenomenon in which the performance evaluations of individual employees tend to improve when, having been presented orally, they must then be reduced to writing. There is no reason to think that the phenomenon will not occur where the evaluations are of corporate rather than individual performance.

To the fullest extent possible, therefore, the better approach may be to minimize the use of paper and to gain access to information through direct face-to-face meetings. In that way, the true richness of feedback can be explored and the participants can be made to feel more at liberty to convey potential problems before they would seem to warrant documentation. Feelings, concerns, gut-level instincts—all of these would likely be more forthcoming if they could be presented orally rather than on paper.

An additional reason exists to minimize the generation of paper, though one is loath to acknowledge it. The reason involves the disadvantage of unnecessary documentation in the event of litigation. While written reports might be used affirmatively in litigation to demonstrate the diligence of audit committee members, the reports might also be taken out of context to show supposedly unpardonable flaws in the financial reporting system. The minimization of written reports reduces the risk.

It is probably too much to ask that an effective communication system be entirely paper-free. After all, there will be a lot to keep track of. Nonetheless, even under the best of circumstances, the efficiency of an organization is probably inversely proportional to the amount of paper it generates. That may be particularly so when it comes to perpetual evaluation of the corporation's financial reporting system and, in particular, the corporate environment.

LEARN THE BUSINESS

To "learn the business" does not mean to study the most recent Form 10-K. Nor does it mean rote memorization of product lines, divisions, or facility locations. What the audit committee really wants to understand is how the organization runs and makes money—what is the system by which the company conceives, creates, sells, collects, and publicly reports. A significant underlying objective in understanding the system is development of an appreciation for those aspects of the system (e.g., budgeting, sales, shipping) in which vulnerabilities leading to potential breakdowns in financial reporting are most likely to occur.

That kind of information is not available from audited financial statements. It is more readily unearthed rather through one-to-one contact with executives and operating personnel. At one public construction company, for example, the audit committee chairman arranged for a series of half-day meetings with executives in five separate areas (finance, construction, human resources, bidding, and estimates) to develop a meaningful understanding of just how the company worked.

Public companies are at bottom simply collections of human beings trying to get along as best they can. An understanding of how individuals interact— the motivations, the pressures, the problems—can contribute mightily to an understanding of underlying vulnerabilities.

 ## MEET WITH OTHERS AND ALONE

The audit committee's function poses something of a dilemma. On the one hand, the audit committee consists of outsiders who by definition are at least once-removed from the company. On the other hand, the audit committee wants to develop an overall sense of the company's financial reporting weaknesses that is more objective and more vivid than that of almost anyone else.

A consequence is that the audit committee should have two types of meetings. One type is meetings with others. "Others" would include the CEO, the CFO, at times key operating personnel, the outside auditor, and internal audit. The purpose of such meetings (and their effectiveness may be enhanced if they are done separately) is to capture the full texture of each individual's experience and views as to what is going on and, more important, where problems may be developing.

The other type of meeting consists of meetings in which the audit committee members confer by themselves. Only in isolation can they candidly express their views as to the strengths and weaknesses of individuals, company systems, and the company as a whole. That is not to say that each meeting must adhere to a rigid agenda—first the CEO, then the CFO, then the internal auditor, then 10 minutes for private discussion. Rather, it means that, as the audit committee seeks to explore potential vulnerabilities in financial reporting, a full spectrum of meeting configurations may be useful.

MEET WHEN NECESSARY

One issue that seems to have attracted more than its share of regulatory attention is the frequency with which audit committee meetings should be held. Should they be held once a year, once a quarter, once a month, before each board meeting, or on an ad hoc basis?

No rule or regulation definitively answers the question, though former SEC Chairman Arthur Levitt made clear his disdain for an audit committee that presumed to fulfill its responsibilities while meeting "only twice a year before the regular board meeting for fifteen minutes." At the other end of the spectrum, Arthur Levitt has presented to the business community his Platonic ideal of an audit committee that "meets twelve times a year."

Here is a commonsense suggestion. While it sounds almost too obvious to mention, a good approach would be to hold audit committee meetings as often as necessary. For example, an audit committee just getting started or at a company whose financial reporting system suffers from a history of problems might want to meet as often as every two or three weeks. As appropriate systems are put in place, once a month or, later still, once a quarter may be just fine. The point is that the frequency of meetings should be driven by the needs of the company—not by a self-imposed edict or by the desire to create an appearance of diligence. Good judgment is probably the best guide.

USE GOOD JUDGMENT

The importance of good judgment brings to mind one final point. All organizations are different. They have different histories. They operate in different industries. They have different cultures. What works for one company may not work for another. It is hard to conceive of a single set of guidelines for effective audit committee oversight that would work optimally at all companies across the board.

Perhaps the most important guideline an audit committee might use to accomplish its objectives is simply the good judgment of its individual members. In the end, the audit committee is trying to measure the pulse of the enterprise throughout the trials and tribulations of its corporate life. The overriding goal is to isolate the financial reporting system from the inevitable pressures that result when things don't go exactly as desired. No regulation, charter, checklist, mission statement, or corporate resolution can effectively guide the audit committee as it seeks to fulfill that goal. The best tool, rather, is the informed good judgment of the individual committee members.

EXHIBIT 5.12 Sample Audit Committee Charter

Purpose

The fundamental purpose of the audit committee shall be to assist the board of directors in fulfilling its responsibility to oversee the company's system of financial reporting. In fulfillment of that purpose, the audit committee shall:

1. Assist board oversight of—

   (i) The integrity of the company's financial statements,

   (ii) The company's compliance with legal and regulatory requirements,

   (iii) The independent auditor's qualifications and independence, and

   (iv) The performance of the company's internal audit function and independent auditor; and

2. Prepare an audit committee report as required by SEC rules to be included in the company's annual proxy statement. [*NYSE Listed Company Manual 303A.07(b)*]

Composition

The audit committee shall be composed of three directors, each of whom shall be independent as defined by applicable rules and the company's corporate governance documents, and each of whom shall be selected by a majority of the independent directors of the board. A majority of the independent directors of the board shall also select the audit committee chair. Neither the chair nor any other member of the audit committee may be removed except by a majority of the independent directors of the board. [*NYSE Listed Company Manual 303A.07(a)*.] Each member of the audit committee shall be financially literate, as such qualification is interpreted by the company's board in its business judgment, or shall become financially literate within a reasonable period of time after his or her appointment to the audit committee. At least one member of the audit committee shall have accounting or related financial management expertise, as the company's board interprets such qualification in its business judgment. At least one member of the audit committee shall also qualify as an audit committee financial expert as defined by SEC Regulation S-K Item 407. [*NYSE Listed Company Manual 303A.07(a) commentary; Regulation S-K Item 407(d)(5)*.]

Duties and Responsibilities

The duties and responsibilities of the audit committee shall be as follows:

1. The audit committee shall be directly responsible for the appointment, compensation, retention and oversight of the work of the public accounting firm engaged (including resolution of disagreements between management and the auditor

regarding financial reporting) for the purpose of preparing or issuing an audit report or performing other audit, review or attest services, and each such registered public accounting firm must report directly to the audit committee. [*SEC Rule 10A-3(b)(2)*.]

2. The audit committee shall receive reports from the independent auditor, prior to the filing of an audit report, regarding—

   (i) All critical accounting policies and practices to be used;

   (ii) All alternative treatments within generally accepted accounting principles for policies and practices related to material items that have been discussed with management, including:

   (a) Ramifications of the use of such alternative disclosures and treatments; and

   (b) The treatment preferred by the registered public accounting firm; and

   (iii) Other material written communications between the registered public account-ing firm and management, such as any management letter or schedule of unad-justed differences. [*Regulation S-X Rule 2-07(a)*.]

3. The audit committee shall, at least annually, obtain and review a report by the independent auditor describing: the firm's internal quality-control procedures; any material issues raised by the most recent internal quality-control review, or peer review, of the firm, or by an inquiry or investigation by governmental or professional authorities, within the preceding five years, respecting one or more independent audits carried out by the firm, and any steps taken to deal with any such issues; and (to assess the auditor's independence) all relationships between the independent auditor and the company. [*NYSE Listed Company Manual 303A.07(b)(iii)(A)*.]

4. The audit committee shall discuss the company's annual audited financial statements and quarterly financial statements with management and the independent auditor, including the company's disclosures under "Management's Discussion and Analysis of Financial Condition and Results of Operations." [*NYSE Listed Company Manual 303A.07(b)(iii)(B)*.]

5. The audit committee shall discuss the company's earnings press releases, as well as financial information and earnings guidance provided to analysts and rating agencies. [*NYSE Listed Company Manual 303A.07(b)(iii)(C)*.]

6. The audit committee shall discuss policies with respect to risk assessment and risk management. [*NYSE Listed Company Manual 303A.07(b)(iii)(D)*.]

7. The audit committee shall meet separately, periodically, with management, with internal auditors (or other personnel responsible for the internal audit function) and with the independent auditor. [*NYSE Listed Company Manual 303A.07(b)(iii)(E)*.]

8. The audit committee shall review with the independent auditor any audit problems or difficulties and management's response. [*NYSE Listed Company Manual 303A.07(b) (iii)(F)*.]

9. The audit committee shall set clear hiring policies for employees or former employ-ees of the independent auditor. [*NYSE Listed Company Manual 303A.07(b)(iii)(G)*.]

10. The audit committee shall report regularly to the board of directors. [*NYSE Listed Company Manual 303A.07(b)(iii)(H)*.]

11. The audit committee shall establish procedures for—

(continued)

EXHIBIT 5.12 (*continued*)

(i) The receipt, retention, and treatment of complaints received by the company regarding accounting, internal accounting controls, or auditing matters; and

(ii) The confidential, anonymous submission by employees of the company of concerns regarding questionable accounting or auditing matters. [*SEC Rule 10A-3(b)(3).*]

12. The audit committee shall have the authority to engage independent counsel and other advisers, as it determines necessary to carry out its duties. [*SEC Rule 10A-3(b)(4).*]

13. The audit committee shall have the power to obtain appropriate funding, as determined by the audit committee in its sole discretion, in its capacity as a committee of the board of directors, for payment of—

(i) Compensation to any registered public accounting firm engaged for the purpose of preparing or issuing an audit report or performing other audit, review or attest services for the company;

(ii) Compensation to any advisers employed by the audit committee under this charter; and

(iii) Ordinary administrative expenses of the audit committee that are necessary or appropriate in carrying out its duties. [*SEC Rule 10A-3(b)(5).*]

14. The audit committee shall have the exclusive power to engage and supervise a Director of Internal Audit and the exclusive power to oversee the company's internal audit function.

15. The audit committee shall inquire into the independence of the outside auditor; preapprove all audit and nonaudit services pursuant to established preapproval policies and procedures; receive from the outside auditor a written statement disclosing all relationships between the auditor and the company that in the auditor's judgment may reasonably be thought to bear on independence; engage in dialogue with the auditor with respect to any disclosed relationships, services, or fees that may affect the objectivity and independence of the auditor; receive from the auditor written confirmation that the auditor in its judgment is independent; and take appropriate action to ensure the independence of the auditor. [*Regulation S-X Rule 201(c)(7); Regulation S-K Item 407(d)(3)(i)(C); ISB No. 1.*]

16. The audit committee shall discuss with the outside auditor, to the extent appropriate, the items identified in PCAOB Audit Standard No. 16. [*Regulation S-K Item 407(d)(3)(i)(B); PCAOB Audit Standard No. 16.*]

17. The audit committee shall make a recommendation to the board of directors as to whether the company's audited financial statements should be included in the company's Form 10-K. [*Regulation S-K Item 407(d)(3)(i)(D).*]

18. The audit committee shall investigate any matter brought to the audit committee's attention within the scope of its duties which, in its judgment, warrants investigation, and possess the power, without the consent of the board of directors, to engage outside professionals for that purpose.

19. The audit committee shall undertake an annual evaluation of its performance and review and assess the adequacy of this charter on an annual basis. [*NYSE Listed Company Manual 303A.07(b)(ii).*]

Operation

The audit committee shall meet at least four times a year and more often when the circumstances require. The audit committee chair shall schedule and preside over audit committee meetings and shall appoint a secretary (who need not be a member of the committee) to take written minutes as appropriate. The audit committee chair may, in consultation with other members of the committee, invite to audit committee meetings other members of the board of directors, members of management, company operating personnel and employees, representatives from the outside auditor, representatives from internal audit, outside professionals, or others as may be appropriate under the circumstances.

CHAPTER SIX

In the Crosshairs:
The Chief Executive Officer

WHEN IT COMES TO THE CHIEF EXECUTIVE OFFICER, let's start with something on which we can all agree. The life of a public company CEO has not gotten any easier. Now it's not enough to grow the business, deliver stellar quarterly results, be an effective public spokesperson, look good at roadshows, protect the environment, and ensure a nonhostile workplace. Now the CEO has to serve as the foremost guardian of integrity of the company's financial reporting system.

The key phrase here is "integrity of the system." As a practical matter, there is simply no way that a public company CEO can be completely knowledgeable as to what is behind every single number in a company's financial statements. Nonetheless, every quarter the CEO must certify that he has reviewed his company's financial report, that it is not false or misleading, and that the financial statements fairly present the company's financial condition. As frightening as the prospect may be, the CEO as a practical matter has no alternative but to rely on the system by which the financial information is generated. That means that, while the CEO can obviously rely on subordinates, he has got to have a pretty good grasp of the financial reporting system and how well it is working.

In today's financial reporting environment, moreover, the repercussions of transgressions are severe. From the perspective of the SEC, when financial misreporting takes place, it is the CEO who is almost inevitably in the cross-hairs. These days, moreover, SEC penalties may include monetary fines, the disgorgement of perceived ill-gotten gains, and a permanent bar from further service as an officer or director of a public company. But the SEC is just one problem. There is also the plaintiffs' class action bar and the possibility, if not likelihood, that the CEO will be named as a defendant. In severe cases, the Department of Justice may get involved, in which case SEC penalties and class action damages are the least of the CEO's problems. For a public company CEO faced with evidence of a serious financial reporting transgression, the sentences can go up to 20 years.

So there is ample incentive for a modern CEO to strive to the utmost for accuracy in financial reporting. The difficult question is how to accomplish it.

 ## CORPORATE GOVERNANCE PAPERWORK

For starters, let's focus on some of the sorts of corporate governance paperwork that are routinely advocated by experts. These include such devices as a code of ethics and executive financial subcertifications.

Certainly there is something to be said for a code of ethics. If nothing else, such a code explicitly reaffirms the organization's commitment to honesty in all of its business activities. As discussed elsewhere, though, it is probably a mistake for a CEO to believe that such a code will do much to discourage financial misreporting where the incentives for misreporting otherwise exist. Against a culture that tolerates or encourages accounting devices to compensate for operational shortfalls, even a splendidly written code of ethics doesn't stand a chance.

The usefulness of written executive subcertifications of financial results is more complicated but not necessarily more assuring. The benefit of subcertifications stems from the notion that, as Samuel Johnson reportedly once said, "When a man knows he is to be hanged in a fortnight, it concentrates the mind wonderfully." The thinking is that, faced with a requirement of a written subcertification of financial results, a lower-level executive's incentive to ensure the accuracy of those results is correspondingly increased. A subcertification may thereby help to instill some level of executive accountability.

But here, too, an executive subcertification may do little to discourage financial misreporting where the incentives for misreporting otherwise exist. One reason is that those engaged in financial misreporting will often bend over backwards to rationalize the acceptability of their conduct. Execution of a subcertification for such an executive poses no problem because the executive has convinced himself that his numbers, while perhaps not absolutely pristine, can still be defended. For those executives whose numbers are beyond defensible, a subcertification would probably pose no barrier whatsoever. Such an executive has probably already lied many times. Once more isn't going to make a big difference.

Viewed from the perspective of risk management, subcertifications can backfire, such as occurs when an executive signs a subcertification under protest and drafts a memorandum to the file to permanently record his discontent. Then, the hapless CEO believes he is protected by documentation as to the integrity of the company's financial results when tucked away in the filing cabinet is a memorandum precisely to the contrary. Unbeknownst to the CEO, the memorandum just sits in a drawer waiting to be subpoenaed by regulators or the class action bar.

The inescapable conclusion is that, whatever the usefulness of codes of ethics, executive subcertifications, or other forms of corporate governance paperwork, integrity in financial reporting requires a lot more.

THE RIGHT CULTURE

Specifically—and there is simply no getting around this—integrity in financial reporting requires the right kind of culture. It requires a culture that places objectivity, candor, and transparency above everything else—above stock price, above quarterly earnings, above everything. A company whose employees are functioning in the right kind of culture will benefit from an almost infinite number of self-correcting mechanisms to prevent financial reports from going astray. A company whose culture is in the other direction will suffer from an almost equal number of opportunities for corruption.

How to instill such a culture? Actions speak louder than words, but words are still important. Here we move beyond the paperwork and focus upon the kinds of things the CEO says in establishing budgets, holding people accountable, and striving for the attainment of financial objectives. The key is for the CEO to make clear his own personal commitment to accurate financial results. The attainment of financial targets may be important, but objectivity in measuring results is more important still. The message needs to be conveyed directly and often, especially when the going gets tough. The basic point is that under no circumstances—none—will the vaguest suggestion of accounting impropriety be tolerated. The subjects of operational shortfalls and accounting methodologies are not even to be discussed in the same conversation. It is a message that requires reaffirmation at all levels. It is a mindset that should permeate everything.

Saying the right thing is a good start, but doing the right thing is even more important. That brings us to a key aspect of integrity in financial reporting: the process by which budgets are established and executives held accountable for attainment of them.

The critical thing here is to avoid hopelessly aggressive financial targets. No doubt, that is easier said than done. For one thing, there is a natural inclination for employees to want to understate projected performance to give themselves some room in case things go wrong. So any suggestion that a CEO can simply accept at face value all projections of future performance is neither realistic nor likely to result in optimum financial performance. For that matter, stretch targets aren't necessarily bad; many people perform best under pressure, and "stretch" but attainable goals may bring forth the intensity of effort that leads to heroic achievement. It is when performance targets become overly aggressive that accounting irregularities can get their start. The delicate challenge for the CEO is to put in place budgets and projections that maximize effort while remaining grounded in reality.

A budget that is established through an unlistening CEO's edict, accordingly, carries with it the potential for disaster. So does a budget that results from an unrealistic preoccupation with sustaining a particular revenue growth curve, attaining the performance expectations of outside analysts, or otherwise satisfying the somewhat arbitrary performance objectives of outsiders. True, the performance objectives of outsiders, including the shareholders who own the company, certainly must be understood and considered. However, to give them the definitive role in establishing budgets is to risk the health of the company's financial reporting culture.

That takes us to the issue of holding executives accountable for performance, and this area is similarly fraught with peril. The main danger—a lesson that has been demonstrated over and over again—is a corporate culture in which failure is viewed as unforgivable. In that kind of environment, it is too easy for an executive preoccupied with keeping his job to rationalize the use of accounting devices to compensate for operational shortfalls. The more pressure on the executive, the more difficult the temptation can be to resist. In the wrong kind of high-pressure environment, the notion of some level of accounting adjustment—often in a way that an executive may rationalize to be completely permissible—looks increasingly attractive. That is precisely how the seed of a massive accounting problem is initially planted.

What is the lesson here? As strange as it may sound, sometimes failure needs to be an option. Executives need an environment in which inability to attain a periodic performance objective is not necessarily a career-terminating event. This does not mean that substandard effort need be tolerated. But it does mean that a CEO should not be delivering the message: "Get to your number, or else."

GETTING INFORMATION

Now we get to a particularly knotty problem. On the one hand, the CEO wants to create pressure for performance because pressure can maximize effort. On the other hand, the CEO wants to keep the pressure from getting out of hand— he wants to install a culture in which, given a choice between reporting failure and dishonesty, an executive will choose to report failure. With all of the penalties of financial misreporting if the CEO gets it wrong, the heroically difficult challenge is striking exactly the right balance.

Another level of complexity makes this challenge even more difficult. The CEO himself may not have a terribly good grasp on exactly what kind of financial reporting environment he is creating. A CEO might, for example, view himself as the quintessence of tolerance while, in truth, those reporting to him are scared out of their wits. So it is not enough to recognize the need for a culture that includes exactly the right mix of pressure for performance and forgiveness of failure. The more difficult question is how to achieve it.

Important are the CEO's willingness to listen and his access to candid information. The CEO has to be willing to seek information from subordinates, think about what they're saying, and accept the possibility that it may contain a kernel of truth. Sometimes, that can be particularly difficult for visionary entrepreneurs who "didn't get here by listening to people." The other aspect of information gathering is equally important: getting information that is candid. The CEO needs to appreciate that, to some extent, almost all information will be biased in favor of making the CEO, the speaker, or both look better than they should. The CEO has to cut through the blather and find out what is really going on.

For information relevant to financial reporting, probably the best starting place, logically, is the CFO. Unlike the CEO, the CFO has hands-on responsibility for understanding what is behind the numbers and the inner workings of the financial reporting system. The CFO will almost always be the primary source for candid information as to the strengths of the system and its potential weaknesses. But relying exclusively on the CFO can create a danger. That is particularly so where the CEO and the CFO are themselves under intolerable pressure for performance. It is all too easy for the CEO and CFO to become companions in squeezing out of the financial reporting system every last drop of profitability—an approach that can allow the CEO and CFO themselves to almost unwittingly slip into some level of accounting manipulation. To the extent the CEO and CFO find themselves exploring creative devices pursuant to which reported earnings can be enhanced, that discussion may displace objective evaluation of weaknesses in the financial reporting system. Indeed, to the extent the CFO's accounting department becomes a facilitator of the attainment of performance targets, the CFO himself may become disconnected from candid information regarding the financial reporting environment. Either way, the usefulness of the CFO as a source for candid information is compromised.

Broader CEO access to information is therefore desirable, and another useful source can be both lower-level financial executives and those executives whose roles have more to do with operations than with financial reporting. Useful information to gather will include how those aspects of the system relevant to financial reporting are operating and whether they are being compromised by pressure for performance. Sometimes, useful information can be gleaned from employees who appear to have nothing to do with financial reporting at all. If targets are only being achieved through frenzied quarter-end devices, lots of employees may know about it outside the finance department.

Another source of information can be the company's audit committee. The relationship here can be somewhat awkward. An important objective of the audit committee, of course, is to seek bad news and to put in place financial reporting systems whereby bad news will flow from stressed-out underlings, bypassing the layers of corporate bureaucracy, to the audit committee itself. In one way or another, blame for such problems can be either directly or indirectly traced to the CEO. In other words, an important objective of the audit committee is to get candid information as to how the CEO is screwing up.

That is obviously a flow of information that can make a CEO nervous, but it is also a flow of information that a well-meaning CEO can turn to his advantage. The simple reality is that an effective audit committee may have access to information that the CEO simply does not. The audit committee, therefore, can be a useful source of information as to how things can be improved. An attentive CEO will appreciate as a potential opportunity the audit committee's access to information that might otherwise be unavailable. This assumes, of course, that the CEO is interested in corporate improvement rather than employee retribution. If the latter should be the case, the CEO's reaction will only make things worse.

Beyond the audit committee, another potential source of candid information may be the outside auditor of the financial statements. This is particularly so now that auditors have gotten more involved with reporting on internal control, which ideally includes the financial reporting environment. The auditor's discoveries on this subject may prove to be a treasure trove of useful data as to where the environment is, and is not, conducive to financial reporting accuracy. The CEO should not hesitate to drill down into the information beyond the written reports themselves. Often, cultural problems will be sufficiently nuanced that their significance can be lost in the dry recitation of formulaic reports.

A somewhat difficult question is presented by the issue of CEO access to corporate environmental information through internal audit. The issue is actually symptomatic of the general uncertainty that surrounds the use of internal audit, and it involves the extent to which internal audit should report directly and exclusively to the audit committee or, in the alternative, report directly to the audit committee with parallel reporting to the CEO or CFO. In some respects, dual reporting may seem to make sense. The concern, however, is whether reporting to the CEO or CFO may impede internal audit independence and candor. For a company led by an optimal CEO, this will not be a problem; both the CEO and the audit committee will share an earnest desire for candid information regarding system problems. Where the CEO is less interested in candid information and more interested in minimizing criticism, the potential exists for some level of internal auditor muzzling.

SIGNS OF CORRUPTION

Of course, an important part of information-gathering is knowing what to look for. Thus, the CEO needs to recognize the telltale signs of accounting corruption. An obvious one is any hint that accounting adjustments are being used as a vehicle to attain periodic performance objectives. Even where executives genuinely believe that the accounting adjustments are proper, it can be exceedingly harmful to the corporate culture to allow accounting adjustments to be viewed as a permissible device by which financial targets are attained.

Another indicator of a potentially troublesome environment may come in the form of reports that departments are offering quarter-end discounts to increase revenue. Putting aside the wisdom of such periodic discounting from a business perspective, a CEO might wonder why sales executives are prepared to compromise margins and profitability in order to increase revenue by quarter-end. A CEO might also wonder whether other devices are being used, such as side deals that go unreported to the accounting department.

In that regard, the cold numbers themselves can suggest an unhealthy financial reporting environment. If, for example, earnings are almost nonexistent in the first month of the quarter, pick up a little in the second, and then go gangbusters in the third, the CEO might wonder why. It may be that the company has, through quarter-end discounting, conditioned its customers to hold off purchases until the end of the quarter in anticipation of steep discounts by desperate salespeople (which itself can be a problem). Or quarter-end earnings spikes may suggest that some level of accounting hanky-panky is taking place.

Problems with cash flow, including the collection of outstanding receivables, can be still another indication of a suboptimal environment. It is much easier to artificially inflate such things as revenue and earnings than it is to artificially inflate cash in the bank. If sales executives are cutting side deals with customers, shipments are being made that do not represent genuine sales, or bad debts are improperly being kept on the books, these improprieties will ultimately manifest themselves in a lack of collected cash. A seemingly inexplicable discrepancy between revenue and cash collections, therefore, can be an indicator of an underlying accounting problem.

 ## WHAT'S THE OBJECTIVE?

All of this sounds great, but the truth of the matter is that, for a typical CEO, pressures for performance, and therefore for financial misreporting, will abound from every direction. Wall Street analysts want to see their publicly reported expectations met. Bankers want compliance with loan covenants. Employees want valuable stock options. Shareholders want an increasing stock price.

All of these pressures come together on the shoulders of a public company CEO. For that reason, among others, it is perhaps useful for the CEO to periodically do a reality check by asking himself about the ultimate objective of financial reporting. And perhaps one way for a CEO to keep focused is to keep firmly in mind that it is *not* the objective of financial reporting to maximize stock price. It is the objective of *operations* to maximize stock price. The objective of financial reporting is to tell the truth—the good, the bad, and the ugly.

A related thought is that, while no CEO wants to see his stock trading below what he believes to be its true value, a stock trading *above* its true value isn't such a great thing either. For a stock trading above value, the possible consequences are two: either a correction and corresponding drop in price or unrelenting pressure to keep the stock price artificially high. Either way, the effects can be debilitating. Sudden stock price corrections are often followed by disappointed investors, angry analysts, bad press, and sometimes shareholder litigation and regulatory investigation. On the other hand, trying to sustain a stock price that is unrealistic can create a level of pressure for performance that corrupts the financial reporting culture. Then we are back to square one— where financial fraud gets its start.

In the end, perhaps the concept of *transparency* is the best guiding star of all for a CEO. It is a transparency that allows candid information to flow from the lowest levels of the organization through the senior executive ranks, to the audit committee, and on to the entire board of directors. It operates to expose potential problems before they affect the accounting, allows the CEO to understand the environment his targets are creating, and prevents a disconnect between investor expectations and the underlying business reality. Ultimately, transparency translates into objectivity and candor in financial reports. More than helping to prevent accounting problems, that kind of environment should help the whole business run better.

PART THREE

Detection

CHAPTER SEVEN

Detection and Its Aftermath

O NE CONSEQUENCE OF REFORM is that the means of detection of financial fraud have been vastly improved. Audit committees have installed early-warning mechanisms and vehicles for information about potential problems to flow upward more easily. Internal audit systems have been made more robust. Outside auditors have developed new approaches and procedures to enhance their detection capabilities. Corporate cultures have changed in ways that encourage resistance among lower-level employees to potentially improper accounting and that encourage escalation when it is found.

WHISTLEBLOWERS

Perhaps the mechanism of detection getting the most recent attention is that of the whistleblower. In a sense, the groundwork for whistleblowing was laid by the Treadway Commission itself in its encouragement of audit committees to vigilantly pursue weaknesses in the financial reporting system and encourage bad news to flow upward. Sarbanes-Oxley undertook a more explicit encouragement of whistleblowing through statutory provisions that sought to protect whistleblowers from retaliation. The popular press contributed a broader awareness of whistleblowing through stories that sought to portray whistleblowers as heroes of corporate America. *Time* magazine at one point proclaimed three corporate whistleblowers as "Persons of the Year."

Still an additional step was taken in the wake of the 2008 financial crisis with the enactment of a potpourri of legislation known as "Dodd-Frank." Dodd-Frank took existing whistleblower mechanisms one step further by calling upon the SEC to put in place regulations pursuant to which whistleblowers would be amply rewarded for their efforts. Pursuant to Dodd-Frank, the SEC established an Office of the Whistleblower designed to receive whistleblower tips and complaints, provide guidance to SEC enforcement staff, and help the SEC determine the size of whistleblower awards. Under Dodd-Frank, whistleblowing can be profitable indeed—under specified conditions a whistleblower may receive up to 30 percent of collected monetary sanctions. Before Dodd-Frank, the main gratification from whistleblowing was a sense of virtue. After Dodd-Frank, it is money.

Dealing with whistleblowers is tricky business. Some are aware of genuine and serious wrongdoing and motivated by an earnest effort to see things set straight. Some, however, are not. Some may simply be disgruntled employees, individuals out to settle a grudge, perennial malcontents, or employees wanting to shake things up by passing on the latest rumor. Of course, after Dodd-Frank, some may aspire to get rich.

With the opportunities for wealth, whistleblowing is becoming a bigger business than ever. One reason is that the traditional plaintiffs' law firms are getting involved with the apparent expectation of earning a share of any whistleblowing reward. This evolution carries with it the possibility to change the nature of whistleblowing considerably. Back when the main motivation was altruism, it was often the case that whistleblowers were driven by the genuine desire to help, which often meant surgical correction of the problem with a minimum of disruption. Now, it may be more profitable for whistleblowers, and their new law firms, to maximize disruption whether it helps the corporation or not.

Certainly the evidence is showing robust whistleblower activity. The SEC's new whistleblower office receives an average of eight whistleblower tips on a typical day, with financial misreporting topping the charts as the most frequently reported misconduct. One of the early SEC officials helping to put in place the SEC's whistleblowing mechanisms has decided to leave the SEC staff to work in private practice—at one of the premier plaintiff law firms where he is leading the law firm's new whistleblower practice. A consequence of all of this is that, now more than ever, audit committees will have enhanced opportunities for financial fraud to be detected. That opportunity carries with it, though, the need to be ready when the bad news surfaces. Where serious fraud is found, it is alarming how fast so many things can go wrong.

 ## THE IMMEDIATE CHALLENGE: RELIABLE INFORMATION

Whether it comes from a whistleblower or in some other way, the first evidence of potential fraudulent financial reporting almost always brings with it a host of unanswered questions. What is the exact nature of the problem? Was it by accident or deliberate? How far back does it go? Are there other problems beyond this one? Who was involved?

It is the last of these—who was involved—that typically creates the first obstacle to getting to the bottom of things. The unfortunate reality is that, given the way financial fraud typically starts and grows, senior management is right away placed on the list of potential wrongdoers. The problem, of course, is that the natural reaction is to seek information from the corporate systems overseen by senior management.

Those seeking to get to the bottom of things, therefore, are immediately confronted with a dilemma. On the one hand, it is senior management that controls the corporate mechanisms through which the truth can be most efficiently uncovered. On the other hand, senior management itself may be complicit.

 ## ENTER THE AUDIT COMMITTEE

For such reasons, when credible evidence of financial fraud has surfaced, effective corporate governance systems will have the information brought quickly to the attention of the audit committee. That is not to suggest that the audit committee has to be alerted to every internal complaint that surfaces. Every month, large public companies may receive innumerable complaints about all sorts of things, many of which can be dismissed out of hand and may not even involve financial reporting. The monthly commencement of unnecessary investigations based on shadowy whistleblower complaints is a formula for perennial chaos.

Still, when the information carries with it some element of credibility and potentially involves fraudulent financial reporting, an alert to the audit committee—even if it is simply to the audit committee chair—is often a good idea. Awareness by the audit committee immediately introduces the independence, financial sophistication, and access to resources that are the strengths of audit committee oversight. Beyond the practicalities of corporate governance, audit committee awareness of credible evidence of financial fraud makes sense as a matter of law: It is the audit committee that, under Sarbanes-Oxley, maintains responsibility for the oversight of the financial reporting system. At the board level, therefore, the audit committee members have real skin in the game.

A PRELIMINARY INVESTIGATION

With the early information having been raised at the audit committee level, the big question is what to do about it. One possibility—and sometimes this is the right thing to do—is to simply meet with carefully chosen members of senior management and raise the evidence. Under some circumstances, that can be the most efficient approach, but it carries with it risk. If serious financial misreporting has indeed taken place and those being questioned are in fact involved, they are unlikely to immediately confess. Instead, they may use their authority to cover their tracks and impede further steps to investigate the problem. Files may be destroyed, emails deleted, employees warned to be parsimonious with information. Evidence can be lost that will take weeks or months to later recreate.

Still, reliable information must be obtained as quickly as possible. An alternative, where immediate discussion with senior management seems inadvisable, is to quickly target sources of accounting or other data that may either corroborate or refute the early information. Exactly who is to perform this task is a judgment call in itself. The General Counsel's office is one possibility, but it must be borne in mind that the General Counsel reports to senior management and may feel a duty to seek input from senior management as to what he or she has been asked to do. Another possibility is the outside auditor, but, unless it is audit season, immediate introduction of an outside auditor combing through books and records may give rise to a managerial reaction that becomes counterproductive. For those companies with viable internal audit systems, one approach is to seek the assistance of the chair of internal audit. The benefits of internal audit include (where internal audit is properly configured) some measure of independence from senior management, expertise, sophistication, and the fact that examination by internal audit is less likely to raise senior-level eyebrows and thereby generate suspicion.

If potentially corroborating information is found, the next step, too, is a judgment call. One possibility is to immediately commence a major investigation, but in many circumstances that will be too much, too fast. A better approach will sometimes be to carefully select those knowledgeable of the potentially corroborating data—ideally, those at lower levels of management—so that the information can be better understood and its background and content explored. Armed with that additional information, it is entirely possible that the next step will be to present the matter to more-senior management. That step, though, needs to be undertaken with care. It carries with it the risk that evidence will thereafter be compromised.

 DIGGING DEEPER

If the preliminary investigative work yields corroborating data and does not explain away the early evidence, the natural reaction is to want to dig deeper. By this point, if the entire audit committee has not been informed, it will probably make sense to do so. More data will need to be collected, and perhaps additional interviews conducted, to get a better sense as to just how bad the situation is. If the situation is indeed a serious one, a broader investigation will be needed.

It is at this point that one of the key provisions of Sarbanes-Oxley comes into play—the power vested in the audit committee to engage, and pay for, its own advisers without the permission or even acquiescence of senior management. Probably the first outside professionals with whom the audit committee would want to consult are its own independent counsel. An important consideration here is that the audit committee engage counsel that it can trust to be on its side. If the evidence potentially implicates senior management—as evidence of fraudulent financial reporting frequently does—the audit committee will not want outside counsel whose allegiances are divided. For that reason, the company's regular outside counsel—regardless of its reputation or expertise— will rarely, and probably never, suffice. It is too awkward to ask regular outside counsel to investigate the management that has been, up to now, paying its monthly bills. That is not to say that the audit committee must never engage any counsel that has done even a moment's work for the company—for some large companies that might rule out pretty much all counsel that knows anything about fraudulent financial reporting. Still, it must be clear that the audit committee's counsel is prepared to objectively and earnestly investigate senior management. If there is a question as to that, then someone else is needed.

A question that sometimes arises is whether counsel should be disqualified from service to the audit committee if it has earlier represented the auditor of the company's financial statements. The answer is that disqualification for that reason is rarely needed. For that matter, almost all of the large law firms with financial reporting expertise have, at one point or another, served as counsel for one or more accounting firms and their disqualification as audit committee counsel might eliminate as candidates those firms with the greatest sophistication, expertise, and resources. Insofar as the auditor's trust in audit committee counsel will be of the utmost importance (see ahead), audit committee counsel's knowledge and background with the accounting profession may even be a significant advantage. Indeed, the interests of the audit committee, the audit committee's counsel, and the auditor should all be completely aligned: objectively evaluating the problem and doing the right thing to set things straight.

 ## ALERTING THE COMPANY'S AUDITOR

Speaking of the auditor, once corroborating information is found of fraudulent financial reporting, if not earlier, the outside auditor should be made aware. There are several reasons. Foremost is the fact that the auditor will expect to be told about such information promptly. The company will soon find that the support of its auditor is critical to digging its way out of the problem, and that support is best earned by establishing up front that the audit committee can be trusted to keep the auditor informed. Failure to alert the auditor of potential financial fraud is not a way to get things started on the right foot.

Another reason involves the auditor's own legal obligations where possible illegal acts have been uncovered at an audit client. Known within the accounting profession as the auditor's "10A responsibilities"—named after the statutory section of the federal securities laws in which the responsibilities appear—they involve the auditor's duty to evaluate whether the audit committee is taking "timely and appropriate remedial actions" in response. Auditors view this responsibility with the utmost seriousness, and a failure to alert the auditor in the first place can right away call into question whether the audit committee's reactions to the problem qualify as "timely and appropriate."

 ## SECURING DOCUMENTS

An immediate task—by this point, there will be an ever-growing list of immediate tasks—will be to see that documents are being adequately secured.

Indeed, steps to secure documents may begin taking place as corroborating information begins to be found or, better still, as soon as the problem initially surfaces.

Ensuring the security of the company's documentary records is critical for a number of reasons. Foremost, if there is in fact a financial fraud, the odds are that some of the most revealing evidence will be found within the company's email system. That email system must be preserved. Should it not be, it may take weeks, months, or even years to put together the puzzle of what actually happened. No audit committee wants to see an investigation drag out endlessly when it could have been brought to a much more prompt conclusion if corporate records had simply been kept.

Another reason for securing documents involves the company's regulators, foremost among them the SEC. Once the SEC staff is informed of the problem, one of its first questions will be whether corporate records have been preserved. If the answer is not affirmative, the SEC's skepticism of the audit committee will immediately increase as it views the committee as inept, corrupt, or both. As with the auditor, winning over the trust of the SEC is critical to efficiently getting things straightened out. A hostile SEC is the last thing the audit committee needs.

SENIOR MANAGEMENT CULPABILITY

One of the more frustrating tasks on the audit committee's early agenda will be the need to evaluate the potential complicity of senior management.

The main point here (more about this later) is that the company obviously cannot be run by crooks. However, determining just who is a participant in fraudulent financial reporting can be difficult—even *after* all of the evidence is in, let alone at the outset. Adding to the frustration is that suspect senior executives may be at the height of their careers with national reputations. Discharging such an executive, or simply placing him or her on a leave of absence, is disruptive and distasteful—and that's before even getting to unfair.

At the same time, it is important to get wrongdoing senior executives out of the company fast. Beyond the fact that a company cannot be run by crooks, of later importance to a successful investigation will be the tone and the environment in which it is conducted. As long as senior wrongdoers are in place, their continual presence will almost inevitably impede candor. Even knowledgeable employees can be expected to be parsimonious in providing information to the audit committee based on the fear that candor will later be met with reprisals. While well-meaning employees would like to believe that the audit committee will protect them, that depends on an audit committee reaction that will be uncertain as the investigation proceeds. Employees will fear that wrongdoers left in place will make it through unscathed and, when the investigative apparatus goes away, candor will be dealt with.

This means that, even at a preliminary stage, the audit committee will want to be alert to evidence of senior management complicity. If it is not uncovered at the outset, the audit committee will continue to be alert and the evaluation of senior management will be an ongoing process. When the accumulated evidence points to senior management guilt, a crisp response will be needed. It may be difficult and it may be awkward, but a company cannot be run by crooks.

INITIAL DISCLOSURE

As the events unfold and additional evidence of wrongdoing is uncovered, the same questions will dominate the agenda. How bad is the fraud? How far back does it go? Who did it?

An additional question that will provide some of the greatest sense of urgency is whether financial statements now on file with the SEC are false. Recall from Chapter 1 the way fraud starts and grows—modestly at first and then, quarter after quarter, worse and worse as the perpetrators try to cover their tracks but end up just digging a bigger hole for themselves. The implication is that, by the time the fraud has surfaced, it may be much bigger than anyone hopes and may very well go back to prior quarters or years. If so, it may be that company financial results and disclosures now on file with the SEC are materially misstated. Once it is determined that existing SEC filings can no longer be relied upon, it will be time to issue a press release to that effect.

One frustrating aspect of such a press release is that, no matter how much it would like to, the company cannot control its timing. Ideally, of course, the company would be able to wait until all the facts are in—the extent of the fraud, who was involved, the corrections to the numbers, and personnel changes. Alas, that is rarely the case. More likely, events will conspire to require a press release while the information is still uncertain at best.

There are several reasons. The first is simply the fact that, if enough is known to render the financial statements unreliable, failure to promptly issue a press release potentially allows innocent shareholders to continue to trade based on fraudulent information. Every week, every day, every hour that goes by, shareholders are continuing to buy and sell the company's stock with a degree of reliance on the company's reported results that the company now understands to be unjustified. That does not mean that the board should be panicked into premature issuance of a press release that, in overstating or incorrectly describing the problem, does more harm than good. Still, if reliance on the information is no longer justified, good conscience requires that the company say so.

If good conscience doesn't do it, there's always the outside auditor. Under the standards of the accounting profession, an auditor is not allowed to sit by and watch financial markets trade based on audited financial statements that, owing to subsequently discovered evidence, now appear to be false. Thus, as soon as the auditor understands that the situation involves materially misstated financial statements, the auditor will begin alerting the board of the need for a press release with corrective information.

Still another source of time pressure for a press release may be the potential for irregular trading in the company's stock. Once an accounting problem has surfaced, it is typically only a matter of time before rumors start to swirl. Making matters worse, accounting irregularities have an unfortunate propensity to surface soon before a previously scheduled date for a company's earnings announcement—the delay of which will only excite suspicions further. Throughout the entirety of the time that it's desperately seeking information on the extent of, and particulars about, the problem, the board will be haunted by the specter that, at any given moment, significant disruptions may occur in trading of the stock. Should that happen, immediate action may be an imperative. The board may be called upon to issue a press release by the end of the day.

To all of this, regulations promulgated subsequent to Sarbanes-Oxley introduce an additional timing consideration. Pursuant to the regulations, once a board of directors determines that previously issued financial statements "should no longer be relied upon because of an error," the board is, within four days after that conclusion, to file a Form 8-K setting forth specified information. The information is to include the date of the board's conclusion as to the financial statements' unreliability and the financial statements at issue, a brief description of the facts (to the extent known), and a statement whether the matter has been discussed with the company's outside auditor. If the matter is first raised by the auditor rather than the company, alternative (and somewhat more onerous) disclosure requirements apply.

Throughout the time period preceding issuance of the initial press release, therefore, the board will be faced with a very real tension between the objective of prompt disclosure and the need for accurate disclosure. It is a tension that will likely exist throughout the entire process.

The content of the press release itself will obviously depend on the particulars of the situation. For its part, the outside auditor of the financial statements, upon a determination that financial statements underlying its audit reports are no longer reliable, will want to see that the press release makes an explicit statement to that effect. The main challenge is to avoid overstating or understating the problem, all the while recognizing that it may be worse than it presently seems. In situations where the known quantification is below accepted materiality levels, there may be a temptation to refer in the press release to a lack of materiality. However, in the absence of reliable data, that temptation should probably be resisted. The SEC staff has historically viewed such preliminary assessments of nonmateriality with skepticism, and can have a harsh reaction if a subsequent disclosure reveals that the problem turned out to be much bigger than initially believed.

Understandably, a company in its initial press release will want to alert financial markets as to what the correct financial results should be. Otherwise, financial markets may simply assume the worst. The countervailing concern is that any corrected results the company provides at a preliminary stage may, upon a more thorough investigation, turn out to be wrong as the problem turns out to be bigger than understood at the time. Thus, a well-intentioned press release providing early quantification may end up understating the problem, thereby making things worse rather than better as the audit committee itself is now inadvertently drawn into some level of additional misreporting. As much as the audit committee might want to share its initial assessment of the financial statement impact of the problem, premature quantification that runs the risk of understatement is best avoided.

INFORM THE SEC?

One question likely to ignite healthy debate is whether the audit committee should, even at a preliminary stage, reach out to the SEC.

To some, the suggestion would seem idiotic. At this point, pretty much everything seems to be going wrong. The company may not be sure that there was even a fraud let alone who was involved in it. The company may not be sure whether its financial statements are materially misstated or, if so, the extent of the misstatement. Even assuming a fraud and a material misstatement, the company probably does not know how far back it goes. And whatever corrective steps the company has taken so far, it is a safe bet that when everything is uncovered it will not be enough.

But there are factors going the other way. One is that, particularly given the financial incentives put in place by Dodd-Frank, it might make sense to assume that, once the audit committee has learned of a potential fraud, somebody has *already* gone to the SEC. For that matter, by the time the audit committee has found out, the SEC may have already started an investigation. If the SEC later finds out that the audit committee itself was alerted, and did not affirmatively reach out to self-report to the SEC staff, it might have a negative reaction. Certainly that is not the way for the audit committee to make a good first impression.

More fundamentally, a critical objective of the audit committee, mentioned earlier, will be to earn the SEC's trust. The reason is that one of the audit committee's main objectives will be to gain the SEC's permission to investigate the problem itself. The audit committee can do it more efficiently, more quickly, and probably with less disruption than an outside investigation by SEC staff. That means that audit committee counsel will at one point be proposing to the SEC that the SEC stand down from its own investigation so that an audit committee investigation may proceed unimpeded.

With that objective in mind, an early call to the SEC can make a great deal of sense. The SEC staff will normally understand that the audit committee at this early stage does not have as much information as it would like. Still, such an outreach can pay great dividends as the investigation proceeds. (See more about this in Chapter 11.)

 ## THE SECURITIES EXCHANGE

The SEC will not be the only regulators interested in what is going on. Regulatory responsibility is also vested in the stock exchange where the company's stock trades. So there is still another item for the audit committee's to-do list: reaching out to the stock exchange to let it know of the problem before the exchange reads about it in the newspapers.

The major exchanges, such as the New York Stock Exchange and Nasdaq, have requirements regarding the reliability of publicly filed financial information and, where financial fraud has surfaced, those requirements may have been violated. The consequences for the company can include delisting. While the deadlines for compliance can be strict, exchange officials often possess some level of discretion to allow a company to get its house in order and bring itself back into compliance. Important to the exchange officials exercising that discretion will be the integrity of the audit committee's processes.

COMPANY LENDERS

Legal compliance is obviously important to a company's viability. But other things are important as well. One of them is cash.

The prospect of running out of cash often takes a typical audit committee, or for that matter a typical board of directors, by surprise. Often both insiders and outsiders alike have grown accustomed to thinking of the company as flush with cash. It may have plenty of cash in the bank. It may have a substantial revolving credit facility. It may have terrific lending relationships. It may have an additional borrowing capacity that has historically proved to be more than enough for the company's needs.

Unfortunately, that can change the moment that financial fraud has surfaced. Among other things, if the company has any debt, it may have violated its lending agreement insofar as the financial statements earlier provided to the bank may have been false. For example, a lending agreement might provide:

> 12. REPRESENTATIONS AND WARRANTIES
>> 12.4 *Financial Statements and Projection.* (a) The Borrower has delivered to the Bank the audited balance sheet and related statements of income and cash flow for the Borrower and its consolidated Subsidiaries as of December 31, 20xx, for the Fiscal Year then ended. . . . All such financial statements have been prepared in accordance with GAAP and present accurately and fairly the financial position of the Borrower and its consolidated Subsidiaries as of the dates thereof and their results of operations for the periods then ended.
>
> 13. EVENTS OF DEFAULT
>> 13.1 *Events of Default.* It shall constitute an event of default if any one or more of the following events occurs for any reason whatsoever:
>>
>> * * *
>>
>> (c) Any representation or warranty made by the Borrower in this Agreement, any Financial Statement, or any certificate furnished by the Borrower or any Subsidiary at any time to the Bank shall prove to be untrue in any material respect as of the date on which made.

No matter how strong a company's relationship with its bank, a bank lending committee will often recoil in horror when fraud has surfaced, and a normal reaction is for the bank to restrict the availability of credit until an investigation is complete and new audited financial statements are available. Such a reaction is particularly unfortunate because the resulting constraints on cash come just when the company's credibility is on the line, it is the subject of significant distrust, and unexpected cash needs arise owing to the need to hire a team of investigative professionals and address unforeseen operational difficulties. Of course, the lack of audited financial statements makes raising cash from alternative sources equally difficult.

 ## D&O INSURANCE

Also relevant to the issue of cash will be the desire of the board of directors to understand the potential problems presented to the availability of insurance under the company's directors and officers liability insurance (D&O) policy.

The extent to which D&O insurance will cover an audit committee investigation into financial fraud is in a state of flux. D&O insurers have talked about it for years but encountered difficulties in providing D&O policies that are both attractive to companies and profitable for the insurers. A company should not assume, therefore, that all of this preliminary investigative activity is covered by its insurance. It may very well not be.

Still, a public disclosure of potentially misstated financial results will almost always lead to class action securities litigation. On top of that may be multiple proceedings from regulatory agencies and perhaps criminal investigations as well. So the availability of insurance for these other purposes is an important issue. A problem here is that, for a variety of reasons, D&O insurance policies typically decline to provide coverage for deliberate fraud. A D&O insurance policy, for example, may contain the following among the policy "exclusions":

> The Insurer shall not be liable to make any payment for Loss in connection with a Claim made against an insured . . . arising out of, based upon, or attributable to the committing in fact of any criminal or deliberate fraudulent act.

However, the extent to which such a clause would completely preclude coverage is not always clear. For example, not all directors and officers named as defendants in the litigation will necessarily be knowing participants in the fraud. And the fraud of wrongdoing executive officers will not necessarily be imputed to innocent directors and officers under the policy. But there is an exception: D&O policies sometimes provide that execution of the insurance application by one of the perpetrators of the fraud may cause that person's knowledge to be imputed to other insured persons and to the company. As a result, coverage may be denied completely.

So among the things that need to be evaluated under the D&O policy are: Who signed the policy? Does it appear that the person who signed the policy is complicit in the fraud? Will his or her conduct be imputed to the corporation or other officers and directors? Is there a "deliberate fraud exclusion" that may nonetheless impede coverage? A typical board of directors will immediately want the best available information on whether they themselves, notwithstanding their own innocence, face financial exposure due to the unavailability of coverage.

When it comes to D&O insurance, the good news is that the reputable insurance carriers normally seek to resolve insurance issues through negotiation rather than litigation—which can only add fuel to the fire in the event that the insurance carrier and the company start criticizing each other. Often, therefore, the insurance carrier will begin funding the litigation defense until an investigation is complete and the problems can be sorted out. Insofar as most litigation arising out of fraudulent financial reporting is resolved through settlement, as a practical matter the potential unavailability of insurance evolves into a negotiating tool influencing plaintiff recoveries.

 ## CLASS ACTION LITIGATION

Under normal circumstances, a company may view securities class action litigation as a horrendous event. It can be disruptive. It can be costly. It can be expensive to get rid of. Even completely meritless claims can be a nuisance.

But where financial fraud has surfaced, securities class action litigation is one of the *least* of the company's problems. It will take months to get off the ground. It will proceed slowly. And the outcome, regardless of the merits, is fairly predictable. The odds are overwhelming that it will be resolved through a negotiated settlement.

Where financial fraud has surfaced, therefore, securities class action litigation is often viewed as tomorrow's problem. Too many other legal problems need to take priority. A sensible board of directors will not let the litigation take up too much of its time. It is perfectly reasonable to turn it over to outside counsel—here, the company's regular outside counsel will do just fine—and let them deal with it.

Still, the specter of class action litigation may hang heavy in the air, and if audit committee concern about litigation becomes too great, the effect can be counterproductive. The reason is that, from the preliminary investigation on, almost everything the audit committee does will run the risk of exacerbating the company's liability in the litigation. Its foremost objective will be to dig out the fraud. That will exacerbate its liability. Another objective will be to identify the wrongdoers and exactly what they did wrong. That will exacerbate its liability. Once the investigation is complete, corrective actions will probably involve a public admission of incorrect financial statements, the termination of responsible executives, a restatement of financial statements, and some kind of public resolution with the SEC. All of that will exacerbate liability.

Why does the audit committee do it? Because it has no choice. The path out of fraudulent financial reporting is to dig out the problem, publicly disclose corrective measures, terminate the wrongdoers, and restore business credibility. Undue concern for the litigation implications can derail that entire process. So the company will be faced with a decision: Does it want to move beyond the problem or does it want to minimize its litigation exposure? Often that will translate into a decision between a business with a litigation problem and no business at all.

 ## NOW FOR A MORE THOROUGH INVESTIGATION

With the preliminary work out of the way, it is time for the audit committee to turn to a more in-depth and comprehensive investigation. For this, the audit committee will look to the outside counsel it has just engaged. The outside counsel will in turn want to hire forensic accountants to dig into the numbers. Thus begins the long, tedious process of investigating financial fraud.

8

Investigating Financial Fraud: Objectives and Approach

F ACED WITH EVIDENCE OF FRAUDULENT financial reporting of uncertain dimension, everyone involved will have a strong intuitive sense that an investigation is necessary. They will be right. However, a strong intuitive sense by itself may not carry the day upon the realization that the investigation may cost millions of dollars and keep the company in legal limbo for months on end. Therefore, let's look beyond the intuitive sense and break down some of the key reasons that an investigation will ordinarily be in order.

The starting point is that the company has now lost faith in its public disclosures of financial performance. That will need to be fixed. And it is not enough to simply alert markets that previously issued financial results are wrong— outsiders will want to know what the correct numbers should have been. The only way to find out is to dig into the numbers and distinguish falsified results from the real ones.

Beyond the need to set the numbers straight, the company will need to identify those complicit in the fraud and deal with them. This is not a matter of revenge or a quest for justice. The fact of the matter is that the company will need to restore its credibility, and it will be unable to do so until outsiders are satisfied that the wrongdoing executives have been identified and removed.

Absent voluntary confessions by everyone involved, an investigation is ordinarily needed to distinguish the guilty from the innocent.

The need for corrective disclosure and the removal of wrongdoers are two important reasons for an investigation. A third is just as compelling: The company needs an audit report on its financial statements. The need for a new audit report arises with the likelihood that, once a company's financial statements have been found to be unreliable, the company's external auditor will want to pull its existing report. As a practical matter, "pulling its report" involves the auditor's encouragement that the company issue a press release that previously issued financial statements are not to be relied upon. Once the company issues such a press release, it will enter what might be thought of as legal free-fall. It will be out of compliance with any number of SEC regulations. It will no longer satisfy the threshold prerequisites for trading on the company's securities exchange. It will be viewed by many, and certainly the plaintiff class action bar, as coming close to having admitted wrongdoing. And everyone on the outside—not to mention its own board of directors—will want answers fast.

A critical step in the restoration of important business relationships and a return to compliance with regulatory requirements is the auditor's report. And, where fraudulent financial reporting has been discovered, an in-depth and comprehensive investigation is often the only way to get one.

AUDIT COMMITTEE OVERSIGHT

A critical issue at the outset of a financial fraud investigation is its structure. A key attribute for which the auditor—as well as the SEC—will be on the lookout is that the investigation is overseen by the audit committee.

The reasons for audit committee oversight are several. In public companies, it is the audit committee that has explicit legal responsibility for oversight of financial reporting, and accounting fraud falls squarely within the subject of financial reporting. In addition, the audit committee, as a matter of statutory design, is structured to be independent and possessed of a level of financial sophistication that makes it the most viable subset of the board of directors to oversee the investigative efforts. It is also the audit committee that has the statutory power to engage and pay outside advisers even without the consent of management—a statutory power that can be vital if management is a participant in the fraud.

That is not to say that other possibilities for board oversight do not exist. And some may question whether, instead of the audit committee, an investigation of financial fraud should be overseen by a "special committee" assembled after the fraud has surfaced. Those advocating a special committee may make the argument that the fraud happened on the audit committee's watch. Therefore, the argument goes, it is better to put together a new committee that is not similarly tarnished.

The argument might have some appeal, but normally not enough to prevail. The fact is that the law places upon the audit committee responsibility for oversight of financial reporting and the law does not provide for audit committee delegation of that responsibility to a different committee of the board. Nor does the fact that the fraud happened "on the audit committee's watch" necessarily call into question the audit committee's objectivity or diligence. The fact is that the fraud also happened on the entire board's watch, and the audit committee was probably kept in ignorance just like everybody else. It is far from an indictment of the audit committee that the fraud has occurred.

There is, in addition, a danger in the creation of a special committee to investigate financial fraud. The danger is that the committee gets put together based less on need and talent and more on board politics. Particularly where senior management has been pulling the fraud strings, the board may not be operating as a cohesive, collaborative body of corporate governance. For that matter, some level of board dissension might have been deliberately sown by the CEO. Under such circumstances, the selection of special committee members can be influenced by political considerations other than getting to the bottom of things. Often, the better approach will be to stick with the approach put in place by the law. The audit committee oversees the investigation.

Some members of management, particularly senior management, will accept the benefits of audit committee oversight of the investigation and recognize the need. Some, however, may not. They may instead insist on an investigation overseen by company management. That is particularly so of a senior executive who is accustomed to maintaining hands-on control of everything. The specter of an independent investigation that he is powerless to influence, let alone control, may be more than he can bear.

The best response is often that an investigation under the influence of management will likely lack the requisite appearance of objectivity that will be critical to its acceptability to others such as the outside auditor or the SEC. True, the investigation may have some credibility to the extent it finds executives guilty. But, to the extent it does not, observers will wonder whether determinations of innocence were the result of managerial influence. The result is that such an investigation is incapable of credibly reaching determinations of innocence—it only has credibility to the extent it finds people guilty. No audit committee—for that matter, no innocent executive—should have an interest in that.

AUDIT COMMITTEE COUNSEL AND ACCOUNTANTS

The audit committee's role is to oversee the investigation, not actually conduct it. For that it needs to look to outside professionals, and there are two types in particular. The one is outside counsel to the audit committee. If the audit committee has not already engaged outside counsel, it needs to do so now. It is audit committee counsel who will conduct the interviews, comb through the financial records, and present factual findings for audit committee consideration. Individual audit committee members may choose to sit in on interviews, and that is their choice. But it is audit committee counsel who will actually conduct the investigation.

The other group of professionals is the forensic accountants. Audit committee counsel, while knowledgeable of financial reporting obligations and investigative techniques, will probably not possess a sufficiently detailed knowledge of accounting systems, generally accepted accounting principles (GAAP), or computerized ledgers. For that, audit committee counsel will look to a category of accountants specifically trained in digging into financial records for evidence of fraud.

 ## WHAT IS THE AUDIT COMMITTEE LOOKING FOR?

What exactly is the audit committee looking for in such an investigation? There are primarily two things. The first, obviously enough, is what the actual numbers should have been. In some cases that may be fairly straightforward. If a company has purchased an asset for $5 million, but recorded it on its books at a cost of $10 million, it is not too difficult to see through that one. Comparison of the debit in the general ledger to the underlying general ledger support should expose the discrepancy. The result: Reduce the asset by $5 million.

But that was an easy one. And, in the world of financial fraud, things are rarely that easy. Often fraudulent entries involve judgment calls where the operative question is not whether the number matches the underlying financial records but whether the judgment behind the number was exercised in good faith. In establishing, say, a reserve for bad debts, an executive will want to look into the future and come to the most realistic estimate of the extent to which current receivables will or will not be collected. The operative question for the investigators is whether the executive exercised his judgment in good faith to make the best estimate allowed by reasonably available information. Sometimes it is not so easy to tell.

Beyond the correct numbers, the second thing for which the investigators are looking is executive complicity. In other words: Who did it? Again, the good faith of those potentially involved comes into play. The investigators are not seeking simply whether executives reported financial results that turned out to be wrong. The issue rather is whether the executives *tried* to get them right. If they did and made an honest mistake or estimated incorrectly, that does not sound like fraud and may not even be a violation of GAAP to begin with.

The main point here is that, when it comes to executive complicity, the investigators are ordinarily looking for evidence of wrongful intent. In other words, they are looking for an intentional misapplication of GAAP or an approach to GAAP that is so reckless as to constitute the equivalent of an intentional misapplication. A useful operational definition is provided by the courts pursuant to the federal securities laws. The operative term there is *scienter* and intellectual justification for that concept is that scienter is the state of mind constituting a prerequisite to the federal securities laws' main antifraud provision. Scienter has the additional benefit of interpretive judicial precedent as to when it does or does not exist.

An important corollary is that the audit committee will not normally want to go so far as to investigate negligence, that is, a failure to use "reasonable care." Negligence generally is not a crime. Indeed, a normal executive will be negligent many times over his or her career—some people are negligent a half-dozen times before breakfast. True, the facts uncovered by an investigation may help inform the board as to how innocent executives might have been more careful, and the board is certainly entitled to take that information into consideration in making management decisions. But an audit committee investigation is an expensive and disruptive means of getting that kind of information. Audit committee investigations are better directed against fraud.

SCOPE OF THE INVESTIGATION

The scope of the investigation should not pose too difficult an issue at the outset. Initially, the scope will be largely defined by the potential improprieties that have been uncovered. So far, so good.

The difficult question becomes: How far should the investigators go beyond the suspicious entries? The judgment calls here are formidable. One of the main issues involves the expectations of the auditor and, beyond that, the SEC. If the scope is not sufficiently broad, the investigation may not be satisfactory to either one. Indeed, an insufficient scope can place the auditor in a particularly awkward spot insofar as the SEC may subsequently fault not only the audit committee for inadequate scope but the auditor's acceptance of the audit committee's investigative report.

An additional complicating factor involves the way fraud starts and grows. An important implication of the "treadmill effect" described in Chapter 1 is that, over time, the manipulations will often get increasingly aggressive as the perpetrators will spread the fraud throughout a number of line items so that no single account stands out as unusual. For example, to prevent a distortion of accounts receivable from getting too large, perpetrators may spread the fraud into inventory, then bad debts, then asset capitalization. The spread of the fraud is analogous to pouring a glass of water on a tabletop. It can spread everywhere without getting too deep in any one place.

What are the implications for the scope of the investigation? Once fraudulent financial reporting has been found, even in just a few entries, the investigators will want to consider the possibility that it is a symptom of a broader problem. If the investigators have been lucky enough to nip it in the bud, that may be the end of it. Unfortunately, if the fraud has gotten big enough to be detected in the first place, such a limited size cannot be assumed. Even where the fraud ostensibly starts out small the need for a broader scope has got to be considered.

Does that mean that every single entry in the general ledger has to be scrutinized? No; in fact, for a company of any size, that would be all but impossible—and certainly not efficient. The better approach involves identification of the malefactors, consideration of other accounting entries where they might have had influence, and attention in particular to entries that are vulnerable to manipulation.

The scope of the investigation, therefore, can start out with its parameters guided by the suspicious entries discovered at the outset. In most cases, though, it will need to broaden to ensure that additional areas are not affected as well. Throughout the investigation, moreover, the scope will have to remain flexible. The investigators will have to stay on the lookout for additional clues, and will have to follow where they lead. Faced with an ostensibly ever-widening scope, audit committee frustration is both to be expected and understandable. But there is no practical alternative.

 ## LACK OF SUBPOENA POWER

Now we get to additional complications in the investigation—as if we needed more. One is the fact that, unlike the SEC or other governmental authorities, the audit committee does not have subpoena power. That means that it can neither legally compel witnesses to show up for interviews nor, even if they show up, place them under oath. The investigators are reduced to requesting the voluntary cooperation of everyone, including the wrongdoers, and imploring them to tell the truth.

How realistic is that? It depends on the individual. But several incentives for executive cooperation exist. One is that, if an executive does not cooperate, he is placing his employment at risk. A board of directors, or in this case the audit committee, should have every expectation that executives will make themselves available to answer questions and, when questions are posed, tell the truth. An executive who declines to do either should not assume that he will remain on the payroll for very long.

An additional incentive is an executive's desire to tell his side of the story. If an executive is innocent, he has every reason to cooperate so that his perspective is understood and his innocence made clear. Not only will such an executive want to tell the truth. He will want to *appear* to be cooperative to show that he has nothing to hide. An innocent executive has little incentive to play hard-to-get.

Is the same true for wrongdoers? It depends on how cagey they are. Certainly even a wrongdoer wants to create an appearance of cooperation and innocence. If the wrongdoing executive believes his persuasiveness will throw the investigators off the trail, all the better. As it happens, such an approach rarely works out in the long run as the executive's story is cross-checked against other sources of information. But for a wrongdoing executive—whose dissembling has worked up until now—that might be far from obvious.

A more formidable challenge is often presented by wrongdoers who have left the company. They may see little upside to a voluntary interview by their former employer since the prospect of termination is no longer a risk. True, they may want to throw the investigators off the scent. They may, however, conclude that the risk of getting caught in a lie is not worth the potential benefit. That is particularly the case if they've engaged their own outside counsel who will foreseeably advise wrongdoers to keep their mouths shut.

For all of these reasons, it is a rare audit committee that actually has the ability to investigate everyone. More likely, some individuals—including key ones—will not cooperate at all. Normally, though, the inability to interview everyone does not preclude investigative determinations. There is sufficient opportunity in the normal case to learn enough to pretty much pin down what happened. It would certainly be easier if everyone cooperated and if the wrongdoers candidly confessed. But that is not the way things typically go.

INDIVIDUAL COUNSEL FOR EXECUTIVE EMPLOYEES

Another complicating factor involves employees who ask to have their own individual counsel represent them in the investigation, including participation in the employee's interviews.

For the audit committee, such a request can pose a real dilemma based on competing considerations. One consideration is simply that of fairness. It is entirely foreseeable that, once the investigation is completed, the investigative determinations will be turned over to governmental authorities—including the SEC or the FBI. An argument can be made that fairness requires the availability of counsel to anyone who seeks it. Certainly counsel is normally made available to employees in a governmental investigation. If the investigative determinations are to be turned over to the government, that suggests counsel should be made available here as well.

At the other end of the spectrum are the competing considerations of practicality and time. The involvement of individual counsel for employees can turn an investigation that would take months into an investigation that would take years. For one thing, the lawyer may ask to participate in every conversation with his or her client. In a complex investigation into accounting irregularities, for many employees that simply will not work. Critical to investigative efficiency is the ability to simply stop by an employee's cubicle and to ask, for example, for an explanation behind a particular debit and credit. If a lawyer has to get involved, simply scheduling such a discussion may take weeks. An investigation conducted on such terms will not move forward. There is no practical way to involve lawyers for every employee in every discussion.

And that assumes that an employee, once represented by counsel, will approach things the same way he would have before. That should not be assumed. Some lawyers, well-meaning no doubt, will caution clients against candor and admonish the client that, absent a mental picture constituting specific recollection of an event, the best approach is to simply say, "I don't recall." Investigators trying to conduct interviews under such circumstances have encountered employees professing complete failures of recollection of multimillion-dollar ledger entries made just a short time before. What could have been learned in one or two minutes of questioning now becomes a topic that requires days or weeks of additional investigation. Interviews become not much more than an exercise of running into brick walls.

How does the audit committee deal with all this? First, many employees will conclude that it may not make sense to request counsel at all. They will intuitively understand that, from the perspective of the audit committee investigators, someone who shows up with a lawyer can make a very bad first impression. If that individual then answers questions in an obviously guarded way, the bad impression can get worse. At the same time, both the audit committee and its investigators will not be trying to blame someone who does not deserve it and will understand that someone appearing without counsel has to be given some latitude. Often an individual appearing without counsel has the opportunity to make a much better impression than one who is represented.

As to those executives who do want counsel, the audit committee should keep in mind that, while the company may have indemnification obligations, employees do not have a legal right to the participation of counsel at their interviews. To the contrary, the board of directors has every right to expect that employees will candidly report to the board on subjects falling within the scope of employment. So where an executive insists upon legal representation, one approach is to strike a middle ground. If counsel can make itself readily available, it may participate in formal interviews. However, the scope of counsel's representation is defined to exclude so-called "cubicle discussions," that is, less formal conversations that necessarily arise during the course of the investigative work. Within the constraints of a normal fraud investigation, the participation of counsel in all such discussions is simply not feasible.

All of that having been said, the audit committee should understand that executives will probably have the right to have their individual counsel paid by the company. Public company bylaws typically provide for indemnification of the company's officers and directors to the maximum extent permitted by the law of the company's state of incorporation. For example, state law might provide that a corporation may indemnify

> any persons, including directors and officers, who are, or are threatened to be made, parties to any threatened, pending or completed legal action, whether civil, criminal, administrative or investigative . . . by reason of the fact that such person is or was a director, officer, employee or agent of such corporation, or is or was serving at the request of such corporation as a director, officer, employee or agent of another corporation or enterprise [such as a corporate subsidiary]. The indemnity may include expenses (including attorneys' fees), judgments, fines and amounts paid in settlement . . . provided such director, officer, employee or agent acted in good faith and in a manner he reasonably believed to be in the corporation's best interests. . . .

Even if the company suspects an executive has not acted in good faith, it is difficult to resist advancing defense costs prior to an actual adjudication of wrongdoing, particularly where the bylaws provide that indemnification "shall," rather than "may," be provided to the fullest extent permitted under state law. Moreover, the practicalities of the situation may favor indemnification and advancement of defense costs insofar as a failure to do so may result in public litigation by the departing executive back against the company.

Thus, the company may find itself in the ironic position of financing the legal fees of executives who were in fact responsible for the fraud. The company can, and under the law often must, require an undertaking of repayment from such an executive. But collection is not always assured. By the time the executive's guilt has been determined, his list of creditors may be long.

 ## CONDUCTING INTERVIEWS

An executive interview itself is not a particularly mysterious process. Audit committee counsel, a forensic accountant, a more-junior lawyer, and the executive himself sit down in a conference room. The audit committee counsel, assisted by documents or not, asks questions—typically starting out with broad topics and then working to more specificity. The executive answers the questions. From time to time, the forensic accountant jumps in on more technical issues. The executive answers those questions as well.

While the mechanics are straightforward, the mood is something else. For the investigator's part, he would like as relaxed and conversational a mood as possible. His goal is candor, and a stressed-out executive terrified of the entire process is not consistent with that objective. A skilled investigator, therefore, will do everything possible to put the executive being interviewed at ease.

But good luck with that. For one thing, the executive obviously knows that there is a massive investigation going on. Some within the company will inevitably be characterizing it as a witch hunt. And the executive may very well be aware that crimes have been committed and anything he says can be used against him.

If that were not enough, fairness often requires that audit committee counsel start the interview with something akin to "Miranda warnings" in which the executive is warned about the context of the investigation. That context includes that audit committee counsel represents the audit committee, not the executive being interviewed; that, while the interview is protected by the attorney-client privilege for the moment, the executive does not control that privilege and the audit committee may decide to waive it; and that audit committee waiver may involve turning over the interview results (including a memorandum documenting everything the executive says) to the outside auditor, the SEC, or other governmental authorities. As if to corroborate all of this, the junior lawyer is invariably sitting by a laptop prepared to take down every word the executive speaks. But by all means, the executive should feel free to relax.

THE INVESTIGATION REPORT

When it comes to the optimal form of investigation report, probably the biggest issue is whether the report should be in writing.

Often the immediate reaction is: obviously not. If a written report is prepared and then requested by, and turned over to, the outside auditor, the SEC, the Department of Justice, the company's securities exchange, or others, it may very well lose its status as a document subject to the attorney—client privilege. Once privilege is lost, the report may be obtainable by plaintiffs' counsel in the securities class action litigation that has inevitably been commenced. If the investigation has in fact uncovered wrongdoing, it may be viewed by all as a confession providing a roadmap of exactly what the fraud consisted of and who did it. Plaintiff's counsel can be expected to contend that the only remaining issue is the calculation of prejudgment interest.

So those opposing a written report will have some good arguments. But there are also arguments going the other way. And a key question is whether a written report can actually be avoided.

The preparation of some kind of written report is pretty much inevitable. If, for example, the audit committee declines to provide a written report and instead seeks to report orally, the auditor can be expected to document the audit committee's oral report as best it can and to supplement the audit committee's oral report with the auditor's own observations. The end result of such an approach is that there is indeed a written report—it is simply that the audit committee has lost control of its content. At the same time, similar oral reports may end up being made to the board of directors, the SEC, the Department of Justice, the relevant securities exchange, or others—with each audience dutifully taking notes. Thus, rather than a single, definitive written report, the accuracy of which is controlled by the audit committee, there may be dozens, each with its own variations based on the note-taking abilities of the individuals within the separate audiences. An audit committee that thinks through the alternatives will often conclude that a single, definitive written report—the content of which can be controlled by the audit committee—is preferable to the alternatives.

It is true that a written report may provide a clear trail for subsequent litigants. But, even if the report is not written, subsequent litigants may be able to discover the investigation's findings through other means. Litigants may seek, for example, interview notes, memoranda, notes taken by anyone who learned what was going on, the testimony of audit committee members, and so on. The investigation of accounting fraud is an undertaking of enormous complexity, and no audit committee can get through it without its investigative team generating tons of evidence. The issue for the audit committee is whether it wants to pull all of the data into a single, definitive report that fairly and objectively captures the events—or whether it wants to defer to others to present things in a way that may be less objective.

Beyond the desire to ensure accuracy, an additional consideration is the preferences of those interested in the investigation's findings. As a general matter, those wanting to understand what happened will seek a report in writing. The auditor, for example, will often prefer a written report (see Chapter 10). The same is true of the SEC (see Chapter 11). Indeed, as to the SEC, it is established policy that a key question in evaluating whether an audit committee deserves credit for regulatory cooperation is: "Did the company produce a thorough and probing written report detailing the findings of its review?"

On balance, therefore, an audit committee will frequently conclude that a written report is the way to go. A written report allows the audit committee to control the content and to ensure the report's objectivity and accuracy. A written report is normally the strong preference of those interested in the investigative findings, such as the auditor and the SEC. And, if a fraud has taken place, the plaintiffs in litigation will probably find out anyway.

With all of that out of the way, it is time to get down to the nitty-gritty. It is time to dig into the books and records to find the false numbers.

CHAPTER NINE

Finding the False Numbers

W ITH THE INVESTIGATIVE STRUCTURE and approach in place, it is time to dig into the numbers. The objective is finding and correcting those entries that are false.

 ## A DAUNTING TASK

It is difficult to state the objective without immediately acknowledging how tough it can be. A public company in a single year may have thousands upon thousands of accounting entries. Those perpetrating the fraud may have worked hard to break apart, disguise, and bury the entries that are false. Unless it has been nipped in the bud (a rarity), the fraud may go back for years. And there may be little reason to think that it is limited even to a single country. The fraud of a multinational public company may have been deliberately scattered through multiple countries around the globe.

Nor can the audit committee expect immediate cooperation and candor from those involved. Senior executives who are involved may be educated, articulate, persuasive, and by this point highly experienced in rationalizing and explaining away falsified accounts. Lower-level participants may not like it one bit, but may be concerned that exposure of the fraud, and with it their own complicity, will cost them their jobs and possibly put them in prison. If accounting manipulation at the company has become cultural, it may have taken on a life of its own as midlevel executives have independently hidden, and then tapped into, reserves. Thus, no single individual within the company may have any idea how bad the fraud has actually gotten. Even the ringleaders themselves may not know.

Making things worse, the law can actually operate as an impediment to uncovering the truth—particularly where the fraudulent entries reside outside the United States. For understandable reasons, numerous commercially developed countries, particularly in Europe, have put in place strict "privacy laws" they may operate to impede investigation. Those laws are to be respected, and the audit committee will want to see that they are obeyed. That is without even getting to the fact that some privacy laws impose criminal penalties that, if violated, could turn the audit committee lawyers and forensics accountants themselves into lawbreakers.

GETTING STARTED

As they say, a trip of 1,000 miles starts with a single step. So, too, begins an investigation into fraudulent financial reporting.

The first step is the most obvious one: examining in depth and from every possible perspective the accounting entries that have created the suspicions to begin with. The audit committee lawyers and forensic accountants will want to take a comprehensive and in-depth look at everything that has surfaced so far. Employees anywhere in the proximity of the entries will be interviewed. Supporting documentation will be retrieved and scrutinized. Executives at all levels will be asked about their knowledge of the entries and other potentially suspicious goings-on.

The operating hypothesis at this point will recognize that falsified accounting entries rarely occur in isolation. Those asking the questions will be listening not just to learn about the particular accounting entries at hand. They will be listening for evidence of additional, buried entries that need looking into. The initial interviews will include open-ended questions about the company's approach to financial reporting and executive attitudes regarding public candor and disclosure. In other words, a big part of the investigation will be efforts to learn about the company's financial reporting culture. True, terrified employees cannot be counted on to immediately volunteer their participation in criminal wrongdoing or a culture that has run amuck. But they will give clues. Often without meaning to, knowledgeable employees will reveal clues of accounting transgressions and aspects of the financial reporting culture that, to experienced investigators, provide additional avenues of insight into potential wrongdoing.

That is not to say that such clues are the only thing the investigators have to go on. They will also have in mind the way that financial fraud typically gets its start—the treadmill and cultural corruption described in Chapter 1. Important aspects of that corruption typically involve the need to compensate for quarter-end or year-end earnings shortfalls right before an earnings announcement is to go out the door. One way to get a head start on the best places to look for the fraud is to simply place oneself in the position of an executive facing precisely that kind of problem. If it were several days before the end of a quarter and you needed to generate a few extra pennies of earnings, what would you do?

If you were an executive in such a fix, there would be several things you would want to rule out right away. One is the manipulation of any accounting entries that are black-and-white or easily detected. So, for example, you probably would not try to increase earnings through the manipulation of cash. For one thing, it would be difficult to manipulate cash in such a way that would generate extra earnings within a few days. But beyond that, cash is an asset that the outside auditor will ordinarily examine and test at year-end. And the testing itself is not necessarily rocket science—it can be as direct as a comparison of the company's internal records with corroborating information from the outside bank. Further, a manipulation of cash, once discovered, can be difficult to defend: Very little judgment is involved in determining the correct amount of cash in the bank. So, if you want to commit accounting fraud, cash manipulation offers little opportunity and high risk.

So where do you turn? *Hmmm* . . . . You want an entry that fits the following criteria. First, it needs to hit the bottom line right away—you've only got a few days. Second, it cannot be readily susceptible to auditor detection. Third, it's best if the entry can be quietly adjusted now and then corrected in some subsequent quarter. The overall objective (to the extent that you are thinking it through) is to falsify an entry to gain an immediate earnings boost and then to quietly adjust it back to normal as soon as you can. If the entry can be corrected before the year-end audit, all the better.

What do you do? What entries drop right to the bottom line and are hard to detect and second-guess? Entries that require judgments about the future! An entry involving, say, a reserve for future events would fit the bill perfectly. An adjustment of reserves can drop right to the bottom line and thereby generate earnings in less than a day—indeed, the ledger entry can be done within minutes. Unlike cash, there is no objective outside source of corroborating information—the level of reserve is really a judgment call based on the expectation of future events. And how could an outside auditor, even assuming the entry is not quickly corrected, presume to know more about future events than the executive making the judgment call in the first instance? So, to compensate for the earnings shortfall, an adjustment to reserves it is.

The point of this exercise is this. Some accounting entries are more a candidate for fraudulent manipulations than others. So, even without knowing much about the particular fraud at issue, investigators speaking with company employees know where to probe and what kinds of questions to ask. Among the candidates for financial manipulation (see Exhibit 9.1) are the following.

Revenue Recognition

Revenue recognition is almost always one of the first places to look for financial fraud. The reason is that, if a company executive is facing a shortage of earnings at period-end, the first accounting solution that often occurs to him is simply to find a way to increase revenue. Initially, an approach might be used that seems innocent enough—for example, accelerating shipments on

EXHIBIT 9.1   Potential Financial Fraud Areas

Revenue recognition

- Premature recognition of sales
- Phantom sales
- Improperly valued transactions

Reserves

- Bad-faith estimates
- Onetime charges

Inventory

- Overvaluation
- Nonexistent inventory

Expenses

- Delayed expense recognition
- Improper capitalization of expenses

Other

- Related-party transactions
- Acquisition accounting

orders that are completely legitimate. However, as the quarters progress and the executive finds himself digging a deeper and deeper hole, devices to find additional revenue can get more aggressive. Thus, in some subsequent quarter, the executive may find himself keeping the quarter open for a day or two to add still more revenue or, after that, recognizing revenue on orders that have not even been received.

Revenue recognition can thus provide a trap that is both all too tempting and ultimately inescapable for the unwary executive. It will often occur to the executive first. Early efforts may not seem to be, and may not be, fraudulent at all. But going forward the hole gets deeper and the adjustments become more aggressive. At one point, the executive finds himself over the line. One study of financial fraud cases found that, over a two-year period, issues involving revenue recognition were implicated 40 percent of the time.

As the executive becomes increasingly desperate, creative thinking may result in the discovery of more innovative ways that revenue can be manipulated. One, for example, involves "bill-and-hold transactions"—transactions in which revenue can be recognized even though the product has not been shipped. Under generally accepted accounting principles (GAAP) proper revenue recognition on bill-and-hold transactions involves compliance with a laundry list of criteria. An increasingly desperate executive might find himself allowing revenue recognition on such bill-and-hold transactions even though one or two of the criteria have not actually been met.

Other opportunities are presented by "consignment sales." As a matter of business practice, consignment sales typically involve the delivery of a product to another location—such as a retailer—with an obligation to take back the product in the event it is not sold. Under GAAP, revenue is not normally to be recognized upon delivery to (in this case) the retailer—it is rather to be delayed until the product is actually sold. Still, the product has been shipped. It can be tempting for a desperate executive to contrive documentation incorrectly showing that a consummated sale has taken place.

An additional opportunity for revenue recognition manipulation can involve sales discounts. The need for additional revenue may result in special discounts being offered to purchasers that make little economic sense and that, if truthfully reported to the accounting department, may result in little or no increase of earnings. So the discounts, or some aspects of their terms, are not candidly reported. Again, financial results are artificially manipulated upward.

If all else fails, there's always barter transactions. These are genuinely a device of last resort—they can be complicated, messy, and an overall headache for everyone involved. Still, a barter transaction—meaning an exchange of one physical asset for another (rather than for cash)—historically has created the opportunity for manipulation since, for example, the values of the exchanged items may have been less than concrete. The accounting principles applicable to barter transactions are complicated and recent rule changes have made manipulation more difficult. A further downside is that a significant barter transaction—particularly at quarter-end—may attract the attention of the auditors. But, for an executive who is genuinely desperate, one does what one has to do.

Reserves

As illustrated at the outset, an area ripe with opportunity for manipulation involves the use of reserves. Although the term *reserves* is used broadly, in this instance we are talking about pools based on an estimate that either reduces the value of an asset (e.g., an allowance or reserve for bad debts) or establishes a liability for costs expected to be incurred in the future (e.g., damages relating to a lawsuit).

The reason reserves may be candidates for manipulation is that reserves by their nature often involve some element of prediction. The precise number, therefore, can never be known. Under GAAP, the appropriate reserve level is determined according to the best estimate of management based on its reasoned and informed judgment.

With regard to some reserves, the opportunities for manipulation are fairly constrained. If, for example, a company has consistently experienced a 90 percent collection rate on its receivables over the last 20 years, it is hard to argue that suddenly the reserve should be reduced from 10 percent to 2 percent absent any demonstrable changes that would dramatically improve collections. Frequently, though, the appropriate reserve is not clear. That is particularly the case in new or evolving industries, where the track record of performance is either nonexistent or short.

One type of reserve that has generated more than its share of regulatory scrutiny—and that has been a particular hot button with the SEC—involves reserves in the form of restructuring charges taken at the time of a merger or corporate reorganization. Restructuring charges are supposed to cover one-time costs, such as the costs of consolidating two companies, relocating or eliminating redundant operations, or paying severance to terminated employees. The charge is generally recorded and labeled as a special or unusual charge in the company's financial statements.

The danger inherent in such reserves arises from the potential desire by management to overstate the restructuring charge (i.e., create an excess reserve) so that the excess can be used to bolster income in future periods. Many believe that Wall Street analysts tend to ignore or discount the effect of restructuring charges as onetime or extraordinary, so the company's managers may reason that they are better off taking a hit to income up front and later reversing the excess reserve into income, thereby improving profits.

Inventory

For those defrauders interested in tradition, inventory manipulation is the vehicle of choice. One of the most famous frauds of the past century—McKesson-Robbins during the 1930s—turned on inventory fraud. It was specifically because of the inventory fraud at McKesson-Robbins that audit standards were rewritten to enhance auditor observation as to inventory.

Today, inventory remains rich with opportunity. One reason is the need to record inventory at the lower of cost or market. Although cost is objectively verifiable, market value sometimes is not. GAAP also necessitate judgments as to the time at which recorded inventory levels should be reduced or perhaps written off entirely.

Another problem with inventory involves the clumsiness inherent in physical inspection and verification. Although audit standards generally call upon an auditor to undertake some level of physical observation of inventory, even here the auditor relies on techniques of statistical sampling and random tests. In the event of fraud, such tasks are never foolproof. Fraud perpetrators have been known to go to such extremes as filling boxes with bricks, sealing the boxes, and labeling them falsely. Another device has been to borrow inventory at year-end, place falsified labels upon the boxes, place the boxes on the shelves so they are available to be counted, and then return the inventory to its rightful owner once the auditors have left. Other methods used to circumvent the physical inspection and verification process include manipulating inventory counts at locations not visited by the auditor and falsifying records regarding inventory reported to be in transit.

Expenses

Expense manipulation isn't usually the first choice, but sometimes it gets used to help cover tracks. The manipulation of expenses can be more difficult than, say, the manipulation of reserves, because expense amounts are normally objectively verifiable and, under GAAP, there is typically not much room for discretion. Nonetheless, expense recognition can be delayed, thereby artificially enhancing profitability.

One aspect of the recording of expenses, moreover, is more susceptible to fraud than the others. That involves the distinction between expenditures that are to be expensed and expenditures that are to be capitalized. Insofar as the distinction under GAAP can involve judgments regarding the nature of the cost or its future benefit to the organization, the opportunity for manipulation is enhanced.

 ## THE GENERAL LEDGER

Let's get back to the search for the fraud. With a good sense of those areas of the financial statements most vulnerable, and whatever clues we've gleaned from an initial set of interviews focusing on those entries initially arousing suspicion, we can turn attention to a place with the potential to provide a cornucopia of useful information. That is the accounting system's general ledger.

For an audit committee on the search for fraud, there are several great things about the general ledger. One is that virtually all sophisticated financial reporting systems have one. Another is that, as the primary accounting tool of the company, it reflects every transaction the company has entered. Unless the fraud has been perpetrated simply through last-minute topside adjustments, it is captured in the general ledger somewhere. The issue is knowing how to look.

The important thing here is to keep in mind (yet again we go back to the origin of financial fraud in Chapter 1) the way that fraud starts and grows. That means that ledger entries entered at particular points of time—say, the final days leading up to the end of a quarter—are more likely to reflect falsified information than entries made at earlier points. Beyond that, a fraudulent general ledger entry in the closing days of a quarter may reflect unusual characteristics. For example, the amounts involved (having been determined, as they were, by the need to cross a certain numerical threshold rather than by a legitimate business transaction) may by their nature look a bit strange. Perhaps they are larger than might be expected or rounded off. It also may be that unusual corporate personnel were involved—executives who would not normally be involved in general ledger entries. Or, if the manipulating executives are not thinking far enough ahead, the documentation behind the journal entries may not be complete or free from suspicion. For example, a nonroutine, unusually large ledger entry with rounded numbers that was atypically made at the direction of a senior executive two days before the end of a quarter might arouse some suspicions.

Forensic computers can be deployed to look for fraud. Based on years of accumulated experience, savvy forensic accountants at the big accounting and consulting firms have developed computerized searching tools that, once plugged into a company's general ledger system, will at high speed start combing through thousands of entries and kicking out those that for any number of reasons look unusual or suspicious. Armed with that data, the forensic accountants may then seek backup documentation and undertake other efforts to look for those entries that were not legitimate when made.

It is a virtue of the general ledger that, once a suspicious entry has been identified, the ledger itself will contain a wealth of data to be explored (see Exhibit 9.2). Among such data may be the source for the amount recorded (a manually prepared journal entry may look more suspicious than an entry made through an automated sub-accounting system), the individual employee responsible for physically keypunching the entry into the accounting system, the date on which the entry was made, an explanation, and other backup data supporting the entry. That is not to suggest that the general ledger will provide all of the answers, but it does provide an excellent place to start.

Indeed, once a suspicious general ledger entry has been identified, determining its legitimacy can be fairly straightforward. Sometimes it might involve simply a conversation with the employee who physically made the entry. The background here is that senior executives seeking to perpetrate financial fraud often suffer from a significant handicap: They don't know how to work the computers. To see that a fraudulent entry is made, they have to ask some employee sitting at a computer screen—who, if properly trained, may want to understand the support for a nonroutine transaction coming from an unusual source. Of course, if the employee's boss simply orders him to make the entry, resistance may be awkward. But, if suspicions are aroused, the direction to enter the entry

---

EXHIBIT 9.2   General Ledger Clues

- The journal entries that the company recorded to implement the fraud
- The dates on which the company recorded fraudulent transactions
- The sources for the amounts recorded (e.g., an automated sub-accounting system, such as purchasing or treasury, versus a manually prepared journal entry)
- The company employee responsible for entering the journal entries into the accounting system
- Adjusting journal entries that may have been recorded

may stick in the employee's memory, giving the employee the ability to later describe in convincing detail exactly how the ledger entry came to be made. Or, concerned about the appearance of his own complicity, the employee may include with the journal entry an explanation that captures his skepticism. The senior executive directing the entry may be oblivious to all this. He thinks he has successfully adjusted the general ledger to create the needed earnings. Little does he know that within the ledger entry the data-entering employee has embedded incriminating evidence.

The general ledger may reflect as well large transactions that simply by their nature are suspicious. The audit committee's investigators may want to ask the executive responsible about such a transaction's business purpose, the underlying terms, the timing, and the nature of the negotiations. Transaction documentation might be compared to the general ledger's entry to make sure that nothing was left out or changed. If feasible, the forensic accountants may even want to reach out to the counterparty to explore whether there are any unrecorded terms in side letters or otherwise undisclosed aspects of the transaction.

An investigation will not ordinarily stop with clues gleaned from the general ledger. For example, frequently a useful step is to assess the extent to which a company has accounted for significant or suspicious transactions in accordance with their underlying terms. Such scrutiny may include a search for undisclosed terms, such as those that may be included in side letters or pursuant to oral agreements. In searching for such things, the investigators will seek to cast a wide net and may try to coax helpful information from knowledgeable company personnel outside the accounting function. As one habitually skeptical accountant once put it, "I like to talk to the guys on the loading dock. They'll tell you anything."

While such forensic accounting techniques—and there are many others— can be undertaken independently of what employee interviews turn up, usually the two will go hand in hand. For example, an interview of one employee might yield suspicions about a particular journal entry, which is then dug out of the accounting system and itself investigated. Or a search of the general ledger may yield evidence of a suspicious transaction, resulting in additional interviews of employees. Before long, the investigative trail may look like a roadmap of Paris. Clues are discovered, cross-checked against other information, and explored further. Employees are examined on entries and, as additional information surfaces, examined again. As the investigation progresses, shapes start to appear in the fog. Patterns emerge. And those executives not being completely candid look increasingly suspicious.

In the meantime, investigators will be dispatched to look at still another source of potential information. That is the treasure trove of clues that are likely to be found within the company's email system.

 ## EMAIL SEARCHES

It is simply astonishing the extent to which perpetrators of financial fraud will email each other about their accounting manipulations. But, astonishing or not, it happens.

Why do employees do such a stupid thing? Well, it may not seem so stupid at the time. For one thing, the employees themselves might not realize that the accounting adjustments they are discussing would be viewed in a more objective environment as fraudulent. That is particularly so if they are being overseen by senior executives whose ostensible integrity is beyond question. Such entries may be mixed in as part of the normal quarter-end closing process in which the distinction between legitimate adjusting entries and those more questionable is hazy. To the extent certain kinds of adjustments have gone on for years, there may be a completely understandable inclination to assume their legitimacy. A junior accountant hired just out of college by a prestigious company may be less likely to question the way things are done if only because he doesn't know any better.

How do the audit committee investigators go about searching the email system? One way to start is simply to search for terms normally associated with financial fraud. Among the more obvious terms, for example, might be "fraud," "cooking the books," "rainy-day reserves," or "cookie-jar reserves." Believe it or not, all of those terms can be used by defrauders. And a good clue is the perennial email, "We should not be discussing this subject by email." Not all the clues, of course, will be that obvious, and searches through emails often must be accompanied by additional interviews. But, again, it is astonishing how often the email evidence will be fairly clear.

 ## TERMINATING SENIOR WRONGDOERS

With all these techniques being pursued in parallel, the investigators will make steady progress. Still, that progress is rarely as fast as anyone would like. One reason is that the investigators, even with all their experience and ingenuity, will be encountering a significant headwind. That headwind is the lack of candor on the part of those who have a good sense of where the bodies are buried.

For the guilty senior executives, that is not surprising. They have probably lied many times about their accounting manipulations and gotten pretty good at it. Over the years, they may have found themselves giving false explanations about financial results to the board of directors, the audit committee, outside investors, lenders, and analysts—not to mention the internal auditors and external auditors who may have sought supporting detail. As the years have gone by, false explanations regarding financial performance may have become perfectly natural. They may have become more natural than telling the truth.

For less-senior employees, lack of candor about accounting manipulations may come less naturally but, in context, may be nonetheless understandable. In a sense, such employees are in trouble no matter what they do. Of course, if they have doubts about their own innocence, that can be a significant impediment to a level of candor that would put their doubts to the test. However, even genuine belief in individual innocence will not necessarily result in candor with the audit committee investigators. That is particularly the case if the more-senior wrongdoing executives are still in place. Knowledgeable employees, even if innocent, will be all too aware of the possibility that at some point the investigation will end, the investigative team will be disbanded, and the audit committee will retreat back into its more distant role. If senior wrongdoing executives are still in place, the opportunity for revenge will be at hand. Far better for even innocent employees, therefore, to keep their mouths shut as long as there is any possibility that senior executives will survive. That is particularly so if the senior executives find ways to communicate to employees that they are doing their best to keep track of who is saying what.

This means that one of the most important objectives for the audit committee investigators will be an early determination regarding the complicity or innocence of senior executives. Senior executives whose innocence has been established can be called on to encourage employees to speak candidly and provide full cooperation without fear of retribution down the road. In contrast, those senior executives found to have been complicit in the fraud are best removed quickly. The mere fact of their continuing presence at the company can be expected to chill the candor of the dialogue with the audit committee investigators.

The urgency of the need to come to up-front determinations on the complicity of senior executives can result in a significant level of discomfort for the audit committee itself. The audit committee, for example, may have been interacting with a complicit senior executive for years. Over time, the committee members may have developed respect for his ostensible integrity and trust in his judgment. Now, they are being told by newly hired investigators—who, by virtue of their independence, they may have never met before—that this trusted executive needs to be terminated at once. Some degree of audit committee skepticism and reluctance is understandable.

And the senior executive will not make things any easier for the audit committee. He can be expected to protest that it's all a mistake, the investigators are confused, nobody understands the accounting system better than he, and the "evidence" is vague at best. To some degree, much of this may be true. To the extent that it is, the duty of candor of the investigators themselves to the audit committee requires they acknowledge where ambiguities exist in their investigative analysis. The members of the audit committee, therefore, may be torn. They may be concerned about a "rush to judgment" and whether the senior executive has received the fair hearing and due process that his years of hard work and loyalty to the company have earned. Making things worse, his termination may need to be a noisy affair—the securities laws may require a press release—and the result will be not only the termination of his career but in all likelihood additional investigation and severe reaction by the SEC and, in particularly egregious cases, the Department of Justice. On the other hand, the audit committee members will appreciate that, as long as a senior wrongdoer is left in place, complete cooperation by employees cannot be expected. Loyalty, and even the desire for additional due process, cannot overcome the need to set things straight as quickly as possible.

The termination and removal of wrongdoing senior executives can constitute a watershed in the investigation. Once complicit senior executives are removed, it will be obvious to employees at all levels that the truth is going to come out. In a sense, overly cautious employees will now want to change sides. If a senior executive can be terminated, so can any employee—unless he quickly establishes his own integrity by immediately volunteering what he knows. At this point, the process of plodding through the general ledger, searching through emails, and employing other investigative techniques gets a sharp boost. Employees start telling the investigators all they can about where to look and what happened. The time needed to complete the investigation has now been shortened exponentially.

CHAPTER TEN

Getting a New Audit Report on the Financial Statements

A S A COMPANY WORKS THROUGH the problems following the discovery of financial fraud, one realization will loom larger and larger in the audit committee's mind: To a significant extent, the company's fate now lies in the hands of its outside auditor. Without an unqualified audit report, a company can find it almost impossible to function with any degree of normalcy. Lenders, regulators, its securities exchange, suppliers, customers, employees—each of these will remain exceedingly skeptical of management until the company's integrity is reestablished and its credibility restored. The audit report represents independent confirmation that the company has taken the right steps toward getting its financial house in order, in providing reliable financial data, and in restoring some level of institutional integrity.

For a board desperate to move beyond the problem, procurement of an unqualified audit report often becomes the key to a return to normalcy. Unfortunately, it can also seem like the quest for the holy grail. Auditors, too, are capable of emotional reactions to the discovery of fraud, especially when the fraud has developed in such a way that they can be counted among the victims. Just at the moment the company's need for an audit report is at its utmost, the auditor may be looking to the door. Auditor resignation in such a circumstance is far from unknown.

For that reason, the board's focus will soon shift to the auditor. In particular, it shifts to one of the biggest obstacles the board will face: getting a new audit report on its financial statements.

EARLY INVOLVEMENT OF THE AUDITOR

Once an early indicator of potential fraudulent financial reporting takes on any element of credibility, an audit committee will not want to delay in alerting the outside auditor of the financial statements. One reason may simply be a practical one. The audit committee may not know who within the company was involved and may lack the internal resources to conduct a preliminary investigation from within. The audit committee may want to seek the assistance of the auditor because, as a practical matter, the audit committee has nowhere else to turn.

Beyond the practicalities, there is an additional reason for early involvement of the outside auditor. The relationship between the company and the outside auditor is about to undergo a period of great stress (see ahead). It will be critical for the audit committee to keep the outside auditor's trust—or, if that trust has dissipated, to regain it—and candor with the auditor will be key. Any sense by the auditor that it has been kept in the dark, even for a brief period, may factor significantly into whether the auditor is willing to keep the company as a client.

SECURITIES EXCHANGE ACT SECTION 10A

An auditor who receives information of possible illegal acts materially affecting financial statements is not completely left to its own judgment as to how to respond. Rather, as part of the "tort reform" of the mid-1990s, an amendment was added to the Securities Exchange Act of 1934 specifically directed to an auditor's response where such evidence has surfaced. Within the accounting profession, it is known simply as "Section 10A." Its impact often catches audit committees completely by surprise.

The basic gist of Section 10A calls upon the auditor to evaluate whether an audit committee, faced with evidence of possible illegal acts affecting the financial statements, is doing the right thing. The technical provisions are complicated (see Exhibit 10.1), but the statute boils down to a requirement that the auditor evaluate whether the audit committee is taking "timely and appropriate remedial actions." If the auditor is satisfied that the audit committee is taking "timely and appropriate remedial actions," the auditor may allow the audit committee to proceed accordingly. If, however, the auditor is *not* satisfied that the audit committee is taking "timely and appropriate remedial actions," the statute provides for auditor notification directly to the SEC. To provide that notification, the statute gives the auditor 24 hours.

What are the "timely and appropriate remedial actions" the absence of which may result in 24-hour notification to the SEC? The statute does not say. It is left entirely to the discretion of the auditor.

The congressional determination behind Section 10A—which was vigorously debated before its enactment—was that an audit committee not properly

---

EXHIBIT 10.1   Section 10A (Excerpt)

(2) *Response to Failure to Take Remedial Action.* If, after determining that the audit committee of the board of directors of the issuer, or the board of directors of the issuer in the absence of an audit committee, is adequately informed with respect to illegal acts that have been detected or have otherwise come to the attention of the firm in the course of the audit of such accountant, the registered public accounting firm concludes that:

(A) the illegal act has a material effect on the financial statements of the issuer;

(B) the senior management has not taken, and the board of directors has not caused senior management to take, timely and appropriate remedial actions with respect to the illegal act; and

(C) the failure to take remedial action is reasonably expected to warrant departure from a standard report of the auditor, when made, or warrant resignation from the audit engagement; the registered public accounting firm shall, as soon as practicable, directly report its conclusions to the board of directors.

(3) *Notice to Commission; Response to Failure to Notify.* An issuer whose board of directors receives a report under paragraph (2) shall inform the Commission by notice not later than 1 business day after the receipt of such report and shall furnish the registered public accounting firm making such report with a copy of the notice furnished to the Commission. If the registered public accounting firm fails to receive a copy of the notice before the expiration of the required 1-business-day period, the registered public accounting firm shall:

(A) resign from the engagement; or

(B) furnish to the Commission a copy of its report (or the documentation of any oral report given) not later than 1 business day following such failure to receive notice.

(4) *Report After Resignation.* If a registered public accounting firm resigns from an engagement under paragraph (3)(A), the firm shall, not later than 1 business day following the failure by the issuer to notify the Commission under paragraph (3), furnish to the Commission a copy of the report of the firm (or the documentation of any oral report given).

responding to fraudulent financial reporting should not be left to its own devices. Under the statute, therefore, an auditor whose client is failing to take the proper steps can be expected to make a so-called "Section 10A report" to the SEC disclosing the auditor's dissatisfaction with the audit committee's response. The statutorily specified 24-hour time frame gives the auditor very little room to maneuver once dissatisfaction with the audit committee's response has been determined. As a result, often unbeknownst to the audit committee, the entirety of the auditor—client relationship is now on a hair-trigger.

One consequence is that, as it proceeds through the investigative process, the audit committee will want to listen carefully to the auditor's views and concerns. Unsophisticated audit committees sometimes operate under the presumption that, while things are not going perfectly, they are going well enough. Unbeknownst to the audit committee, behind the scenes the auditor is in a high level of distress but constrained by the circumstances to conveying only temperate expressions of dissatisfaction. The audit committee learns only after it is too late that those temperate expressions of dissatisfaction should have been listened to with greater attentiveness.

While Section 10A vests in the auditor great latitude in forming a judgment regarding the extent of an audit committee's "timely and appropriate remedial actions," the auditor's judgment is not exempt from scrutiny by the SEC. Thus, the auditor has to assume its judgment regarding the audit committee's "timely and appropriate remedial actions" will, once the investigation is complete, be the subject of after-the-fact SEC consideration. In a sense, the effect is to make the auditor strictly responsible for the adequacy of the audit committee's investigation. Woe to the auditor that issues an audit report based on an investigation or other audit committee actions that the SEC subsequently concludes to have fallen short of "appropriate." This is one reason that the auditor will be sensitive to the tone and substance of the audit committee's interaction with the SEC and to whether the SEC appears to be satisfied with the steps the audit committee is taking. If there appears to be stress between the two, that can constitute a significant impediment to the auditor's ability to issue an audit report.

Mindful of its obligations under Section 10A, the accounting profession over time has adopted an approach that appears to favor investigative reports fulfilling key criteria such as oversight by the audit committee, the involvement of independent counsel, and auditor transparency into the investigative findings. Boiling it down, among the criteria appear to be these:

1. An internal investigation of potential accounting irregularities at a public company should be overseen by the board's audit committee.

2. The investigation should be undertaken by a substantial law firm of good reputation that has no meaningful history of reporting to management. Regular outside counsel, or defense counsel in related litigation, will rarely suffice.

3. The law firm under normal circumstances should arrange for forensic accountants to provide assistance.

4. The investigation may initially focus on particular issues but is not to be impeded by unreasonable constraint. The investigators are to have license to pursue all evidence of potential improprieties no matter where they may lead.

5. The investigators should consult with the auditor at the outset to ensure that the proposed scope of the investigation will be sufficient to be relied upon for audit purposes. Throughout the course of the investigation, the auditor should be periodically apprised of the extent to which the scope remains adequate or needs to be expanded.

6. The audit committee, as a matter of substance and tone, must express a willingness to actively oversee the investigation and assume responsibility for its results. It is the audit committee that is to select and engage the law firm responsible for conducting the investigation, and it is the audit committee to whom the investigators are to directly report.

7. The audit committee is to see that all company personnel are encouraged to cooperate with the investigation in both substance and spirit. Company personnel are to make themselves available on request, to cooperate to the fullest extent possible, to make available all requested documents, and to be truthful and candid with the investigators.

8. The audit committee should consider the need to put in place procedures to ensure that executives or employees potentially involved in misconduct are not informed or updated as to investigative progress or tentative results. Executives should not have the opportunity to interfere with the investigation or have any prior substantive contact with individuals being interviewed on the subjects into which inquiry is being made.

9. The audit committee, in conjunction with its counsel, should consider the extent to which initial disclosure regarding the investigation and its subject matter may be needed. Draft press releases should be made available for review by the auditor.

10. The investigation may proceed with all available dispatch, but is not to be compromised by inordinate management pressure, upcoming deadlines for the filing of a Form 10-K, or other artificial constraint. The auditor will not permit the scope, quality, or depth of an investigation to be compromised by deadlines.

11. The auditor will often seek "complete transparency" between the conduct of the investigation and the information available to the auditor. In other words, the auditor may not accept, as justification for lack of access to information, assertions of attorney-client privilege or work product. The auditor will ordinarily want to determine, as a matter of its own judgment, those investigative materials it will want to review. The auditor may view a failure to provide those materials as a scope limitation to the audit.

12. The audit committee should consult its counsel as to its responsiveness and cooperation with the staff of the SEC in connection with an SEC investigation. That issue should be discussed as well with the auditor insofar as the audit committee may request the auditor to accompany company personnel in SEC presentations.

13. On particular issues, investigators may find evidence going both ways— both incriminating and exculpatory. The audit committee should understand that the auditor will consider incriminating evidence in assessing appropriate remedial action and its willingness to accept representations from particular individuals.

14. Upon the investigation's completion, the investigators should provide a report setting forth, among other things:

    a. The circumstances giving rise to the investigation
    b. The investigation's scope
    c. The persons interviewed
    d. Sources of documents reviewed
    e. The underlying facts
    f. Determinations as to wrongful intent
    g. The necessary adjustments to the company's financial statements (if feasible)
    h. Proposed remedial action

    The auditor and the audit committee should discuss whether the report should be in writing with appropriate cognizance being taken of the needs and desires of relevant regulators. The audit committee should understand that, regardless of whether a written report is prepared, the auditor will normally document important aspects of the report in its workpapers.

15. Upon the investigation's completion, the auditor will assess the reasonableness of the scope, findings, and conclusions of the investigation and the extent to which the investigation can be relied upon for the purpose of issuing an audit report.

16. The auditor will separately assess the extent to which the company has taken "timely and appropriate remedial actions" pursuant to Section

10A of the Securities Exchange Act of 1934. An important aspect of that assessment will often involve the extent to which company personnel have been forthright and candid with investigators and company stakeholders.

17. The company will be called upon to provide representations with regard to the investigation and any financial statements affected by its conclusions. The audit committee and investigators should be mindful, throughout the investigation, that the auditor may not be in the position to accept audit-related representations from members of management as to whom there is evidence of wrongful conduct.

18. Throughout the investigation, and upon its completion, the audit committee and its counsel should assess the extent to which additional public disclosure is appropriate. Such disclosure should be reviewed by the auditor prior to its issuance.

The more criteria an audit committee can fulfill, the greater the likelihood that the investigative conclusions will be acceptable for the purpose of issuing a new audit report on restated financial statements—which is one of the key objectives of the entire process.

Insofar as Section 10A is included within the federal securities laws, it is technically not applicable to private companies. However, an analogous requirement of auditor evaluation of a company's response to possible illegal acts, applicable to public and nonpublic companies, is contained within generally accepted auditing standards (GAAS) themselves. While the two are not exactly the same, they are close enough so that both public and nonpublic companies can expect the auditor to scrutinize carefully the company's response to potential fraudulent financial reporting.

THE IMPACT ON PREVIOUSLY ISSUED FINANCIAL STATEMENTS

For an auditor who learns that a client has perpetrated a financial fraud, the situation is enormously complicated—and many competing considerations need to be evaluated at once.

For the auditor, the starting place will be some of the most obvious questions. How bad is the fraud? How far back does it go? Who did it? Does it potentially affect previously issued financial statements underlying an audit report? How did we miss it?

While these are generally the same questions everyone else will be asking, the auditor may bring particular urgency owing to an obligation under GAAS. That obligation involves the need for the auditor, upon learning of fraudulent financial reporting, to evaluate the reliability of financial statements underlying previously issued audit reports on which the public or others may be relying.

This evaluation of financial statement reliability is, to say the least, difficult. On the one hand, the auditor will want to formulate a judgment without delay. On the other hand, the circumstances will often impede any definitive conclusion. Nor does it suffice for the auditor to simply assume the worst and encourage the audit committee to make a public announcement that overstates the problem. Rather than overstate or understate the problem, the objective will be to encourage disclosure that describes the situation as accurately as the circumstances allow. Here, again, the auditor has to assume that the auditor's judgment will later be scrutinized by the SEC. The SEC will have the benefit of hindsight. At the time the judgment has to be made, the auditor does not.

If the auditor concludes that previously issued financial statements underlying an audit report are no longer sufficiently reliable, the auditor will want to encourage the audit committee to make appropriate disclosure to that effect. For public companies, such disclosure will often take the form of a press release that seeks to strike the delicate balance between accurate disclosure of the problem and avoidance of undue panic in the streets. Where the determination is made that previously issued financial statements lack the requisite reliability, the key phrase to be included in the press release will often be that the financial statements and related audit report "should not be relied upon."

Of course, the auditor is not the only one called upon to form a judgment regarding the reliability of earlier-issued financial statements. It is the company, and in particular its audit committee, that will have primary responsibility for that evaluation and the content of any public disclosure that is to be made. Securities law regulations mandate that a company, within four days after determining that financial statements "should no longer be relied upon because of an error," is to disclose certain information, including the date of its conclusion regarding nonreliance and "a brief description of the facts . . . to the extent known." If the company's disclosure is prompted by a notification from the outside auditor, the regulations require additional information regarding the auditor's views.

THE DIFFERENCE BETWEEN AN AUDIT AND A FORENSIC INVESTIGATION

The involvement of the outside auditor means that two separate teams of accountants—typically from different firms—will be involved in the examination of the accounts. A source of perennial audit committee confusion is the difference in the function of each.

The main difference between a conventional audit and a forensic investigation involves the principal assumption that constitutes the engagement's predicate. In a normal audit, the predicate is that, absent evidence to the contrary, management of the company, while perhaps not perfect, is approaching its financial reporting in good faith and seeking to prepare financial statements that fairly present the financial position of the company in accordance with generally accepted accounting principles (GAAP). The basic approach to the audit, therefore, involves the auditor's receipt of draft financial statements from the client; the selection of samples of financial data to be subject to audit testing; testing of the sampling of accounts; communication to the company of financial statement amounts that, based on the audit testing, need to be adjusted; and the formulation of a judgment regarding whether the financial statements, as adjusted, present fairly the financial position of the company.

None of this is to suggest that an auditor is entitled to accept everything at face value. An auditor is called upon to make a judgment about the risk of a material misstatement due to fraud and in light of that judgment to design appropriate audit tests. Still, absent evidence to the contrary, the auditor will generally not assume management to be dishonest. The technical term describing the approach is "professional skepticism." At its core, professional skepticism encourages the auditor to be a skeptic but not to assume the falsity of everything everybody says.

In a forensic investigation, that approach changes to the complete opposite. Once it has been established that the bookkeeping has been infected by fraudulent financial reporting, the issue for the forensic accountant is: How deep and widespread does it go?

Therefore, in the eyes of a forensic accountant, anyone might be a suspect. Members of the board of directors, senior executives, those in middle-level management, right down to a truck driver transporting potentially fictitious goods—all may be initially subject to the forensic accountant's exacting scrutiny. True, most may not stay suspects for long. But at the outset, the forensic accountant takes nothing for granted.

This means that all suspicious areas—and even many areas that are only potentially suspicious—will be investigated. Whereas, in the absence of evidence to the contrary, the outside auditor would ordinarily start with the presumption regarding, say, the genuineness of documents, forensic accountants may exhaustively search for evidence that either validates key documents or establishes their falsity. Similarly, forensic accountants will be suspicious of the veracity and completeness of the statements of company personnel made during the investigation. For those within the company, credibility is something that now must be earned.

COORDINATION BETWEEN THE FORENSIC ACCOUNTANTS AND THE OUTSIDE AUDITOR

Another source of audit committee confusion, if not frustration, involves the need for separate audit testing once an investigation is complete. An oft-asked question is: Why does the auditor need to do additional testing at all? Why can't the auditor, once the forensic accountants are finished, simply issue its audit report and be done with it?

The answer lies in the realization that forensic accountants, rather than seeking to conduct an "audit" of the sort that results in an audit report on financial statements, are in substance trying to get things in sufficient order so that an audit can be subsequently undertaken. In other words, the forensic accountants are not conducting an audit. They are trying to get the books and records to a level of reliability such that a proper audit can then be commenced. Once the forensic accountants and other tools of investigation have rooted out the fraud and corrected the falsified entries, it is then the job of the auditor to separately undertake its audit procedures, pursuant to GAAS, to come to a judgment about whether the financial statements, now benefitting from the forensic accountants' work, present fairly the financial position of the company in accordance with GAAP.

There is no rule *prohibiting* the forensic accountants, upon completion of their investigation, from thereupon taking the additional steps necessary under GAAS to formulate a judgment about conformity to GAAP and issuing an audit report to that effect. Indeed, in situations in which, for whatever reason, the company and its outside auditor have parted ways, forensic accountants have been known to do exactly that. Still, the formulation of a formal opinion and issuance of an audit report is not a normal part of the forensic accountant's engagement or within the scope of its work.

This means that, where fraudulent financial reporting has been uncovered, two different sets of accountants—the forensic accountants and the outside auditors—will be examining the financial statements and underlying accounts at almost the same time. Logically, the work of the forensic accountants needs to come first. Until the forensic accountants have rooted out the fraud, there are no theoretically correct financial statements for the auditor to audit. However, the urgency that normally accompanies an audit committee investigation often results in a desire that the auditor commence its audit procedures as soon as it feasibly can.

One consequence of all this is that coordination between the forensic accountants and the outside auditor can be a challenge. While both share a common objective—the issuance of properly stated financial statements—the pressures and difficulties of the environment can sometimes lead to stress between the two. From the auditor's perspective, there may be a lack of enthusiasm over the fact that a team of forensic accountants from a different accounting firm (by the way, a competitor) will be combing through the books and records to figure out just who missed what. The forensic accountants undertaking that investigation, moreover, will probably have a fairly good sense of audit standards and will be almost unable to avoid second-guessing the diligence with which they were applied.

A natural consequence would be for the auditor and the forensic accountants simply to avoid each other. That, though, is a luxury that neither can afford. Each needs the other. The forensic accountants need the auditor because the auditor has possession of knowledge and workpapers that can get the forensic investigation off to a more efficient start. Information about period-end adjusting journal entries, conversations with management regarding suspicious transactions, even important aspects of the audit chronology—all of these will be just sitting in the auditor's historical workpapers waiting for the forensic accountants' review.

But the need for information is not simply a one-way street. The auditor also needs information from the forensic accountants. In particular, as extra protection regarding the integrity of its new audit, the auditor needs to know the results of the forensic accountant's investigation. Was the CEO in on the fraud? Was the CFO? Which individuals within the accounting department were involved in the fraud? These are all key questions that, to the extent not determined during the audit, will need to be answered before the auditor is prepared to issue a new audit report. For the auditor, simply turning away from the forensic accountants and offering no cooperation is not an attractive option.

A truce will therefore be established. The auditor will normally allow the forensic accountants access to its workpapers to assist in the speed and efficiency of the forensic investigation. And the audit committee will agree that formulation of a conclusion as to the adequacy of the auditor's prior work is not an objective of the audit committee investigation. That is not to say that no aspect of the investigation will turn up evidence that might ultimately be used against the auditor. The mere fact that the auditor did not catch the fraud probably makes the discovery of some such evidence inevitable. But the audit committee will agree that, with regard to the auditor, it will not try to make things worse than they already are.

STRESS BETWEEN THE AUDITOR AND ITS CLIENT

Beyond the interactions of the forensic accountants and the auditor, a more serious source of stress may be present. That is the stress between the auditor and its client.

The source of the stress will be the fact that, from the auditor's perspective, company personnel deliberately falsified information, forged documents, fabricated entries, or undertook any number of malevolent actions to deceive the auditor into issuance of an audit report on falsified financial statements. The falsifications were in all likelihood accompanied by face-to-face meetings in which company executives directly lied to audit engagement team personnel. No one likes to be the victim of a lie. That is particularly the case for an outside auditor whose acceptance of the company's falsified information has now in all likelihood made the auditor itself a target in regulatory investigation and litigation.

On the other hand, audit committee members or other board members may be wondering why the auditor failed to catch it. Even sophisticated businesspeople often lack an in-depth understanding of the extent to which a normal audit relies upon selective sampling and judgments based on information provided by the company and may not understand how even a properly conducted audit can be defeated by fraud. As events progress, frustration may evolve into seething resentment as the forensic accountants dig out more and more problems, the auditor insists on more in-depth audit testing, and things seem to drag on and on.

Often, therefore, each side of the relationship—the auditor and the audit committee—will have an eye on relationship termination. If the auditor becomes concerned that the audit committee is not doing the right thing—not taking "timely and appropriate remedial actions" in the language of Section 10A—the auditor may conclude that nothing is to be gained by continued association with the company. For its part, the audit committee may suspect that the auditor's more extensive procedures reveal an internal determination that it will *never* issue an audit report and is just going through the motions. While that will rarely if ever be the case, the audit committee will wonder whether things could be more efficiently completed if the current auditor were replaced with a new one.

BENEFITS OF CONTINUING THE AUDIT RELATIONSHIP

If the stress between the auditor and the company increases to the point where there is a parting of the ways, normally it is the company that has the most to lose.

For the auditor, the downsides of the loss of the audit client are fairly limited—to the extent they exist at all. In purely financial terms, the auditor may have long ago lost any hope that this engagement would turn out to be a profitable one. The auditor by this point is probably paying enormous amounts in legal and other fees owing to regulatory investigation and litigation. In the meantime, any number of state boards of accountancy may be waiting in the wings to commence state law proceedings calling into question whether those individual auditors who missed the fraud should have their state licenses revoked. Beyond that, the auditor's prior association with the company may be the subject of severe criticism in the financial press. True, a strong sense of duty will contribute to the auditor's sense of professional obligation to see the task through to the end. But, in purely financial or reputational terms, the costs may appear to exceed the benefits.

From the company's perspective, the loss of the incumbent auditor can be a disaster. Once fraudulent financial reporting has surfaced, the procurement of an audit report as fast as possible is of the utmost importance. No matter how long the incumbent auditor seems to be taking, its replacement with a new auditor will probably take longer. If the incumbent auditor is replaced, moreover, a new auditor may want to scrutinize and second-guess areas of the financial statements *unaffected* by the fraud. A new auditor will not necessarily accept at face value the old auditor's judgments in the application of GAAP.

Breaking it down, typical reasons for favoring continuation with the incumbent auditor are these:

1. *Speed.* The incumbent auditor can do it faster. In the absence of evidence to the contrary, the incumbent auditor to some extent will generally be able to rely on audit work it has already performed. Conversely, in order to be able to render an opinion on the financial statements, any new auditor may need to perform extensive audit procedures beyond areas affected by the accounting irregularities. Such additional efforts can be particularly time consuming where the irregularities have affected multiple years.

2. *Information.* Often, the auditor's workpapers will contain documents that shed light on the origin of and parties responsible for the fraud. For example, an auditor may have copies of documents that turn out to have been altered or evidence of misrepresentations made to the auditor by company personnel. Termination of the auditor may hinder the investigation by delaying or even precluding audit workpaper access.

3. *Concurrence.* If a company opts to engage a different auditor, it increases the risk that the former auditor will later publicly contest the restatement. Such disputes can cast further doubt on the integrity of the company's financial statements at a time when the company can ill afford additional uncertainty.

4. *Prior-year audit reports.* When financial fraud is determined not to extend back to multiple years, a company may wish to continue to rely on prior years' audit reports. For example, applicable regulations generally require a company to keep on record a total of three successive years of audited financial statements. If the company terminates its incumbent auditor or otherwise isolates the auditor from the investigation findings, the auditor may withhold its consent to incorporate its audit reports from prior years. Conversely, an auditor that is sufficiently familiar with the investigation findings should be in a position to reaffirm previously rendered audit reports on years unaffected by the fraud.

5. *New auditor reluctance.* At this particular moment in its corporate history, the company is not exactly a dream audit client. At least some members of management have probably committed fraud. Among the victims of the fraud is the incumbent auditor. It is not necessarily the case, therefore, that termination of the incumbent auditor will be followed by an onslaught of other auditors fighting to pick up the engagement. Depending on the circumstances, each of the other Big Four accounting firms (if your incumbent auditor is a Big Four firm, already you're down to three) may decide it

is better to let this one pass. If the company has separately engaged one or more other accounting firms for nonaudit services that are prohibited by SEC independence rules, those other firms may not be realistic candidates to be engaged as auditor. Termination of the existing auditor—at least until another firm is lined up—can therefore leave the company in the completely untenable position of having no auditor at all.

RESPONSIBILITY FOR RESTATED FINANCIAL STATEMENTS

Notwithstanding the involvement of armies of auditors and forensic accountants, the ultimate responsibility for preparing proper financial statements remains with the company. Before the auditor issues an audit report on the restated financial statements, it will require appropriate members of the company's management to provide written representations that the financial statements are management's responsibility and have been fairly presented in accordance with GAAP. Management must, therefore, fully understand and take responsibility for any corrections.

Although it may seem obvious that management should be knowledgeable about its own financial statements, the time-sensitive, pressure-filled environment of an investigation into financial fraud usually is unfamiliar territory to management personnel. In some cases, high-level financial managers, new to their positions as a consequence of recent personnel changes, may be dedicating most of their time to other newly obtained responsibilities. Often, irregularities are identified and quantified initially by the forensic accountants rather than company personnel, who may find themselves largely left out of the picture. However, even in instances in which well-respected forensic accountants have identified, quantified, and documented restatement adjustments, management must ensure that the company maintains appropriate documentation of the nature and composition of such adjustments and takes responsibility for concluding that such adjustments are appropriate.

RESTATEMENT REQUIREMENTS

If fraud is found to an extent that requires adjustment of the financial statements, the proper vehicle of correction is a *restatement*. Not every issue that surfaces, however, will require a restatement. Indeed, restatement to accommodate certain kinds of issues is forbidden by GAAP. Thus, one task facing the company will be to determine which issues require restatement and which do not.

As a general matter, the issues uncovered during an investigation will fall into one of five categories:

1. *Errors.* Errors are unintentional misstatements of amounts or disclosures in financial statements. Errors may involve
   ▪ Mistakes in gathering or processing data from which financial statements are prepared
   ▪ Unreasonable accounting estimates arising from oversight or misinterpretation of the facts
   ▪ Mistakes in applying accounting principles relating to the amount, classification, manner of presentation, or disclosure in the financial statements
2. *Irregularities.* Irregularities (under revised audit standards they are now called *fraud*) are intentional misstatements arising from fraudulent financial reporting practices, such as
   ▪ Manipulation, fabrication, or alteration of accounting records or supporting documents from which financial statements are prepared
   ▪ Misrepresentation in the financial statements of events, transactions, or other information
   ▪ Intentional misapplication of accounting principles relating to the amounts, classification, manner of presentation, or disclosure in the financial statements
3. *Illegal acts.* Illegal acts involve violations of laws or governmental regulations.
4. *Inaccurate estimates.* Subsequent events may demonstrate that accounting estimates used in preparing the financial statements have proved to be inaccurate. Examples of accounting estimates that can be called into question include inventory valuation reserves, bad debt reserves, loss contract reserves, percentage-of-completion revenue recognition estimates, sales returns and allowance reserves, and warranty reserves.
5. *Changes in accounting policies.* Accounting policies represent the methods adopted by a company to account for transactions in accordance with GAAP. Sometimes two or more acceptable methods of accounting exist for certain types of transactions (the use of FIFO or LIFO to account for inventory being a good example).

It is the category into which an item falls that determines whether the financial statements are to be "restated" for the item or not. Material misstatements arising out of newly discovered errors, irregularities, or illegal acts are generally to be corrected through a restatement. On the other hand, the identification of good-faith but ultimately incorrect estimates underlying the financial statements does not mandate restatement. Under GAAP, changes in estimates generally should be accounted for in the period the company changes its estimate and, in certain circumstances, in future periods. (See Exhibit 10.2.)

The distinctions between these different types of accounting issues can be imprecise. Distinguishing between an incorrect estimate that is the result of an error (which requires a restatement) and an incorrect estimate that is the result of reasonably unforeseen subsequent events (which does not) can be subtle. The context in which the distinctions must be made virtually guarantees that all such determinations will be heavily second-guessed. Thus, the restatement process may involve much discussion and debate among the audit committee, management, the auditor, counsel, and the forensic accountants.

Further complicating the process may be a natural desire on the part of the audit committee to seize the opportunity to change preexisting accounting policies even though those preexisting accounting policies have already complied with GAAP. For example, to increase its credibility with the financial community, the audit committee may decide to adopt new accounting policies that, while still complying with GAAP, are more conservative than those previously used.

If a company elects to change from one proper accounting policy to another, the nature and justification for the change and its effect on income are to be disclosed in the financial statements in the period in which the company

EXHIBIT 10.2 Restatement Guidance

Accounting issues that require restatement:

■ Misstatements arising out of errors
■ Misstatements arising out of irregularities
■ Misstatements arising out of illegal acts
■ Misstatements arising out of bad-faith estimates

Accounting issues that do not require restatement:

■ Misstatements arising out of a revision of earlier good-faith estimates
■ Misstatements arising out of a change in accounting principles

makes the change. Although GAAP provide for certain exceptions, companies generally are to report most changes in accounting principles by recognizing the cumulative effect on net income of the period of the change rather than as a restatement of prior-period results.

RESTATEMENTS AND MATERIALITY

Assessment of the need for a restatement is complicated by another consideration. Financial statements must be restated only where the prior misstatement is one that is *material*.

Assessments of materiality have always been a challenge, and the challenge has increased within the last several years. Historically, materiality assessments have typically focused upon the application of certain numerical thresholds. By convention, potential adjustments below 5 percent were less inclined to be viewed as material. Potential adjustments above 10 percent were more inclined to be viewed as material.

In August 1999, the staff of the SEC tried to jolt the financial community into assessments of materiality that focused less on numerical thresholds and more on the potential significance of the item to investors. The SEC's pronouncement was entitled "Staff Accounting Bulletin Number 99" or "SAB 99," and its gist was that "there are numerous circumstances in which misstatements below 5 percent could well be material." For SAB 99, assessment of materiality did not involve simply the application of numerical thresholds, but "qualitative factors" that "may cause misstatements of quantitatively small amounts to be material." Among such factors was "how the misstatement arose." According to SAB 99, deliberate misstatements were more likely to be viewed as material. SAB 99 provides: "It is unlikely that it is ever 'reasonable' for registrants to record misstatements or not to correct known misstatements—even immaterial ones—as part of an ongoing effort directed by or known to senior management for the purposes of 'managing' earnings."

In promulgating SAB 99, the staff of the SEC had its heart in the right place. It arguably made sense to prevent companies, prior to the issuance of their financial statements, from failing to correct known misstatements of less than 5 percent solely in an attempt to sustain a company's stock price. However, applied to the potential need to correct financial statements that have already been issued, the logic behind SAB 99's view of materiality becomes less workable. Suppose, for example, that a company discovers that in the previous year it mistakenly reported earnings 1 percent higher than it should have because of an honest blunder in counting inventory. Insofar as the prior financial statements now include a "known misstatement," does that render the financial statements "materially" misleading? Does it make a difference if, rather than being accidental, the inventory misstatement was deliberate? Does it matter if the discrepancy happened two years, rather than one year, before?

At the moment, SAB 99's impact on such questions is unclear. Without actually saying so, SAB 99 by its terms appears primarily intended to address assessments of materiality in financial statements yet to be issued rather than in financial statements that have already gone out the door. For now, suffice it to say that materiality assessments as to already-issued financial statements can be exceedingly challenging.

A different challenge as to materiality comes up when a series of misstatements has occurred over successive years that, while not material to the financial statements in any one year, when accumulated add up to an adjustment that would be material. To address this issue, the SEC staff has issued "Staff Accounting Bulletin No. 108" or "SAB 108." SAB 108 acknowledges that, in such an instance, there are two ways of looking at materiality. One, known as the "rollover approach," quantifies a misstatement based on the amount of the error originating in each of the successive years. For example, the materiality of a $20 misstatement in each of five years would be evaluated based on the materiality of the misstatement in each of the years in which it originated. The other approach, known as the "iron curtain approach," quantifies a misstatement based on the impact of a correction at the end of the current year. In the $20 example, the misstatement would be quantified as a $100 misstatement based on the current-year financial statements.

Which are you supposed to use in assessing materiality? The answer is both. The point of SAB 108 is that, as the standard itself puts it, "the registrant should quantify the current year misstatement in this example using both the iron curtain approach (i.e., $100) and the rollover approach (i.e., $20)." As a result, "if the $100 misstatement is considered material to the financial statements, after all of the relevant quantitative and qualitative factors are considered, the registrant's financial statements would need to be adjusted." If the accumulation of prior years' nonmaterial errors results in a material error in the current-year financial statements, the appropriate adjustment would be to "the prior year financial statements . . . even though such revision previously was and continues to be immaterial to the prior year financial statements." All the more reason to avoid a misstatement to begin with.

THE AUDIT PROCESS

Once the new audit has commenced, management is often taken aback by the auditor's adoption of new procedures in conducting the actual audit testing. The audit process, never a complete pleasure even under the best of circumstances, can become more exasperating once the auditor has been told that it was earlier the victim of lies. The auditor will understandably want to be more thorough and cautious during the reaudit, to the point where genuinely innocent employees may get frustrated as their integrity seems to be repeatedly called into question.

That frustration may be increased insofar as company personnel fail to appreciate exactly what the auditor is trying to accomplish during the new audit. Common misconceptions among company personnel about a reaudit include:

- The auditor will confine itself to revisiting only those prior-year issues that the company has called to its attention.
- The auditor can fully rely on work done and conclusions reached by the forensic accountants, so the auditor will not have to perform much additional work.
- The auditor will only require the company to provide the same level of documentation as customarily requested in prior audits.
- The company will only be dealing with the same personnel from the auditing firm that performed past audits of the company.

In general, company employees should expect audits of restated financial statements, particularly those resulting from prior fraudulent financial reporting, to involve heightened auditor skepticism, more extensive evidence-gathering, and expanded audit teams. All in all, it will generally be an entirely unpleasant experience for everyone involved.

Evidence of a new approach in the audit, moreover, will be everywhere. The auditor might seek additional documentary evidence from outside the company. For example, if the fraud involved improper revenue recognition, the auditor may request expanded confirmations from the company's customers on issues such as contract terms, the existence of side letters, acceptance criteria, delivery and payment terms and timing, the extent of any continuing company obligations, and cancellation or return provisions.

Such an additional level of audit scrutiny can be burdensome and frustrating. The auditor may request documents that are voluminous, that have been sent to off-site storage, or, even worse, that cannot be found. The auditor may demand to see original documents when previously it accepted photocopies. The company may be asked to prevail upon its customers to research and confirm (or perhaps reconfirm) details about the customer's business with the company dating back years. Management may believe it has provided the auditor sufficient explanation or documentation, yet the auditor may seek still more. Even innocent senior executives may get the feeling that their overzealous auditor no longer trusts anything anybody says.

Such a characterization usually is something of an exaggeration, but it does highlight an important dynamic that occurs in instances of financial fraud. Auditors, always obligated to conduct independent audits with an attitude of professional skepticism, must consider how the fraud previously escaped detection both by the company's internal control system and by the auditor. Once the auditor concludes that one or more members of management consciously committed fraud, the auditor may question the reliability of every representation or piece of evidence received from those individuals. The auditor may also question the reliability of every representation or piece of evidence prepared by their subordinates.

All of this is made more difficult for company personnel by the auditor's likely introduction of new audit team personnel to supplement the previous engagement team, with which company personnel may have been comfortable. The auditor may introduce personnel not previously involved in the company's audit commensurate with the newly increased risk. The addition of new accountants to the audit team, moreover, may not only take place among those individuals at the company's offices. Beyond those in the field, the audit capability may now include significant participation by the most senior technical representatives of the accounting firm's national office. In all likelihood, company personnel will notice constrained flexibility and discretion in those areas that require some level of judgment. Correspondingly, the process of decision-making may be slowed. To some extent, company personnel may get the impression that the CPAs in the field are very much in regular, close communication with those at the auditor's national headquarters. In many instances, that impression will be correct.

THE AUDITOR'S EVALUATION OF THE AUDIT COMMITTEE'S INVESTIGATION

In a process characterized by stress, perhaps the most stressful moment arrives with the auditor's determination whether to accept the audit committee's investigation as the predicate for the issuance of a new audit report.

It is the critical determination in the entire process. If the auditor finds that the investigation is adequate, the auditor can move forward with completion of its own audit testing and the issuance of a new audit report. With a new audit report, credibility can be restored and the company can again begin to function with some semblance of normalcy.

If, however, the auditor's conclusion is otherwise—that the investigation is not satisfactory—the company has taken a giant step backward. The weeks or months of intense investigative effort will not have accomplished their principal objective. The company's public market credibility, assuming it has any left, will be further eroded. SEC and other regulatory scrutiny may increase. And the company's goal of putting the problem behind it will recede further into the distance.

Indeed, in some situations the auditor's unwillingness to accept the audit committee's investigation may have an even worse impact. If the audit committee's investigative professionals—outside counsel and the forensic accountants—have conducted the investigation in a way that calls into question their own sophistication, expertise, objectivity, or thoroughness, the credibility of the entire investigative apparatus may be compromised beyond repair. A foreseeable solution is replacement. That means the audit committee's engagement of new outside counsel and, if necessary, the engagement of new forensic accountants. Then the investigation starts over.

The auditor's evaluation of the investigation, therefore, is a process on which the audit committee will want to focus throughout the entirety of the effort. A sophisticated audit committee will be attentive to any indications of auditor discontent. Where such indications should surface, the audit committee will want to see that they are swiftly rectified to the auditor's satisfaction. Any auditor suggestion that the process is lacking will optimally be raised immediately with audit committee outside counsel and the forensic accountants so that corrective measures are not delayed.

One impediment to this attentiveness can be concern regarding the waiver of attorney-client privilege—with the result that the auditor is not provided transparency into the investigation as it unfolds. Those raising the issue of attorney-client privilege may be well intentioned, for it is true that, depending on the law at issue, revelation of investigative results to the outside auditor may indeed result in a privilege waiver. Even where waiver is not assured, the risk is often higher than prudent defense counsel would like. Nonetheless, on balance, the audit committee will almost always conclude that assertion of attorney-client privilege to preclude the auditor's access to information is counterproductive. Without transparency into the investigation, the auditor cannot be expected to find it acceptable. The issue, therefore, becomes not whether the auditor gains access to the information but simply the timing. If the auditor is to gain access at some point in the investigation—as the auditor inevitably will—it makes little sense to hold off until the end given the risk of auditor dissatisfaction and the inability to promptly put in place corrective measures as the investigation proceeds. Sophisticated audit committees will conclude that it is far better to provide the auditor with complete transparency throughout the investigative process and thereby to minimize the risk of auditor dissatisfaction at the end.

A separate issue is whether the auditor should be provided with a written report of the investigation's processes and determinations. Often the desire to avoid a written report will be motivated by the same concerns regarding auditor transparency into the investigative process—the potential waiver of attorney-client privilege and the fact that the report may thereby become available to the plaintiffs in the inevitable class action litigation about the fraud. Here, again, the concern is understandable but probably outweighed by other considerations.

Increasingly, the accounting firms appear to be favoring written rather than oral reports, owing largely to unfortunate experiences with oral reports. While the circumstances have varied, the experiences have involved a common theme: superficial oral assurances of management innocence that, when the auditor later got into the details, proved to be unfounded. In one instance, for example, the auditor was assured of the absence of unlawful conduct only to discover vivid evidence of managed earnings when the details underlying those oral assurances became available. In another, the auditor received similar assurances of innocence, then encountered evidence of fraud in the underlying interview memoranda. In another, the investigators sought to excuse apparent misconduct through an explanation that, when reduced to writing, came across as patently absurd. In other words, auditors have come to learn that investigative blemishes can surface much more readily in a report that is written. Beyond that, auditors are keenly aware of the extent to which recollections of investigative conclusions may fade once an audit report has been issued and that the SEC may turn the absence of a written report against an auditor through the suggestion of an inadequate predicate for an audit report. For the accounting profession, the reasons for seeking a written report are many.

Even a well-prepared written report, though, will not necessarily be taken at face value by the auditor. Rather, the auditor will want to subject the report, as well as the investigative process itself, to some level of audit scrutiny and testing.

For this purpose, the auditor may bring in its own separate team of forensic accountants to "shadow" the team of forensic accountants engaged by the audit committee. The shadowing may involve participation in witness interviews, interaction with the forensic accountants regarding the scope and thoroughness of their work, and participation in audit committee meetings. Auditor scrutiny of the investigation may also involve testing of the audit committee's examination of emails and the extent to which each email potentially relevant to fraudulent financial reporting has been adequately investigated. Based on the selective sampling that is the foundation of the audit process, the auditor may start with the entire population of emails and select a representative sample for inquiry and examination. That inquiry and examination may involve questioning audit committee counsel and the forensic accountants as to how the selected emails were investigated and the extent to which they did or did not reveal a fraud. The audit committee will want to appreciate from the outset that the auditor may pluck from thousands of emails a sampling and go so far as to ask about investigative steps into, say, the particular wording of a single sentence.

REPRESENTATIONS TO THE AUDITOR

One issue that rarely creates a major problem in a normal audit, but that can pose quite a significant problem after financial fraud has been discovered, is the auditor's need to obtain management representations.

The auditor's procurement of management representations is mandated by audit standards. Before the audit report is issued, the auditor is to obtain a "representation letter" setting forth, among other things, the representations of responsible executives that the financial statements are set forth in accordance with GAAP and that the auditor has been provided with all pertinent information. That representation letter is to be signed by executives whose knowledge of the financial reporting system is such that an adequate basis for the representations exists. Beyond the formal representations of the representation letter, any number of executives and accounting personnel will make separate representations during the course of the audit that the auditor will document in its workpapers.

What can be routine in a normal audit, however, can become more of a problem once fraud has been discovered. Suddenly, the normal procurement of management representations can be difficult or even impossible insofar as executives from whom the representations would normally be obtained—such as senior financial executives or the CEO—may have been terminated or, even if not terminated, may no longer be viewed as completely reliable. In instances in which key management personnel have been terminated, the company may have filled newly vacated positions with individuals not previously associated with the organization.

New members of management may add credibility to the company, but they can also pose a challenge to the audit process. The auditor will seek from management written representations covering all previous years upon which the auditor is to express an opinion. Executives new to the company may resist taking responsibility for the propriety of financial reports about which they know little. Under audit standards, management's unwillingness to furnish written representations can constitute a limitation on the scope of the audit sufficient to preclude an unqualified opinion. It is also enough to cause the auditor to disclaim an opinion or to withdraw from the engagement.

Needless to say, an auditor disclaimer or resignation is the last thing management wants. Neither is likely to restore the confidence of shareholders, creditors, regulators, or others. The need for management representations can therefore delay the release of audited financial statements if not dealt with early in the audit process. At the outset, company management and its auditor should do their best to achieve a clear understanding of the personnel from whom the auditor will seek written representations and exactly what those representations will consist of. Of course, even the best of planning in this area may be ruined if the investigation finds fault with individuals from whom the auditor had planned to obtain representations.

Beyond the normal representations of management, the auditor may seek additional representations regarding the adequacy of the audit committee's investigation and the disclosure of investigative results and underlying evidence to the auditor. Thus, for example, the auditor may ask the audit committee to represent to the best of the committee's knowledge and belief that: (1) the auditor has been provided with access to all relevant documents and information in connection with the investigation, (2) the investigation is complete, (3) the investigation is sufficient for the audit committee to determine the appropriateness of inclusion of the financial statements in a filing with the SEC, and (4) the company has taken (or is taking) timely and appropriate remedial actions. Some audit committee members may bristle that they personally must attest to such things, but here again we find another instance in which normal audit procedures change once financial fraud has been uncovered. In fairness to the auditor, moreover, responsibility for the scope and depth of the investigation falls to the audit committee, which is the logical candidate to attest to the investigation's adequacy. For their part, the audit committee members are protected by the fact that they are only providing information as to their knowledge and belief. They are not providing a guarantee.

AUDITOR INDEPENDENCE

Amid all the uncertainty of the new audit and investigative process, one matter is a virtual certainty—lawsuits will be filed. One question that often arises involves the effect of such lawsuits on the auditor's ability to continue in its capacity as the company's independent auditor.

Public accountants are governed by a code of professional ethics and laws that require them to be "independent" of the companies whose financial statements they audit. Litigation concerning the propriety of a company's previous financial statements and the accompanying audit report can potentially interfere with the auditor's independence. For one thing, litigation that names both the company and the auditor as codefendants can potentially turn the auditor and management into adversaries—and thereby chill the objectivity and candor that, under audit standards, best characterize the audit relationship. Often, both the company and the auditor will come to the strategic recognition that lashing out against each other in litigation is counterproductive. Still, the potential for compromised independence poses a risk to issuance of a new audit report.

Whether independence is in fact compromised involves a complex area of audit standards and SEC rules that is to be governed by the particular circumstances at issue. As a general matter, the following may be evidence of impaired independence:

- The commencement of litigation by present company management against the auditor alleging deficiencies in audit work on the company's financial statements
- The threat of litigation by present management of the company against the auditor under certain circumstances involving alleged audit deficiencies if the auditor deems the filing of such a claim to be probable
- The commencement of litigation by the auditor against present management alleging management fraud or deceit

Conversely, litigation by shareholders or others against the company and its auditor, or against either one alone, normally does *not* in and of itself impair the auditor's independence. Even such third-party litigation, however, can lead to an impairment of auditor independence under certain circumstances. Independence may be compromised if, for example, the company files a cross-claim against the auditor alleging that the auditor is responsible for financial statement deficiencies. A cross-claim filed by the auditor alleging fraud by present company management may also impair the auditor's independence.

On the other hand, the existence of cross-claims filed by the company, its management, or any of its directors merely to protect the right to legal redress in the event of a future adverse decision in the primary litigation (or, in lieu of cross-claims, agreements to extend the statutes of limitations) need not impair the auditor's independence, unless there was thereby created a significant risk that the cross-claim would result in a settlement or judgment in an amount material to the accounting firm or the company.

Another issue sometimes giving rise to questions about independence is whether the forensic accountants from the company's incumbent auditor may themselves undertake the necessary forensic investigation on behalf of the audit committee. On this subject there is not complete uniformity of views. Some are of the view that it is actually *preferable* for a forensic accountant team from the same firm as the auditor to undertake the forensic aspect of the investigation. In that way, the thinking goes, the audit engagement team can be satisfied that the forensic accountants, coming from the same accounting firm, had the utmost motivation to get things right and the audit engagement team has all the more opportunity to see to it that things were done to the audit engagement team's satisfaction. Others are of the view that a separate firm performing the forensic work adds the appearance of objectivity and credibility to the investigative conclusions.

The issue of auditor independence is often complicated, and the complications only increase once a company has fallen victim to financial fraud. The nuances, including the complexities of the litigation environment, preclude the formulation of hard-and-fast rules governing auditor independence in all possible circumstances. Accordingly, the best approach is probably to raise the issue of independence at the outset of the reaudit so that both the auditor and company management are completely familiar with the risks and can develop a common understanding of how those risks will be addressed.

CHAPTER ELEVEN

The Securities and Exchange Commission

O NE OF THE BIGGEST CHALLENGES upon the discovery of fraudulent financial reporting is evaluating the best way to deal with the Securities and Exchange Commission. From the moment financial fraud is discovered, critical decisions must be made regarding the company's approach and strategy. Should the company self-report to the SEC or wait for a subpoena? Should it cooperate with the SEC or resist? Should it confess or defend?

Making such decisions particularly difficult is the need to make them at an early stage when the information is typically vague and uncertain. There may be serious doubt as to whether the early evidence constitutes fraudulent financial reporting at all or, even if it does, whether it is significant enough to affect any SEC filings. A further complication involves the SEC's ability to judge the company's approach with hindsight. If a company believes it has justifiably concluded that potential evidence of fraud is in fact an honest mistake, but it turns out otherwise in the end, the SEC's ultimate reaction may be harsher than the company would like. Still another complication involves the ramifications of SEC interaction upon other problems with which the company will be dealing. The outside auditor, for one, will be exceedingly attentive to the company's approach to the SEC and can be easily distressed if things seem to be going awry. The company's approach to the SEC may also have an impact upon the company's defense of the inevitable securities class action litigation. And, in serious cases, the SEC may be cooperating with the FBI and the Department of Justice. If the Department of Justice gets involved, company executives and others could end up going to prison.

All in all, the company's approach to the SEC is fraught with tough judgment calls and risks. Careful balances must be struck with serious consideration given to both negative consequences and overall objectives.

STRUCTURE OF THE SEC

Established by Congress in 1934 to administer and enforce the federal securities laws, the Securities and Exchange Commission consists of five members appointed by the president with the advice and consent of the Senate for staggered five-year terms. By law, no more than three members of the Commission may be from the same political party, meaning the political party in power often has a majority. The five commissioners themselves normally come from a variety of backgrounds, including law, business, academia, government, and law enforcement.

Below the level of the Commission itself, the main business of the SEC is divided into five divisions. The Division of Corporation Finance oversees the process of corporate disclosure in SEC filings, periodically reviews and comments on the substance of corporate SEC filings, and generally seeks to enhance the quality of disclosure by companies seeking access to public capital markets. The Division of Trading and Markets provides day-to-day oversight of the major securities market participants, including the securities exchanges, securities firms, clearing agencies, securities information processors, and credit rating agencies. The Division of Investment Management oversees and regulates the investment management industry, including mutual funds, professional fund managers, analysts, and investment advisers. The Division of Risk, Strategy and Financial Innovation seeks to identify developing risks and trends in financial markets.

The fifth division—and the division of immediate interest here—is the Division of Enforcement. It is the Division of Enforcement that is charged with responsibility for enforcement of the federal securities laws and it is the division likely to be most directly and intensely involved with a company that has discovered fraudulent financial reporting. Often interacting with the Division of Enforcement will be a separate part of the SEC—the Office of the Chief Accountant (OCA)—which assists the Commission in establishing accounting principles and overseeing the private sector standards-setting process. The Enforcement Division and OCA will often work together: The Enforcement Division will take the lead in investigation and penalties; OCA will assist with determinations as to any difficult issues of generally accepted accounting principles (GAAP) interpretation. That is not to say there is a bright-line distinction between the functions of each. The Enforcement Division can be counted upon to come to its own views as to when GAAP were violated. At the same time, OCA may formulate policy as to appropriate remedies for certain kinds of financial reporting violations.

The five SEC Commissioners, the five divisions, and OCA are all headquartered in the SEC's home office in Washington. However, much of the work—particularly for the Enforcement Division—is conducted through 11 regional offices located in strategically selected cities throughout the United States: Boston, New York, Philadelphia, Atlanta, Miami, Chicago, Denver, Salt Lake, Fort Worth, San Francisco, and Los Angeles. The location of the particular SEC office ending up with jurisdiction over a particular company's financial fraud is often a function of the location of the company, the workload at the various offices, the seriousness of the potential securities law violations, the company's profile, and which office learned about it first.

WHETHER TO SELF-REPORT

One of the first issues to confront a company upon discovery of evidence of potential fraudulent financial reporting is whether to self-report to the Division of Enforcement.

Few decisions in dealing with the SEC carry with it more importance than this one. Self-reporting to the SEC can help establish exactly the right tone at the outset for subsequent interaction with the SEC and make a first impression that will pay significant dividends down the road. On the other hand, once a company has self-reported, there is no turning back. Should subsequent investigation reveal that the problem did not involve fraudulent financial reporting at all, or perhaps involved something of no great consequence, the SEC cannot be expected to simply close the file and go on to something else. If self-reporting is to do the most good, it is best done right at the outset. Then the company will live with the consequences of that judgment for a long time.

Making the determination of self-reporting all the more difficult is the number of considerations that must be weighed in the balance. One is that, by the time the company learns of potential financial fraud, the SEC may already know about it. As mentioned in an earlier chapter, new incentives for

whistleblowers means that those suspicious of corporate wrongdoing are taking it upon themselves to go to the SEC with ever-increasing frequency. At the
same time a company is wringing its hands over whether to self-report, the
SEC may have already opened up a file. For that matter, it may be waiting to see
whether the company does the right thing and self-reports. A failure to do so,
when the SEC staff thinks it should, can be a significant negative.

At the same time, a company does not want to overreact and jump to
conclusions. Early evidence that looks like financial fraud may turn out to
involve nothing at all, or a problem that has already been effectively addressed.
Even if an instance of accounting manipulation has taken place, that does not
mean that it had any significance let alone resulted in a material misstatement
of financial results. A possible consequence of overreaction is a full-scale SEC
investigation that lasts for years and in the end turns up nothing—or, even
more frustrating, turns up some problem completely unrelated to the initial
evidence that by itself would not have justified significant regulatory reaction.
Even a company with its heart in the right place will be understandably reluctant to invite the Enforcement Division to comb through its records if only
because of uncertainty over what will turn up.

A further complication involves the reaction to self-reporting of the SEC
staff itself. While SEC policy generally favors those who self-report, a lot turns
on SEC leadership at the time, the particular individuals ending up with responsibility for the investigation, the profile of the company at issue, and numerous
other factors whose significance may be nuanced but nonetheless important.
Experienced practitioners are all too aware of the frustration of trying to predict
the reaction of SEC staff to a given scenario. Those frustrations are omnipresent
when the stakes are so high.

All of that having been said, if the available evidence points to a potentially
serious financial fraud, self-reporting will frequently be the best approach. One
reason—again, we go back to Chapter 1 and the way financial fraud starts and
grows—is that evidence of financial fraud, particularly if it implicates the company's culture or tone at the top, is often just the tip of the iceberg. The company
has to appreciate the distinct possibility that the evidence will get worse. If that
is the case, the SEC will inevitably find out at some point. It is better that it find
out early and from the company itself.

An additional consideration is a strategic one. The company gets to select
where it will self-report. This provides company counsel—or, more precisely,
audit committee counsel—the opportunity to take into account its recent experience with the various SEC regional offices and the extent to which particular enforcement personnel within them can be expected to react in a fair and

balanced way. If recent experience suggests that a particular regional office has a demonstrated proclivity to be unreasonably punitive, self-reporting provides the opportunity for that office to be avoided. That is not to say that all of the regional offices are equally up for grabs—reporting a New York–based accounting problem to the Los Angeles office might come across as a bit much. And reporting a problem to the Boston office does not mean that Washington will decline to grab hold of it. Still, self-reporting provides the opportunity for some level of selection and greater opportunity to get things started on the right foot.

THE "SEABOARD FACTORS"

While SEC staff reaction can never be predicted with certainty, it is official SEC policy to reward self-reporting. That policy was put in place in connection with an investigation of Seaboard Corporation, an investigation in which the company worked hard to cooperate with SEC staff. At the conclusion of the investigation, the SEC opted to credit the company's cooperation and to formulate policy regarding its reasons for doing so. It accordingly issued the so-called "Seaboard factors," setting forth in detail those factors the SEC will take into consideration in fashioning remedial actions and penalties. The Seaboard factors in their entirety, prominently included among which is whether the company took efforts to "promptly, completely and effectively disclose the existence of the misconduct to the public, to regulators and to self-regulators," are as follows:

1. What is the nature of the misconduct involved? Did it result from inadvertence, honest mistake, simple negligence, reckless or deliberate indifference to indicia of wrongful conduct, willful misconduct, or unadorned venality? Were the company's auditors misled?
2. How did the misconduct arise? Is it the result of pressure placed on employees to achieve specific results, or a tone of lawlessness set by those in control of the company? What compliance procedures were in place to prevent the misconduct now uncovered? Why did those procedures fail to stop or inhibit the wrongful conduct?
3. Where in the organization did the misconduct occur? How high up in the chain of command was knowledge of, or participation in, the misconduct? Did senior personnel participate in, or turn a blind eye toward, obvious indicia of misconduct? How systemic was the behavior? Is it symptomatic of the way the entity does business, or was it isolated?

4. How long did the misconduct last? Was it a one-quarter, or one-time, event, or did it last several years? In the case of a public company, did the misconduct occur before the company went public? Did it facilitate the company's ability to go public?

5. How much harm has the misconduct inflicted upon investors and other corporate constituencies? Did the share price of the company's stock drop significantly upon its discovery and disclosure?

6. How was the misconduct detected and who uncovered it?

7. How long after discovery of the misconduct did it take to implement an effective response?

8. What steps did the company take upon learning of the misconduct? Did the company immediately stop the misconduct? Are persons responsible for the misconduct still with the company? If so, are they still in the same positions? Did the company promptly, completely and effectively disclose the existence of the misconduct to the public, to regulators and to self-regulators? Did the company cooperate completely with appropriate regulatory and law enforcement bodies? Did the company identify what additional related misconduct is likely to have occurred? Did the company take steps to identify the extent of damage to investors and other corporate constituencies? Did the company appropriately recompense those adversely affected by the conduct?

9. What processes did the company follow to resolve many of these issues and ferret out necessary information? Were the audit committee and the board of directors fully informed? If so, when?

10. Did the company commit to learn the truth, fully and expeditiously? Did it do a thorough review of the nature, extent, origins and consequences of the conduct and related behavior? Did management, the Board or committees consisting solely of outside directors oversee the review? Did company employees or outside persons perform the review? If outside persons, had they done other work for the company? Where the review was conducted by outside counsel, had management previously engaged such counsel? Were scope limitations placed on the review? If so, what were they?

11. Did the company promptly make available to our staff the results of its review and provide sufficient documentation reflecting its response to the situation? Did the company identify possible improper conduct and evidence with sufficient precision to facilitate prompt enforcement actions against those who violated the law? Did the company produce a thorough and probing written report detailing the findings of its review? Did the

company voluntarily disclose information our staff did not directly request and otherwise might not have uncovered? Did the company ask its employees to cooperate with our staff and make all reasonable efforts to secure such cooperation?

12. What assurances are there that the conduct is unlikely to recur? Did the company adopt and ensure enforcement of new and more effective internal controls and procedures designed to prevent a recurrence of the misconduct? Did the company provide our staff with sufficient information for it to evaluate the company's measures to correct the situation and ensure that the conduct does not recur?

13. Is the company the same company in which the misconduct occurred, or has it changed through a merger or bankruptcy reorganization?

Taking into account the various considerations, the decision whether to self-report and thereafter cooperate often boils down to this. If a company discovers that wrongdoing executives have deliberately defrauded shareholders, almost inevitably the right approach will involve self-reporting, self-investigation, and cooperation with the SEC staff. That is the surest and quickest way for the company to accomplish its main business objective—putting the problem behind it as fast as humanly possible. Both the business needs of the company and the demands of integrity in financial reporting will thus dictate precisely the same course of action: independent investigation, the removal of wrongdoers, and corrective disclosure. Through cooperation and candor, the company can virtually turn the SEC staff into an ally in attaining those objectives.

If that is the course the company selects, the company wants to bend over backward to allow the SEC staff to become satisfied as to the genuineness of the company's investigative effort. Once satisfied, the staff may choose to stay out of the company's way until the company's own investigation is complete. Thus, the staff may postpone its own requests for interviews, taking of testimony, or rigorous review of documents to allow the company's investigation to proceed unimpeded. If the company produces a thorough and credible written report, that report may itself be accepted by the staff as a reliable account of what happened. In that circumstance, the SEC largely accepts the company's investigative results, evaluates the extent of its remedial actions, and undertakes little additional investigation of the company on its own. Sophisticated investigators, at the outset of an investigation, may establish such an SEC staff reaction as an important objective of the investigative effort.

HOW TO SELF-REPORT

For all of the difficulties in deciding *whether* to self-report, the act of self-reporting is straightforward. Once the best place to self-report has been determined, it can be as simple as picking up the phone, calling an SEC staff representative, and informing the representative that the company has discovered potential evidence of an accounting problem and wanted to call the SEC staff so the staff was aware of it. The staff member may ask about the circumstances and details, but will likely understand, particularly at such a preliminary stage, that the information is vague, an audit committee investigation is just getting under way, and therefore the committee is not at this point in a position to share any substantive details though information will be forthcoming as it becomes available. The entire call can take as little as five minutes.

While the call may be abbreviated both in terms of time and information, there are certain points critical to sending the right message and for which the SEC staff member can be expected to listen. One is that it is the audit committee that is in control. The SEC staff member will want to hear that it is audit committee counsel, not company counsel, that is making the call. The staff member will also want to hear that it is the audit committee that is spearheading the investigation. The staff member may ask about the involvement of management, and will expect to hear that management is not involved in the investigative process. The staff member will also expect to hear a pledge that as information is uncovered it will be made available to the SEC staff. The staff member will also inevitably ask about preservation of documents and expect to hear that effective steps have been taken.

If audit committee counsel is concerned for whatever reason that the company's relationship with the SEC may be a bit shaky (there may have been, for example, a history of stressful interaction between the two), an additional step can be for the members of the audit committee to personally travel to the appropriate SEC office for an initial meeting with the staff. The goal of such a meeting is not to provide investigative detail—at this stage, there probably is not much to be provided. The goal rather is to persuade the SEC staff that the audit committee is determined to do the right thing. That is, such a meeting provides the staff the opportunity to meet face-to-face with the audit committee members, evaluate the genuineness of their commitment to get to the bottom of things, and assess whether the audit committee can be trusted. Audit committee members might understandably be a bit intimidated by the prospect, but such an overture can buy a lot of goodwill from SEC staff.

KEEPING THE INITIATIVE

Self-reporting to the SEC is a good start, but the audit committee will have to work to keep the initiative. That will involve a demonstrable effort to objectively and thoroughly investigate, make corrective disclosure, remove defrauders from their positions, and otherwise set things straight.

The company has to be careful every step of the way. Particularly at the outset, the SEC staff will be looking for indications as to whether the investigation is a genuine one or only an attempt to cover up. Accordingly, each interaction with the staff must be handled carefully. From initial contact, through early communication, responses to staff inquiries, the representation of witnesses, and the production of a final report, the audit committee must be careful to cultivate the sense that this is an investigative process that the SEC staff can trust.

The good first impression made by self-reporting therefore needs to be followed up with a crisp program of self-investigation with regular efforts to keep the SEC staff apprised of ongoing progress and developments. The staff will, early on, want to know who is going to be interviewed, who the participants in the interviews will be, and the types of records being kept. With regard to document searches, the SEC staff may want the opportunity to review the locations from which documents are to be extracted, the "search terms" to be deployed in hunting through company emails, and the processes by which the information will be evaluated. Those processes may include deployment of a vast network of email reviewers simultaneously scrutinizing company emails with quality checks being performed by more experienced attorneys. If the SEC staff is to defer to the audit committee's approach and processes, it will want to be satisfied that the approach and processes can be relied upon.

The SEC staff may also want to learn what the company is uncovering—as it is uncovering it. For some, particularly those accustomed to more adversarial SEC practice, it may seem awkward, or idiotic, to voluntarily reveal to the SEC potential evidence of wrongdoing before completing the investigative steps necessary to understand whether a particular piece of evidence actually involves wrongdoing. Such a reaction is understandable, but the alternative is unlikely to satisfy the SEC staff. The need for logistical efficiency means that any number of clues are being investigated simultaneously and the SEC staff will not want to wait until everything is finished before gaining some insight as to what the audit committee's investigation is uncovering. The result is that, just as the SEC staff will be trusting the audit committee to candidly report evidence as it is uncovered, audit committee counsel will need to trust the SEC staff not to overreact or jump to conclusions based on reports of early clues and evidence that has not yet been run to ground. The critical component of the interaction obviously is trust. SEC staff has to trust audit committee counsel. Audit committee counsel has to trust SEC staff. The need for a good first impression is all the more obvious.

As for the logistical means of updates to the SEC staff, one common vehicle is periodic phone calls. If the desired level of trust has not yet been earned, the staff may seek frequent calls—perhaps as frequently as multiple times per week. As the staff's level of comfort grows, weekly calls may suffice or, as things go on, calls that are less frequent until perhaps the level of trust is sufficiently high that the need is eliminated altogether—the staff is content to await the investigation's ultimate conclusions. The components of a typical call may include progress on the review of documents, the status of witness interviews, accounting issues being explored, important evidence being uncovered, and remedial steps being planned or taken.

One difficulty is sometimes presented where the SEC's staff seeks the ongoing production of investigative work product as it is prepared. That is not so much a problem if the staff seeks, for example, company emails—the staff will get them sooner or later, and an electronic transmission of uncovered emails is not much of a distraction to the investigative effort. The case is different, though, if the SEC seeks, say, notes of witness interviews or memoranda to be prepared once an interview is complete. Producing notes is hazardous for a number of reasons, among them that they are frequently understandable only by the note-taker. That problem might be alleviated through the production of interview memoranda, but the problem here is the time and effort necessary to prepare on an ongoing basis memoranda of sufficient reliability and accuracy. In all likelihood, to maximize speed and efficiency, the investigators themselves will be using rough drafts with the expectation that, when the critical investigative work is done, memoranda can then be finalized. Completing such paperwork on an ongoing basis for SEC staff can simply prolong the time that shareholders are kept in the dark, which is contrary to one of the main objectives of the whole undertaking.

The good news is that sophisticated SEC staff will normally understand these concerns and, if they trust the investigation, be willing to defer the production of such investigative work product until later. If the audit committee proposes to make available to the SEC its investigative results in a more comprehensive form—such as a detailed written report—the SEC staff might not find it necessary to press for interview memoranda and other underlying investigative material at all. Again it comes down to trust. If the SEC staff is skeptical of the investigative effort, it may call for every shred of investigative material immediately.

As to corrective disclosure, it is entirely possible that the audit committee will come to a juncture in which it recognizes that previously issued financial results should no longer be relied upon. Such a determination will probably be followed with a press release to that effect, and the SEC staff will want to learn when such a press release is coming. A prudent approach is to provide such a press release in draft form to the staff prior to issuance and to solicit staff input on its content. SEC staff will probably be reluctant to "bless" the press release in any way—a point that the staff will typically make explicitly—but, nonetheless, the opportunity is thereby presented for the audit committee to learn of any staff concerns. Willingness to run a press release by the SEC staff also reinforces the appearance of the audit committee's desire to do the right thing.

 ## THE AUDITOR'S WATCHFUL EYE

Reinforcement of the message that the audit committee wants to do the right thing is important not only to the SEC. It is important also to the outside auditor.

The reason stems from a judgment that the auditor will need to make when the audit committee's investigation is complete: whether the investigation is adequate for the auditor to rely upon as a predicate for issuance of a new audit report. For the auditor, it is a determination that is fraught with peril. If the auditor relies upon the investigation, but afterward it turns out the investigators missed something, the auditor is at the front of the line of those who may pay a heavy price. The SEC staff has made clear that it will hold the auditor strictly accountable for its judgment about reliance on the audit committee's investigation. True to its word, where an auditor has in complete good faith relied upon an audit committee investigation that turned out to have missed something, the Enforcement Division has faulted the auditor for accepting the investigation in the first place. For the auditor, the consequences can include significant reputational damage, bad newspaper headlines, litigation accusations of "turning a blind eye," and the contention that the accounting firm was itself a participant in a cover-up. The determination whether to rely on the audit committee's investigation is one of the most difficult decisions the auditor will face.

The involvement of the SEC's staff—and in particular the staff's reaction to the audit committee's investigation—is important evidence that the auditor will want to take into account. If the staff is getting regular reports, seems satisfied with the investigative procedures, and otherwise appears to trust the good faith, objectivity, and thoroughness of the audit committee's approach, that can be a significant source of comfort to the auditor. If the auditor's reaction is the same, the audit committee has gone a long way to attaining one of the key business purposes of its investigation, which is a new audit report.

If, however, the SEC staff demonstrates dissatisfaction with the audit committee's investigation, the situation for the auditor is both different and involving much greater risk. One obvious concern would be that the SEC, from its unique vantage point, is concerned that the investigation is missing things or not evaluating the evidence with the objectivity that GAAP require. If that is the SEC's reaction, it stands to reason that perhaps it should be the auditor's reaction as well. Worse than that, SEC staff dissatisfaction with an audit committee investigation may result in the staff's unwillingness to accept the investigation at its conclusion. The consequence of nonacceptance is that the SEC staff largely disregards the determinations of the audit committee and moves ahead with its own investigation. The auditor is then faced with the dilemma that the subsequent SEC staff investigation may turn up new problems that the audit committee's investigation did not. If that should happen, the auditor ends up exactly where the auditor does not want to be: facing an SEC staff accusation that it prematurely issued an audit report in reliance on an audit committee investigation that should not have been trusted. This is a dilemma not only for the auditor but for the audit committee as well. Whereas an audit committee investigation might take months, an SEC investigation will frequently take years. If the auditor concludes that it is necessary to await the conclusion of the SEC investigation before issuance of an audit report, the company may be forced to function in the operational and legal limbo resulting from a lack of audited financial statements for the entire time. It is a fair question whether a company would find it possible to do so.

The point is that creating the right tone with the SEC staff is critical to the company's efforts to work its way out of the problem. An adverse reaction by the SEC to the substance or tone of the audit committee's investigation can be close to an insurmountable impediment.

PRESENTATION TO THE SEC STAFF

Regardless of the means and format of periodic reporting to the SEC staff, at some point the staff will expect a formal presentation of the audit committee's investigative conclusions.

That presentation can be made in several ways. The SEC staff's first choice is ordinarily a comprehensive and detailed written report. In fact, that preference is formally baked into SEC policy through the Seaboard factor that poses the question whether the company made available to the staff "a thorough and probing written report detailing the findings of its review." The advantages and disadvantages of a written report are discussed in more detail in Chapter 8. Suffice it to say that on the "advantages" side of the ledger is the ability to better satisfy the SEC.

Another means of presentation, less preferable than a written report but sometimes nonetheless sufficient, is a slide demonstration accompanied by oral presentation. Properly prepared, a slide presentation can capture the critical aspects of an investigation and its findings. A downside is that the bullet-point format of a typical slide presentation by its nature captures less detail and it is not unknown for critical details to have ended up, consciously or otherwise, slipping through the cracks. A slide presentation can be effective, but the audit committee should be prepared to address an increased level of SEC staff skepticism and scrutiny. The likelihood that the SEC staff will accept a slideshow as a complete and reliable account of events is significantly less than if the audit committee produces a comprehensive and detailed written report.

Another possibility is an oral presentation to the SEC staff unaccompanied by any written presentation whatsoever. The perils here are many. One is an even higher level of SEC staff skepticism based in part on a concern that, if the company is prepared to come clean with investors, why is it unwilling to write down its findings for the SEC? Another is the increased opportunity for important details to go unmentioned—now exacerbated by the lack of a concrete record of precisely what the audit committee is communicating. It is a rare audit committee that views a purely oral presentation to the SEC staff as either optimal or likely to attain the audit committee's objective.

As to the substance of the investigative report itself, the SEC staff will be primarily focused on the same things as the audit committee and outside auditor: the extent of GAAP violations, evaluation of the "wrongful intent" (i.e., scienter) of the participants, and the audit committee's plans for remedial actions. It is true that, beyond wrongful intent, the SEC might also have in mind whether certain individuals, such as CPAs on the accounting staff, were negligent. But, for reasons discussed elsewhere, that is beyond the scope of a typical audit committee investigation and for good reason. Nor is it clear that the SEC staff would be willing to defer to the audit committee's judgment as to findings of negligence in any event. If the SEC wants to evaluate negligence, it will ordinarily be left to its own investigative judgments based on the evidence.

As to remedial actions, the SEC staff will ordinarily be looking for several things. One of the main ones is the company's plans for corrective disclosure. The foremost objective here is a clear and crisp statement as to which financial results turned out to have been misstated and what the correct numbers should be. The staff will normally expect such disclosure to take the form of amended SEC filings with "restated" financial results. A trustworthy audit committee will speak with candor and objectivity in correcting prior misstatements, and the SEC staff will want to hear that such is the audit committee's intent.

Another form of remedial action involves those executives found to have possessed "wrongful intent." The SEC staff's expectations here will be driven by the fact that executives possessed of wrongful intent resulting in financial fraud have presumably violated any number of federal securities laws, including the antifraud statutory and regulatory prohibitions. Where wrongful intent has been found in a senior executive, the staff will expect him to be terminated if he has not been already. One consequence is that, given the manner in which fraud starts and grows, a company may end up losing a wide swath of its senior management and finance personnel.

One frustrating and potentially unjust aspect of the staff's expectations involves lower-level company personnel who were drawn into complicity. The frustration involves the fact that—again, we turn back to the way financial fraud starts and grows—such personnel may not have even realized they were crossing a line at a time when they were given little choice by their superiors. A 26-year-old accountant who was asked to make a journal entry by her boss may not be aware that she is being asked to do anything wrong. However, as additional entries accumulate, she may become suspicious. What does she do, quit? Does she blow the whistle? Should she run to the CEO—who may be behind the whole thing? That is a lot to ask of a junior-level employee, particularly if this happens to be the employee's first job and she is completely unacquainted with normal business practice let alone the regulatory attitudes of the SEC. It is all too easy for such a young employee to realize only too late that she has stepped over the line. Then it is difficult for her to know where to turn.

It is certainly possible that such an employee might, depending on the circumstances, be found to possess wrongful intent. Does that mean that she is beyond rehabilitation and must be terminated—a termination that likely will mean the end of her new career? The SEC staff's official position has been: Yes. Informal statements by staff members of the Enforcement Division have suggested that the staff will not permit lower-level employees to escape harsh remedial measures. The staff has sought to reinforce this message with its insistence that it will pursue wrongdoers "up, down, and sideways" and in the end "there is no such thing as a good soldier." Ultimately, an important goal is to see that the staff is satisfied with the extent of the audit committee's remedial actions. But one hopes that the SEC staff will be willing to look into the particulars of a situation and recognize that not all investigative determinations are a matter of black and white. Certainly audit committee members can be forgiven for an inclination to view such things in more human terms.

 ## POST-INVESTIGATION ACTIONS BY SEC STAFF

Ideally, the audit committee's presentation to the SEC will constitute the main event in getting an SEC investigation behind it. If the audit committee has satisfied SEC staff expectations through an objective and thorough investigation, ongoing cooperation, comprehensive and detailed report, and crisp remedial action, the staff may conclude—with an eye in particular on the Seaboard factors—that no further investigation of the company is warranted. That conclusion may be communicated formally by the SEC staff. Or it may be communicated less formally. In some instances, such a conclusion has not been communicated at all. After a time, the SEC staff has simply stopped phoning.

Such is not the case for those individual executives found to have been wrongfully complicit in fraudulent activity. If the audit committee's investigative determinations include such a finding, the SEC staff can be expected to further scrutinize their emails, take their testimony, and commence formal proceedings against them.

 ## A NEGOTIATED RESOLUTION

If the SEC decides to seek regulatory redress and a negotiated resolution is decided on, the outcome will typically involve different penalties for different people, depending on their status and complicity. Senior executives who were knowingly involved in deliberate wrongdoing can expect severe punishment (see Exhibit 11.1). Penalties may include insistence by the SEC on removal from the company, a bar against further service as an officer or director of a public company, an injunction against further violations

EXHIBIT 11.1 SEC Penalties (Individuals)

Company	Executive	Penalty	Date
TheStreet, Inc.	CFO	Injunction, $125,000 penalty, $34,240 disgorgement, and three-year bar as officer or director	12-18-2012
GlobeTel	CEO	$1.2 million penalty, $1.5 million disgorgement, and permanent bar as officer or director	10-18-2012
Huron Consulting Group	CFO	Cease-and-desist order, $50,000 penalty, and $178,000 disgorgement	7-19-2012
Waste Management	CFO	Injunction, $2.5 million penalty, and permanent bar as officer or director	7-29-2011
NutraCea	CEO	Injunction, $100,000 civil penalty, $350,000 disgorgement, and permanent bar as officer or director	1-20-2011
Vitesse Semiconductor	CFO	Injunction, $162,300 disgorgement, and permanent suspension from practice as an accountant before the SEC	12-10-2010
Delphi Corp.	Treasurer and Vice President	Injunction, $50,000 penalty, $50,000 disgorgement, and five-year bar as officer or director	9-22-2010
Merge Healthcare	CEO	Injunction, $90,000 penalty, $382,000 disgorgement, $117,807 prejudgment interest, and five-year bar as officer or director	11-4-2009
Qwest Communications	Sales Vice President	Injunction, $250,000 penalty, $1.8 million disgorgement, and five-year bar as officer or director	7-26-2005
Dollar General	CEO	Injunction and $1 million penalty	4-7-2005

Company	Executive	Penalty	Date
Lucent Technologies	Vice President	Injunction, $110,000 penalty, and permanent bar as officer or director	5-17-2004
Xerox	CEO	Injunction, $1 million penalty, $6.7 million disgorgement, and five-year bar as officer or director	6-5-2003
Xerox	CFO	Injunction, $1 million penalty, $4.2 million disgorgement, and permanent bar as officer or director	6-5-2003

of the securities laws (which is punishable by a finding of contempt), and a stiff fine. The SEC may also refer the matter to the U.S. Attorney's Office for criminal prosecution.

For those who were not deliberate wrongdoers but merely negligent, the SEC may seek penalties that are less severe. These might include a cease-and-desist order against further violations.

For CPAs or lawyers involved in financial fraud, the SEC has an additional series of punishments owing to its ability to proceed pursuant to a rule known as Rule 102(e). This is the rule by which the SEC brings proceedings against wrongdoing professionals, and the consequences for a professional can be serious. Among the frequently employed remedies of the SEC is a permanent or temporary ban from public practice before the Commission. For many professionals, such a penalty can effectively end their careers.

As to the company itself, the penalties resulting from a negotiated resolution with the SEC may include many of those mentioned earlier—including an injunction and a fine (see Exhibit 11.2). The remedy sought by the SEC may be supplemented by a corporate-governance component. Among other things, the SEC may insist that the company bring in additional outside directors, reconfigure its audit committee, hire a new CFO, and substantially reorganize its internal control system over financial reporting.

As a general matter, the SEC will seek to understand the circumstances of a particular situation and try to use its enforcement mechanisms to fashion a result that fits the underlying problem. Many of its penalties may seem harsh. Frequently, though, they will be preferable to a prolonged battle with the SEC.

EXHIBIT 11.2 SEC Penalties (Companies)

Company	Penalty	Date
Huron Consulting Group	Cease-and-desist order and $1 million penalty	7-19-2012
Thor Industries	Injunction, $1 million penalty, and order to hire an independent consultant to review internal controls	5-13-2011
Office Depot	$1 million penalty	10-21-2010
Dell	Injunction and $100 million penalty	7-22-2010
United Rentals	Injunction and $14 million penalty	9-8-2008
Biovail Corp.	Injunction and $10 million penalty	3-24-2008
Nortel Networks	Injunction and $35 million penalty	10-15-2007
HealthSouth	Injunction, $100 million penalty, and monitor	6-9-2005
Dollar General	Injunction and $10 million penalty	4-7-2005
Time Warner Inc.	Injunction, $300 million penalty, and monitor	3-21-2005
Qwest Communications	Injunction and $250 million penalty	10-21-2004
Halliburton Co.	Cease-and-desist order and $7.5 million penalty	8-3-2004
Symbol Technologies	Injunction, $37 million penalty, and monitor	6-3-2004
Lucent Technologies	Injunction and $25 million penalty	5-17-2004
WorldCom	Injunction and $750 million penalty ($500 million cash and $250 million stock)	7-7-2003
Xerox	Injunction, $10 million penalty, and monitor	4-11-2002

 ## THE WELLS PROCESS

If the company or individual company executives are not successful in coming to a negotiated resolution with the SEC staff, a formal proceeding may follow. If it has not already, the staff may seek a Formal Order of Investigation (not hard for the staff to get), the main effect of which is to authorize the staff to issue subpoenas. The staff may then undertake additional fact-gathering to supplement whatever evidence it feels the audit committee has not adequately provided.

Once its own investigation is substantially complete, the SEC staff may make a "Wells call," or a call in anticipation of such a Wells call, to counsel for those from whom further relief is being sought. A Wells call is simply a phone call in which Enforcement staff contacts defense counsel and advises counsel that the staff is considering a recommendation to the five commissioners that administrative or judicial proceedings be commenced. The purpose of the call is to allow defense counsel the opportunity to make a "Wells submission," which looks much like a legal brief, in which the company or the executives explain their view as to the reasons prosecution is not warranted.

That initial call marks the beginning of a process that may end up going on for weeks or months. After the initial call, defense counsel may request a meeting with the staff to learn the details of the potential charges so that a written submission in defense may adequately address the staff's issues. Upon receipt and review of the defense submission, the staff may think of additional charges and a subsequent meeting to discuss the additional charges may be arranged. Following that meeting, a new defense submission may be submitted, which in turn may lead to still more charges and still additional defense submissions. Ultimately, the participants may end up in a big conference room at the SEC's Washington headquarters with defense counsel and senior representatives of the staff—which may by this point include the Director of Enforcement, accountants from the OCA, lawyers from the SEC General Counsel's office, regional staff representatives, and others—all sitting around a very large table and debating the extent of securities law violations and appropriate regulatory reaction. Defense counsel and in turn the SEC staff may even present slideshows to each other.

If the staff remains unconvinced, the staff goes to the five SEC commissioners and seeks authority to commence judicial or administrative proceedings. Once the staff takes this step, the individual commissioners need to begin the process of acquainting themselves with the underlying facts and staff recommendation in anticipation of a meeting at which the commissioners will be called upon to vote on whether proceedings should or should not be commenced. In preparation for that meeting, each commissioner will be provided with a set of written materials regarding the recommendation (including the Wells submissions), and each commissioner will typically meet beforehand with members of his or her individual staff to discuss the facts and evaluate Enforcement's recommendation. On the day of the vote, the commissioners will gather in a nonpublic meeting room at commission headquarters in a session that may also include members of their individual staffs, the key staff members from the Division of Enforcement, lawyers from the SEC General Counsel's office, and accountants from the OCA (and maybe the Chief Accountant as well). The meeting may begin with a presentation by a lawyer from the Division of Enforcement as to the underlying facts and the reasons for Enforcement's recommendation. Robust discussion may follow in which each commissioner is given the opportunity to ask questions and to undertake in-depth inquiry. When the process is complete, a vote is taken.

If the vote is to go forward (as it usually is), two types of proceedings are possible: judicial or administrative. If the proceeding is judicial, the litigation will be commenced in federal district court and the trial will take place before a federal judge or jury. If the proceeding is administrative, the litigation will be commenced pursuant to administrative regulation and the trial will take place before an administrative judge—who also happens to be an SEC employee. The staff's decision whether to commence judicial or administrative proceedings is often a strategic one and itself may be the subject of internal staff debate. As a general proposition, the staff seems to have a preference for judicial proceedings where large-scale fraud is involved.

Once judicial or administrative proceedings have been commenced, the investigative process begins anew as the normal *discovery* process of litigation enables the parties to seek documents, obtain testimony, and otherwise prepare for trial. During the discovery process, the SEC staff and counsel for the defense will fall into more traditional roles as adversaries and act in every respect as a plaintiff and a defendant in normal litigation. The pretrial discovery process may take anywhere from months to years; as a general proposition, discovery in SEC administrative proceedings tends to get completed faster than in federal district court. Once the discovery process is complete, a trial takes place. And with that, justice is done (pending appeal).

A company that has perpetrated a financial fraud will rarely want to go to trial with the SEC for several reasons, a big one being that it will probably lose. In fact, the company would probably prefer not even to get into the Wells process to begin with, hence the preferability of audit committee internal investigation and self-imposed remedial action.

CHAPTER TWELVE

Criminal Investigations

THINGS CAN CERTAINLY CHANGE over time. It seems not so long ago that *Fortune* magazine was criticizing criminal prosecutors for a perceived unwillingness to take on fraudulent financial reporting. The reason, *Fortune* complained, was not a lack of evidence of wrongdoing but a lack of prosecutorial zeal. Even in the face of egregious misconduct, the magazine concluded that "hardly anyone ever went to prison."

If that was a valid criticism, it is no longer. Today, almost anyone potentially caught in a web of deliberately falsified financial results has to consider the possibility of a criminal investigation. The reasons for the shift are many, but generally involve the increased profile of fraudulent financial reporting and a corresponding reallocation of governmental resources to criminal proceedings. One factor that should *not* have played a significant role in changing prosecutorial attitudes is the law. Fraudulent financial reporting has been a criminal violation of the federal securities laws since the 1930s.

This chapter examines the role of prosecutors in ferreting out and prosecuting misconduct based on public company fraudulent financial reporting. The chapter starts with the considerations potentially relevant to a prosecutor in evaluating whether to commence a criminal investigation. It then turns to the typical phases of a criminal investigation and possible company responses at each phase. Then it discusses the responsibilities of the company to gather information in order to comply with the demands of the government, to monitor the progress of the investigation and evaluate the company's exposure to criminal prosecution, and ultimately to present its best case to avoid indictment.

WHETHER TO COMMENCE A CRIMINAL INVESTIGATION

In the federal system, the decision to start a criminal investigation is entirely within the discretion of the United States Attorney in each federal district. As a result, a criminal investigation of fraudulent financial reporting can originate in all sorts of ways. An investigation may be initiated because of a whistleblower, an anonymous tip, information supplied by a conscientious or guilt-ridden employee, or facts discovered in the course of a routine audit of the company's financial statements. The company's public disclosure of financial misstatements may itself lead to the commencement of a criminal investigation.

For the prosecutor, the decision whether to open an investigation can be difficult. The main reason is the need for the prosecutor to establish criminal intent, that is, that the perpetrator not only got the accounting wrong but did so willfully. Often, bad accounting will be the result of judgment calls, which can be defended as exactly that—executive determinations that, while easy to second guess with the benefit of hindsight, were made in good faith at the time. Thus, a prosecutor evaluating the viability of a criminal prosecution will be looking for evidence of conduct so egregious that the perpetrator *must* have known it was wrong.

That is not to suggest that evidence of a wrongful intent is the only consideration. A prosecutor's exercise of his or her prosecutorial discretion may consider all kinds of factors in deciding whether criminal inquiry is warranted. Those factors may include the magnitude and nature of the accounting misstatements, whether individuals personally benefited from the misstatements or acted pursuant to the directive of a superior, whether documents were fabricated or destroyed, the probable deterrent or rehabilitative effect of prosecution, and the likelihood of success at trial. The availability of governmental resources may also play a role.

Where the putative defendant is a corporation, partnership, or other business organization, a more settled set of factors come into play. These factors were outlined for U.S. Attorneys in January 2003 by then–Deputy Attorney

EXHIBIT 12.1   Securities Act of 1933

Section 24. Any person who willfully violates any of the provisions of this title, or the rules and regulations promulgated by the Commission under authority thereof, or any person who willfully, in a registration statement filed under this title, makes any untrue statement of a material fact or omits to state any material fact required to be stated therein or necessary to make the statements therein not misleading, shall upon conviction be fined not more than $10,000 or imprisoned not more than five years, or both.

General Larry Thompson. The "Thompson memorandum," as it became known, was superseded in August 2008 by a memorandum written by then–Deputy Attorney General Mark Filip. According to the Filip memorandum, factors relevant to the determination whether to charge a corporation or other business organization include:

- The nature and seriousness of the offense, including the risk of harm to the public, and applicable policies and priorities, if any, governing the prosecution of corporations for particular categories of crime
- The pervasiveness of wrongdoing within the corporation, including the complicity in, or the condoning of, the wrongdoing by corporate management

EXHIBIT 12.2   Securities Exchange Act of 1934

Section 32(a). Any person who willfully violates any provision of this title (other than Section 30A), or any rule or regulation thereunder the violation of which is made unlawful or the observance of which is required under the terms of this title, or any person who willfully and knowingly makes, or causes to be made, any statement in any application, report, or document required to be filed under this title or any rule or regulation thereunder or any undertaking contained in a registration statement as provided in subsection (d) of Section 15 of this title or by any self-regulatory organization in connection with an application for membership or participation therein or to become associated with a member thereof, which statement was false or misleading with respect to any material fact, shall upon conviction be fined not more than $5,000,000, or imprisoned not more than 20 years, or both, except that when such person is a person other than a natural person, a fine not exceeding $25,000,000 may be imposed; but no person shall be subject to imprisonment under this section for the violation of any rule or regulation if he proves that he had no knowledge of such rule or regulation.

- The corporation's history of similar misconduct, including prior criminal, civil, and regulatory enforcement actions against it
- The corporation's timely and voluntary disclosure of wrongdoing and its willingness to cooperate in the investigation of its agents
- The existence and effectiveness of the corporation's preexisting compliance program
- The corporation's remedial actions, including any efforts to implement an effective corporate compliance program or to improve an existing one, to replace responsible management, to discipline or terminate wrongdoers, to pay restitution, and to cooperate with the relevant government agencies
- Collateral consequences, including whether there is disproportionate harm to shareholders, pension holders, employees, and others not proven personally culpable, as well as impact on the public arising from the prosecution
- The adequacy of the prosecution of individuals responsible for the corporation's malfeasance
- The adequacy of remedies such as civil or regulatory enforcement actions

However a prosecutor gets there, once he or she determines to commence a criminal investigation, those that are its targets will view it as a priority over everything else. The government's powers to investigate are broad, and, once a determination to go forward is made, the full resources of the government, including the FBI, can be brought to bear. The criminal sentences resulting from a successful prosecution can be severe if not excessive, particularly in light of the enhanced criminal sentences put in place by Sarbanes-Oxley. In one widely reported case, a midlevel executive at a company who elected to proceed to trial was convicted and received a prison sentence of 24 years. The fact that the sentence was subsequently set aside on appeal does little to mitigate the concern that such a sentence could be imposed upon a first-time, nonviolent offender whose transgression was a failure to apply generally accepted accounting principles (GAAP).

EXHIBIT 12.3   Phases of a Criminal Investigation

- Grand jury subpoena
- Initial contacts with prosecutor
- Production of documents
- Grand jury testimony
- Plea negotiations (if necessary)
- Trial (if necessary)

THE INITIAL GRAND JURY PHASE

Typically, a company first learns that it is involved in a criminal investigation when it receives a grand jury subpoena, in most instances a "subpoena *duces tecum*," compelling the company or its employees to furnish documents to the grand jury. In an investigation of fraudulent financial reporting, such a subpoena for documents may encompass all the files underlying the company's publicly disseminated financial information, including the records underlying the transactions at issue and emails.

For a company and its executives, the need to respond to the subpoena presents both an opportunity and a dilemma. The opportunity stems from the company's ability, in responding to the subpoena, to learn about the investigation—an education process that will be critical to a successful criminal defense. The dilemma stems from the need to assess the extent to which active and complete cooperation should be pledged to the prosecutor at the outset. The formulation of a response to a criminal subpoena, therefore, constitutes a critical point in the investigatory process. Those involved are thereby placed in the position of needing to make important decisions at an early stage that can have lasting and significant effects.

Once an initial review of the subpoena and its underlying substance is complete, one of the first steps in formulating a response is often for company counsel to make a phone call to the prosecutor to make appropriate introductions and, to the extent possible, to seek background information regarding the investigation. In this initial contact, the prosecutor will be understandably guarded. Nonetheless, some useful information will frequently be shared. A general impression may be gained about the scope and focus of the investigation and the timing of additional subpoenas and testimony. Thereafter, it is not unusual for some kind of initial meeting to be arranged to discuss in greater detail the company's response. One benefit of such a meeting is that some level of additional information may be forthcoming.

From the outset, company counsel will be undertaking a process that will be ongoing throughout the criminal proceedings: learning as much as possible about the prosecutor's case. The reason is that, unlike a civil case, in which broad principles of discovery enable the defendants to learn the details of the adversary's evidence, the procedural rules of a criminal investigation result in much greater secrecy. Less formal methods of learning the details of the prosecutor's case, therefore, are critical.

In these initial contacts, the establishment of a sound foundation for the company's dealings with the prosecutor is an important aspect of the investigation. To state it simply, those dealings must be premised on a foundation of candor. Although it may be appropriate at various stages to decline to discuss sensitive matters, counsel should avoid making a factual statement on any subject about which it may be incompletely or inaccurately informed. This admonition applies to subjects such as the existence and location of files, the burden of producing documents, and the availability of witnesses. It also applies to more substantive matters bearing on guilt or innocence. A relationship with the prosecutor based on trust and confidence is key.

The judgment regarding the extent of cooperation with the prosecutor can be a tough one. Unlike in a civil proceeding, where cooperation with regulatory authorities (such as the SEC) is generally the preferred approach, the decision to cooperate with the government in a criminal investigation may be much more difficult, insofar as a subsequent effort to oppose the government (should such a change of approach be necessary) would be impeded by the loss of a significant tactical advantage—the loss of surprise. In criminal cases, the government is not afforded the same broad rights of discovery available in civil proceedings. It is entirely possible for a prosecutor to have no significant knowledge of the defense position until after the start of a trial.

On the other hand, the privileges available to a corporation are limited. There is, most important, no Fifth Amendment privilege against self-incrimination for companies. Furthermore, almost any kind of evidence, even evidence that would be inadmissible at trial, except for illegal wiretaps or privileged material, can be considered by a grand jury. Therefore, the company's ability to oppose a grand jury investigation is limited, and the prosecutor may even consider a company's extensive zeal in opposition to constitute obstruction of justice. Moreover, the prosecutor's ultimate decision about indictment of the company may be affected by the extent of the company's cooperation. And corporate management may wish to demonstrate cooperation as a matter of policy or public relations.

One issue with which a company will need to wrestle is whether it is appropriate for a public company or its executives to do anything *other* than cooperate with the government. On this issue, it is useful for executives to appreciate that the U.S. system of justice affords those being investigated certain fundamental rights, and it is not unpatriotic to take advantage of them. As to individuals, one of the most basic of these rights is the Fifth Amendment privilege against self-incrimination. Insofar as, in fraud cases, guilt can be established through circumstantial evidence, executives need to keep in mind that it demonstrates no lack of civic virtue to take full advantage of constitutional protections designed to protect the innocent.

A challenge is that many of these judgments regarding cooperation must be made at the outset when the company's information is limited. Often the best approach, at least as a threshold matter, will be one of courteous professionalism—meaning respect for one's adversary and reasonable accommodation pending more informed judgments down the road. Premature expressions of complete cooperation are best avoided as a subsequent change in approach can give rise to governmental frustration and anger.

 ## PRODUCING DOCUMENTS TO THE PROSECUTOR

Once a grand jury subpoena has been received, documents will need to be assembled, and the company will encounter the appropriate scope of document collection. A normal subpoena will be of sufficient breadth to comprehend almost all company files relevant to the subject matter of the investigation. The best approach in gathering documents is probably one of reasonableness though care should be taken that potentially responsive documents are preserved should production be necessary.

To be safe, company counsel will often want to contact the government attorney to discuss the breadth of the subpoena and ways in which the scope of production can be narrowed. The government may be willing to accept a staggered production of documents in which higher priority categories of documents are produced first with lesser priority categories being saved until later—or, perhaps, simply being preserved at the company.

Individual executives may raise the question whether they must produce, in response to a subpoena to the company, files at the company that the individual views as personal. The short answer is that there is no such thing as a "personal" file relating to company business. A failure to produce subpoenaed documents—even where the failure resulted from an individual employee's unwillingness to turn over physical possession—can result in a finding of contempt.

 ## INITIAL CONTACTS WITH COUNSEL FOR INDIVIDUAL EMPLOYEES

Where fraudulent financial reporting has occurred, there will normally be any number of lower-level employees with relevant knowledge and it is not at all unusual for the government to issue personal subpoenas to each. Where the circumstances allow, it often makes sense to find out those to whom subpoenas have been issued as leads can be thereby developed that may assist in determining the scope and focus of the investigation. Such an effort could also provide insight as to those who are viewed as targets and nontargets. A complicating factor here involves the extent to which the company may want to disassociate itself from employees of apparent complicity. Those employees in a position to cooperate with each other may enter "joint defense agreements" allowing for the exchange of information in a way that should protect its privileged nature.

The exchange of witness interview and debriefing memoranda prepared by lawyers presents some risk of disclosure in discovery in a civil case, presenting difficult strategic decisions. If the criminal case is likely to go to trial, counsel will probably want as much information as possible to prepare. If, however, it appears that the criminal case will not go to trial, the need for such materials may be less compelling.

 ## THE TESTIMONIAL GRAND JURY PHASE

Once documents have been produced to the government, a criminal investigation typically proceeds to a new phase: the government's procurement of testimony. During this phase, government prosecutors will either seek to interview corporate employees and other witnesses or subpoena them to testify before the grand jury. Often prosecutors will undertake an initial round of interviews that they will then use to determine those witnesses best called before the grand jury to testify.

A witness called to testify before a grand jury has no right to counsel present in the grand jury room. The witness is thus alone in a hostile and unfamiliar environment that is controlled entirely by the prosecutor. The prosecutor asks questions, typically in a form that is leading. The witness is called on to answer them. Everything the witness says is under oath and recorded for possible use later.

And there is no immediate respite. A grand jury witness does not have the same rights as someone who has been arrested and is being interrogated by the police. The witness has no right to refuse to speak unless he or she can assert a constitutional right or other privilege. The witness has no right to be advised of the Fifth Amendment privilege not to be compelled to testify. The witness has no right to be told that he or she is a potential target. The witness has no constitutional right, at this grand jury stage, to have counsel appointed—no criminal proceeding has yet been initiated and grand jury testimony is not the equivalent of a custodial police interrogation. If the witness *has* engaged counsel, the witness has the right to leave the room to consult. But that obviously can be awkward.

Once a witness has left the grand jury, debriefing by defense counsel is the norm. Some prosecutors have been known to try to interfere with debriefings, but prosecutors have no right to do so. Some prosecutors have also sought to impose an order of secrecy upon grand jury witnesses. There is no authority supporting the prevention of disclosure by a witness to his or her attorney.

A particular challenge to the grand jury witness is the preservation of applicable privileges against testimony. These are obviously important to the company's and the witness's criminal defense. They are also important to the defense of parallel civil litigation. Before the grand jury, four privileges in particular come into play: the Fifth Amendment privilege against self-incrimination, the attorney-client privilege, the attorney work-product doctrine, and the joint-defense privilege.

The Fifth Amendment Privilege

The Fifth Amendment privilege against self-incrimination stands out in importance in a criminal investigation. As mentioned at the outset, the privilege itself is *personal*, meaning that it applies only to natural individuals. For documents, it protects only the compelled production of self-incriminating documents that are the personal property of the person claiming the privilege or papers in the person's possession in a purely personal capacity.

A witness may assert the privilege on the basis that the answers may be incriminating under either state or federal law and may also assert the privilege on the basis that the answers may be incriminating under foreign law, although the authority for that is less clear. The privilege must be asserted in response to each individual question; a blanket refusal to answer is generally not viewed as adequate.

The privilege against self-incrimination can be claimed in any proceeding whether it is civil or criminal, administrative or judicial. As shall be considered later, the privilege may also be asserted at a deposition taken in a civil case. The compelled testimony must expose the witness to possible criminal prosecution. A witness may not refuse to answer because it would place him in danger of physical harm, degrade him, or incriminate a third party.

As a matter of practice, grand jury targets can usually avoid the personally unnerving experience of asserting the Fifth Amendment privilege in front of the grand jurors by providing the prosecutor with a letter confirming the witness's intention to assert the privilege. Justice Department policy states that "if a 'target' of the investigation . . . and his/her attorney state in writing and signed by both that the 'target' will refuse to testify on Fifth Amendment grounds, the witness ordinarily should be excused from testifying unless the grand jury and the U.S. Attorney agree to insist on the appearance." The company may be well advised to utilize this procedure to avoid potential prejudice and embarrassment and to avoid the not-uncommon situation in which an executive is provoked into departing from his Fifth Amendment silence and begins answering questions in the grand jury room.

When a grand jury witness, in response to a question, does not assert the privilege but instead gives an answer that may be incriminating, an express waiver will be deemed to have been made. An unintentional waiver can be exceedingly unfortunate because, once a witness voluntarily reveals incriminating facts, he may not thereafter refuse to disclose the details. Once the waiver has occurred, for each subsequent question the appropriate determination is whether a responsive answer would subject the witness to a "real danger of further incrimination."

A witness who has previously discussed facts relevant to a grand jury investigation with an FBI agent, an investigator, or a government attorney may still assert the Fifth Amendment privilege before the grand jury as to testimony concerning those same facts. Likewise, a witness who has testified before the SEC or in a civil deposition may still assert the Fifth Amendment privilege before the grand jury as to the same facts.

The Attorney-Client Privilege

As in civil proceedings, the attorney-client privilege is applicable in proceedings before a grand jury. The privilege excuses a witness from testifying about (a) a communication, (b) made in confidence, (c) to an attorney by a person who is, or is about to become, a client, (d) for the purpose of obtaining legal advice from that attorney. The privilege is available to corporate clients as well as to individuals. It applies to communications from the attorney to the client as well as those from the client to the attorney.

Of particular significance to grand jury testimony is the fact that the attorney-client privilege may be waived where there has been a voluntary disclosure of otherwise privileged matter. Disclosure made pursuant to court order is not voluntary. Disclosure made pursuant to grand jury subpoena *duces tecum*, in contrast, *is* voluntary, insofar as the claim of attorney-client privilege can be asserted and maintained by a timely objection to the subpoena.

The Attorney Work-Product Doctrine

The attorney work-product doctrine often operates closely with the attorney-client privilege. The doctrine generally protects written statements, private memoranda, and personal recollections prepared or formed by the attorney "in the course of preparation for litigation after a claim has arisen." The privilege is a qualified one, meaning that, upon a showing "of undue hardship" or "substantial need," documents otherwise covered by the doctrine may be ordered produced.

Both the attorney-client privilege and the work-product doctrine are subject to an important limitation. That is the so-called "crime fraud exception." Pursuant to that exception, otherwise-privileged communications that further an ongoing or future crime or fraud are not protected as work product or, for that matter, as attorney-client confidences. To the extent that the privilege has been invoked to prevent disclosure of communications with counsel regarding ongoing misreported items in the company's financial statements, the privilege's applicability may be challenged.

The Joint-Defense Privilege

The joint-defense privilege is applicable when otherwise-privileged information is disclosed to actual or potential codefendants in the course of a joint defense. The privilege applies, at its broadest, to any exchanges made for the purpose of a common defense. These might include discussions between a potential defendant and counsel for other potential defendants, disclosures to agents retained by counsel for purpose of pursuing a common defense, and possibly even to discussions among potential codefendants themselves.

The joint-defense privilege is particularly important in the context of a criminal investigation arising out of financial fraud, given the usefulness of communications among those involved as a means of learning about the focus and scope of the investigation. It is therefore of great importance that, in such a criminal investigation, a sufficient community of interest, at least among some of those involved, will frequently exist so that the joint-defense privilege may be properly invoked. The joint-defense privilege applies even if those sharing the information are not allies in all respects as long as the information disclosed is in furtherance of some common interest. Ordinarily, subjects and targets of a grand jury will have a sufficiently common defense interest so that their disclosures will be covered by the privilege.

The joint-defense privilege cannot be waived by disclosure to third parties without the consent of all parties who share the privilege. Such a disclosure by a member of the defense group would waive the privilege only as it applied to that party. As a practical matter, this may limit the advisability of the company entering into a joint-defense arrangement insofar as nondisclosure might violate otherwise-applicable disclosure responsibilities or render any cooperation with the government less valuable.

Two additional points should be made regarding the joint-defense privilege. First, although the privilege applies to communications between various clients and counsel involved in joint-defense efforts, it is in practice inadvisable for executives themselves to attend all joint-defense meetings. Executives attending such meetings may come away with information they did not know before, and such information can influence the executive's memory of events or may convince the executive to make a proffer with the required information. It is possible that a nervous executive will inadvertently disclose joint-defense material during an interview with the government or in grand jury testimony, and such disclosure can waive the privilege as it applies to that executive. The more prudent approach is to limit the group to defense attorneys and for each attorney to relay joint-defense information to the executive as the attorney feels it appropriate.

Second, any joint-defense group member may waive his right to invoke his privilege by compromising the confidentiality of the information shared, even though such a waiver does not waive the privilege for all participants. Because the attorney-client privilege may be waived even through inadvertent disclosure, it is important to keep tight control on the dissemination of the information to ensure that it not reach parties beyond the joint-defense group.

 ## PROSECUTORIAL STATUS AND IMMUNITY

The government divides witnesses into three categories: targets, subjects, and witnesses. A "target" is a putative defendant, someone as to whom the government has information that at least currently suggests that this person will likely be indicted. A "subject" is a person who played a role in the conduct being investigated, not necessarily in a culpable way, who could possibly have criminal liability or could be merely a witness. His status could change during the course of the investigation and frequently does. A "witness" is one who the government believes has no culpability but who is simply asked to give testimony because he or she happens to have some knowledge that would further the investigation. For example, a secretary who might be called to testify that she typed a particular document for her boss would almost certainly be regarded as only a witness. An employee who can supply background information as to the identity of individuals with various responsibilities or the nature of certain corporate procedures would also be a witness.

For those called on to give testimony to a grand jury, one issue involves the grant of immunity. Two broad categories of formal immunity are recognized: "transactional immunity" and "use immunity." Transactional immunity precludes the government from prosecuting a witness for any offense (or "transaction") related to the witness's compelled testimony. Use immunity precludes the government from using directly or indirectly a witness's compelled testimony in a prosecution of that witness. In the federal system, a grand jury witness who is faced with a Fifth Amendment problem may be accorded statutory use immunity in return for testifying. Use immunity is not available to a company because it is contingent upon an assertion of the Fifth Amendment privilege, which the company does not have.

CORPORATE CRIMINAL LIABILITY FOR EMPLOYEE ACTIONS

Employees who seek to advance the interests of a company in ways that are criminal may cause the imposition of vicarious liability on the company. A criminal investigation of a company's fraudulent financial reporting, accordingly, inevitably poses the risk of criminal liability for the company. Indeed, as the investigation proceeds, the company's liability may be so thoroughly established that the company's stance, to the extent it has been adversarial, will shift to one of cooperation and possibly plea discussions.

Theoretically, a corporation's ability to disassociate itself from the criminal acts of its employees should be aided by the principle of vicarious liability. Under that principle, corporate liability for employees' criminal acts is limited to those instances in which the criminal acts were undertaken within the scope of an employee's authority. But what falls within the scope of an employee's authority is interpreted broadly, so broadly that, even if an employee acts contrary to instruction or policy, the corporate employer may still be liable. Moreover, the law often imposes on an employer the duty to supervise and control the actions of an employee performing almost any job-related activity. Failure to control an employee's conduct can suggest that the employer adopted and ratified the conduct.

It is no impediment to vicarious corporate liability that the offense required a culpable mental state, such as intent or knowledge. For corporate liability to be so imposed, however, the wrongdoing employee must have acted with an intent to benefit the company. This intent-to-benefit rule avoids the anomaly of imposing liability on a company that is the victim, rather than the putative beneficiary, of its employee's criminal conduct. Depending on the particular circumstances, the conduct involved in a deliberate misstatement of a company's financial statements, if serious enough to be the subject of a criminal prosecution, may potentially be found to have been undertaken to benefit the company.

Ironically, a company can also be held accountable for a crime when there is no single employee who could be convicted. This is the result of the collective-knowledge doctrine, pursuant to which knowledge is imputed to a company based on the aggregate knowledge of its employees as a group. Therefore, a company may be found to have knowingly engaged in a crime based on evidence that one employee knew the facts relating to one element of the offense and a second or third employee knew facts relating to additional elements.

 ## CORPORATE INDEMNIFICATION OF COUNSEL FEES

Every state (including Delaware and New York) has legislation providing for corporate indemnification of expenses, including legal fees, of directors, officers, and sometimes other corporate personnel in defending legal actions brought against them in their official capacities. These statutes vary but, generally, in order to be eligible for indemnification, the executive must have acted in good faith for a purpose he believed to be in the best interest of the company. When there is a criminal proceeding, an executive normally must have had no reasonable cause to believe that his conduct was unlawful. However, indemnification may be appropriate even if the executive is convicted. And in Delaware and New York, as well as some other states, if the executive is successful on the merits, the law requires that he shall be indemnified. Frequently, advance payments are authorized with the proviso that the executive must undertake to reimburse the company if it is ultimately determined that he is not entitled to indemnification.

There may be instances in which the prosecutor or an investigator seeks to obtain the cooperation of a corporate executive by encouraging the company to discipline executives who do not cooperate. For example, if an executive indicates that he intends to assert his Fifth Amendment privilege against self-incrimination, the investigator might ask the company to discourage him from doing so. Similarly, a company may wish to discourage an executive from asserting his Fifth Amendment privilege for corporate policy or public relations reasons. There are, however, often reasons for the company to resist such inclinations. There may be some danger of liability if the company fires or disciplines an executive for exercising a constitutional right. And it may be that the executive's commendably cautious attorney is simply seeking immunity as part of a cooperation agreement, so the executive's assertion of the Fifth Amendment privilege may not carry with it an implication of guilt.

SEPARATE COUNSEL FOR TARGETS AND SUBJECTS

When a criminal investigation has a number of subjects or targets, as will frequently be the case where a criminal investigation has been commenced as a result of fraudulent financial reporting, those involved will often be tempted to seek common representation. The temptation is understandable. Inefficiencies in communication and work can seemingly be limited when one lawyer is doing the work for several executives at the same time.

Nonetheless, separate counsel for each executive who is the focus of an investigation is often the better course. A lawyer who represents two or more targets or subjects, including a lawyer who represents an individual target and a corporate target, may have an inherent conflict of interest, and the simultaneous representation of such potential defendants is fraught with danger. For example, it may be in the interest of one of the lawyer's clients to cooperate and testify against the other, but the lawyer cannot recommend that course to his client without violating the interests of the other. Moreover, even if the lawyer should withdraw from the representation of the client in whose interest it is to cooperate, the lawyer may put himself in a situation where at trial he has to cross-examine a former client from whom he has received confidential and privileged information. The lawyer cannot do so and his only course may be to withdraw from the representation of both clients.

Nor does a client "waiver" of a conflict necessarily solve the problem. Judicial precedent allows judges to disqualify lawyers who represent more than one person even if both clients waive any conflict. This means that, if a lawyer represents more than one person and a conflict develops, a judge may disqualify the lawyer from representing either person even if both provide a waiver.

Moreover, the government itself may raise as an issue such simultaneous representations and seek disqualification. The government, for example, may be seeking the cooperation of one executive and be concerned that a lawyer simultaneously representing that executive and another, less cooperative, executive may discourage the cooperation of the first. If the lawyer is also representing a corporation that has little interest in cooperation, the simultaneous representations, from the perspective of the government, can be even more objectionable. If the government suspects such simultaneous representations are affecting the truthfulness of testimony of the lawyers' clients, the government may even consider charges of obstruction of justice. Government efforts to raise such issues, particularly if they arise late in the game, can create problems for everyone involved.

PARALLEL PROCEEDINGS

A company caught up in a federal criminal investigation arising out of financial fraud will want to be alert to the impact upon parallel proceedings. These might include an SEC investigation, state criminal investigations, administrative proceedings, securities class action litigation, tax investigations, or even congressional hearings.

Because of the dual-sovereignty doctrine, it is possible for the federal government and a state to prosecute separately an executive or the company for exactly the same conduct. Double jeopardy prevents the federal government from trying a person twice for the same conduct, but the federal government can try a defendant for the same conduct for which he has been previously tried by a state. Thus, for example, an employee of a public company who causes the dissemination of false and misleading financial statements might be charged by the state with violations of the state laws against the creation of fraudulent business records and might also be charged by the federal government under similar statutes that apply to interstate communication facilities, the mails, or the purchase or sale of securities.

The Department of Justice has a rule that, in normal cases, it will not prosecute a defendant for conduct for which he has previously been prosecuted by a state. But there are exceptions. Moreover, the rule does not apply to state prosecutors. And state prosecutors, who frequently are elected political officials, may feel impelled to bring a parallel prosecution, particularly if it is a case that is likely to generate favorable publicity. Therefore, a lawyer who negotiates with a federal prosecutor on behalf of his client must bear in mind the possibility that he may have a problem with the state prosecutor and must make sure that any agreements with the federal government do not come back to haunt him in negotiating with the state.

Additional complexity is introduced by civil class action litigations. The existence of this parallel litigation is particularly troublesome during the pendency of a criminal investigation insofar as the defense of one may compromise the defense of the other. For example, it may be important to the defense of the criminal proceeding for a particular executive to assert his Fifth Amendment right against self-incrimination. However, unlike in a criminal proceeding, the assertion of that Fifth Amendment right in a civil proceeding may be used as the basis for a negative inference against the defendant. More than that, a civil jury of normal temperament may be expected to have a severely negative reaction to an executive who so declines to testify before it. As a practical matter, an optimum defense to both the civil and the criminal actions may be difficult.

In a ranking of difficult choices, defendants will likely conclude that the preservation of defenses to criminal charges through the assertion of Fifth Amendment rights is far preferable, even at the risk of a weakened position in civil litigation. Hence, a settlement of the class action litigation becomes all the more desirable. It may be of some consolation that, while settlement of such litigation in the wake of fraudulent financial reporting is frequently painful, restitution to shareholders may operate to the advantage of those involved in the criminal investigation in negotiations with the prosecutor.

 ## PLEA DISCUSSIONS AND SENTENCING

In many conspiratorial offenses, the government makes a deal with one of the conspirators and offers him leniency for his testimony against others, including the company. Sometimes this leniency may be immunity from prosecution. A lawyer who seeks to negotiate with the government on behalf of a subject or target hopes his client will be treated as a witness and not a defendant.

If, however, the government is unwilling to offer the executive immunity and the case against the executive is strong, the executive may have no choice but to enter a plea agreement. This is an arrangement with the prosecutor that is a matter of contract and the terms may vary. A typical plea agreement would be one in which the executive pleads guilty to fewer crimes than the government can readily prove and may include an agreement to cooperate fully with the government. Such a plea agreement is not available in every case. In some instances, the executive will be the ultimate target and there will be no one of significance for him to testify against.

The ability of an executive to obtain formal immunity, a nonprosecution agreement, or a plea bargain varies with the strength of the government's case, the executive's perceived culpability, the government's need for his testimony, and the executive's qualities as a witness. Therefore, a lawyer faced with the task of getting the best possible terms for his client will often have an important objective in mind: convincing the government that, to pursue whatever it is seeking to prove against others, the government must have this particular executive's testimony.

Sometimes the prosecutor will want to talk to the executive personally. This conversation is frequently referred to as a "proffer session." Before this is done, the executive will request informal immunity by means of a "proffer agreement," which puts in place some limitations on the prosecutor's ability to use the discussion in a prosecution of that executive. If the discussions prove fruitful and the prosecutor finds the executive to be a valuable and credible witness, the prosecutor may then offer the executive immunity or a plea agreement.

In the federal system, plea discussions will focus extensively on possible sentences under the Federal Sentencing Guidelines. For a time, as to most defendants found guilty of a crime (whether by plea or verdict after trial) under these guidelines, the judge had exceedingly limited discretion in imposing sentence. More recently, the feature of the guidelines that imposed mandatory rules on sentencing judges has been declared unconstitutional and the Federal Sentencing Guidelines are now advisory. Still, to promote uniformity in sentencing, the federal courts have been admonished to follow the guidelines, though, in fraud cases, there has been a fairly high incidence of guideline departures.

The potential impact of the Federal Sentencing Guidelines, though technically advisory, still dominates in the federal system. A sentencing range is computed by starting with the "offense level" (a number assigned to each federal offense), to which points are added that correspond to such things as the defendant's criminal history; certain aggravating factors particular to the offense (including, for example, enhancements for "more than minimal planning" or "breach of trust"); and, for offenses involving fraud (such as accounting irregularities), the amount of loss. The sentencing judge can mitigate the sentence by crediting the defendant with points, but only in a narrowly circumscribed manner.

The fact that the sentencing guidelines result in an increased allocation of points corresponding to the amount of loss is, in this context, potentially unjust. At best, estimating shareholder losses resulting from fraudulent financial reporting is a highly imprecise undertaking. Making it all the more so, the main theories for estimating damages have been devised by plaintiffs' experts in civil litigation whose ostensible objectives included exaggeration of such losses to increase shareholder recoveries and, correspondingly, plaintiff attorney's fees. To the extent that shareholder losses factor into the sentencing guidelines, therefore, the consequences can be devastating. In one case, a CEO was sentenced to what, for him, amounted to life in prison: 25 years. The CEO was a nonviolent, first-time offender.

EXHIBIT 12.4   Criminal Sentences

Company	Executive	Sentence	Date
LocatePlus Holdings	CFO	5 years	2-25-2013
LocatePlus Holdings	CEO	5 years	6-14-2012
U.S. Foodservice	VP of Marketing	3 years, 10 months	12-7-2011
GlobeTel	CEO	4 years, 2 months	7-26-2010
United Rentals	CFO	2 years, 3 months	3-11-2010
Safety-Kleen Corp.	CFO	5 years, 10 months	11-8-2007
Computer Associates International	CFO	7 months in prison and 7 months' home confinement	1-27-2007
Cendant	Chairman	12 years, 7 months	1-17-2007
Computer Associates International	CEO	12 years	11-27-2006
Enron	President	24 years, four months	10-23-2006
Enron	CFO	6 years	9-26-2006
WorldCom	CFO	5 years	8-12-2005
WorldCom	CEO	25 years	7-13-2005
Adelphia	CFO	20 years	6-20-2005
Rite Aid	Chief Counsel	10 years	10-14-2004
Rite Aid	CEO	8 years	8-11-2004
Network Technologies Group	CEO	9 years	4-23-2004
Health Management	CEO	9 years	11-16-1998

For a corporate defendant, the potential sentence can be mitigated if, prior to the offense, the corporation had an effective compliance and ethics program. In substance, the Federal Sentencing Guidelines provide:

To have an effective compliance and ethics program, an organization shall exercise due diligence to prevent and detect criminal conduct, and otherwise promote an organizational culture that encourages ethical conduct and a commitment to compliance with the law. Such compliance and ethics program shall be reasonably designed, implemented, and enforced so that the program is generally effective in preventing and detecting criminal conduct. The failure to prevent or detect an instant offense does not necessarily mean that the program is not generally effective in preventing and detecting criminal conduct.

Due diligence and the promotion of an organizational culture that encourages ethical conduct and a commitment to compliance with the law minimally require the following:

1. The organization shall establish standards and procedures to prevent and detect criminal conduct.
2. The organization's governing authority shall be knowledgeable about the content and operation of the compliance and ethics program and shall exercise reasonable oversight with respect to the implementation and effectiveness of the compliance and ethics program. High-level personnel of the organization shall ensure that the organization has an effective compliance and ethics program. Specific individual(s) within high-level personnel shall be assigned overall responsibility for the compliance and ethics program. Specific individual(s) within the organization shall be delegated day-to-day operational responsibility for the compliance and ethics program. Individual(s) with operational responsibility shall report periodically to high-level personnel and, as appropriate, to the governing authority, or an appropriate subgroup of the governing authority, on the effectiveness of the compliance and ethics program. To carry out such operational responsibility, such individual(s) shall be given adequate resources, appropriate authority, and direct access to the governing authority or an appropriate subgroup of the governing authority.
3. The organization shall use reasonable efforts not to include within the personnel of the organization having substantial authority, any individual whom the organization knew, or should have known through the exercise of due diligence, has engaged in illegal activities or other conduct inconsistent with an effective compliance and ethics program.
4. The organization shall take reasonable steps to communicate periodically and in a practical manner its standards and procedures, and other aspects of the compliance and ethics program, to the

organization's personnel and agents by conducting effective training programs and otherwise disseminating information appropriate to such individuals' respective roles and responsibilities.

5. The organization shall take reasonable steps (i) to ensure that the organization's compliance and ethics program is followed, including monitoring and auditing to detect criminal conduct; (ii) to evaluate periodically the effectiveness of the organization's compliance and ethics program; and (iii) to have and publicize a system, which may include mechanisms that allow for anonymity or confidentiality, whereby the organization's employees and agents may report or seek guidance regarding potential or actual criminal conduct without fear of retaliation.

6. The organization's compliance and ethics program shall be promoted and enforced consistently throughout the organization through (A) appropriate incentives to perform in accordance with the compliance and ethics program; and (B) appropriate disciplinary measures for engaging in criminal conduct and for failing to take reasonable steps to prevent or detect criminal conduct.

7. After criminal conduct has been detected, the organization shall take reasonable steps to respond appropriately to the criminal conduct and to prevent further similar criminal conduct, including making any necessary modifications to the organization's compliance and ethics program.

The organization shall periodically assess the risk of criminal conduct and shall take appropriate steps to design, implement, or modify each requirement set forth above to reduce the risk of criminal conduct identified through this process.

 ## DISCUSSIONS OVER INDICTMENT

As the government's case becomes clearer, it will be incumbent upon counsel to put together a defense. Except in the most hopeless of cases, the lawyer's goal will be to persuade the government to decline an indictment. In most instances, the lawyer will make written and oral presentations to the prosecutors and, where necessary, to the prosecutors' superiors. It is almost always possible to get a hearing within the Department of Justice or the U.S. Attorney's office at supervisory levels, and it is sometimes possible to meet with the Assistant Attorney General or U.S. Attorney ultimately responsible for the case.

Many cases are successfully resolved by persuading the government that its case is not likely to succeed at trial or that it should exercise prosecutorial discretion not to seek an indictment. The prosecutor obviously recognizes that no indictment should be recommended unless the prosecutor is personally convinced that the defendant's guilt can be proven beyond a reasonable doubt. In a case arising out of fraudulent financial reporting, the inaccuracy of the financial statements may be assumed and the discussions may be centered on whether any particular employee acted with the willfulness required for a criminal charge. If no single employee can be charged because of a failure of evidence, the company's position in opposition to an indictment is strengthened.

But even if an executive is likely to be charged, the company may still have arguments against indictment. If the conduct at issue can credibly be characterized as aberrant or if it involved extraordinary efforts to circumvent sound internal controls and compliance procedures, the company may present itself as a victim. The company's early cooperation may be pointed to as evidence of its decision to disassociate itself from the errant executive and as the best argument to avoid indictment. Indeed, there have been ostensibly hopeless cases in which, because cooperation was begun early—sometimes by the company's voluntary disclosure even before the criminal investigation was commenced—indictment was avoided.

Other factors may influence a prosecutor's charging decision. For example, it may be that by this stage all related litigation has been resolved and the victims of the company's accounting fraud have been made whole by settlement or otherwise. Since one of the purposes of a criminal conviction of the company in the federal system—restitution to victims—has already been accomplished, arguably an additional financial penalty in the form of a criminal fine will be borne by innocent shareholders. In other cases, discussion may center on whether there is a strong prosecutorial interest at stake, such as whether a prosecution of the company serves the goals of specific or general deterrence, or whether other mechanisms, such as enforcement by the SEC or private litigation, are sufficient.

Only if all these efforts prove fruitless and the case cannot be disposed of does a trial become necessary.

CHAPTER THIRTEEN

Class Action Lawsuits

S EVERAL MONTHS INTO A FINANCIAL FRAUD CRISIS, it may be that the board of directors will have occasion to be satisfied with its progress. If all has been properly handled, the board will have undertaken an investigation, alerted the public through a press release, terminated the employment of those whose complicity was clear, and handled innumerable problems involving creditors, employees, suppliers, and others. Looking back, individual board members may be genuinely astonished at the alacrity with which difficult issues have been handled.

There is at least one aspect of the problem, however, where speed and efficiency of resolution most notably will not be the case. That is the aspect dealing with class action litigation. For the board, the litigation will likely proceed with exasperating inefficiency, delay, and expense. It is to this process of dealing with class action lawsuits that we now turn.

WHAT IS A CLASS ACTION?

Broadly stated, a *class action* is a type of lawsuit in which a single representative individual is permitted to sue on behalf of an entire group of similarly situated individuals known as a "class." A class action theoretically comes about when an aggrieved shareholder contacts a lawyer and explains that he has been harmed. The law then generally permits that single shareholder to sue on behalf of all similar shareholders.

Although the conceptual justification for class action litigation begins with the predicate of an aggrieved shareholder reaching out to a lawyer to seek redress, the reality is somewhat different. Shareholder class action litigation tends to be prosecuted by a small number of highly specialized law firms and, over the years, these firms have developed practices and relationships that enable them to take the lead in commencing shareholder litigation almost on their own. A practical consequence is that, within days after issuance of a press release revealing financial fraud, the class action lawyers will normally have their lawsuits already prepared.

COMMENCEMENT OF CLASS ACTION LITIGATION

The catalyst for commencement of the litigation will often be the initial press release (see Exhibit 13.1). Among other things, the lawyers may glean from the press release that accounting irregularities have surfaced, that earlier SEC filings are false, which line items on the financial statements are affected, and the board of directors' preliminary information as to how far back the accounting irregularities go. With that information in hand, the class action lawyers will quickly extract from their word processor an earlier complaint filed in a similar case and quickly insert the specifics regarding the particular company at hand. In their haste to be the first to file a lawsuit, the process of revision is not always completely thorough. In one famous instance, class action lawyers described Philip Morris as being part of the toy industry.

EXHIBIT 13.1 Typical Stages of a Securities Class Action

- Initial press release
- Series of complaints
- Consolidated complaint
- Motion to dismiss
- Document productions
- Depositions
- Settlement (if necessary)
- Trial (almost never)

From the perspective of the board of directors, the result will be that, within several days of the issuance of the company's initial press release, the company will begin receiving a number of seemingly duplicative lawsuits in which the only significant difference seems to be the name of the representative shareholder seeking to represent the interests of the class. In truth, a shareholder gains no meaningful strategic advantage over the defendants in rushing to be named the class representative. In the end, only one class of similarly situated shareholders will be certified and only one complaint ordinarily will survive. Rather than trying to get a strategic advantage over the defendants, the interest of a plaintiff in rushing to be named the class representative is to get an advantage over the other plaintiff shareholders—or, more precisely, their lawyers. For a class action plaintiff's lawyer, having one's client named the class representative opens the door to the lion's share of the legal fees.

 ## POTENTIAL DEFENDANTS

Although the class action complaints may not be precisely identical, in all likelihood they will focus on the same general defendants. The main candidates of those who may be named in the class action complaints are as follows:

- *The company.* The corporate entity will almost inevitably be named a defendant. Also named may be a parent company or holding company. The plaintiffs will argue that the corporate entity or entities are responsible for the wrongdoing of their individual officers and directors.
- *Officers who have resigned, been terminated, or placed on leave.* It may be that the initial press release will have identified particular officers who have resigned, been terminated by the board, or been placed on paid or unpaid leave. The plaintiffs' lawyers will infer from any such corporate action the officers' complicity in wrongdoing.
- *The CEO and the CFO.* Prime candidates to be included as defendants are the chief executive officer and the chief financial officer. The plaintiffs will infer from their positions some level of complicity. Also, they will have signed what have now turned out to be incorrect SEC filings, such as a Form 10-K or Forms 10-Q.
- *Particular officers.* Beyond the CEO and CFO, other officers may be named as defendants depending on the nature of the fraud (as described in the press release) and a particular officer's proximity to it. For example, if the fraud involved improper revenue recognition on consignment sales, the plaintiffs

may seek to include as a defendant the officer or officers with responsibility in that area. Similarly, if the fraud involved improprieties at some remote location, those responsible for operations or the financial reporting function of that location may be named.

- *Outside directors.* These days, outside directors tend not to be included as defendants. Historically, all outside directors would be named as defendants almost as a matter of course. Congress's passage of federal securities law tort reform in the mid-1990s, however, has operated as an important impediment to the inclusion of the entire board—at least in the absence of evidence suggesting an individual director's knowledge or complicity.

- *Underwriters.* Where the company has publicly issued stock within the last three years, the underwriters may be included. For the corporate issuer, this is particularly unfortunate insofar as typical underwriting documents will provide for corporate indemnification of the underwriter in the absence of the underwriter's own wrongdoing.

- *Selling shareholders.* An issuance of public stock within the prior three years may also open the door to the inclusion as defendants of shareholders who participated as sellers in the offering. Plaintiffs may seek to show their complicity based on inferences drawn from their natural desire to see the stock price sustained or increased during the period prior to their sale.

- *The outside auditor.* Several years ago, inclusion of the outside auditor in an accounting irregularities case occurred as a matter of course. Today, the inclusion of the outside auditor as a defendant—at least in the first complaint—has become less automatic. As with the inclusion of outside directors, the federal securities law tort reform legislation in the mid-1990s erected barriers to naming the outside auditor, at least without particularized facts showing auditor complicity. However, the auditor may not be left out forever. An important objective of the plaintiffs will be assembling detailed evidence sufficient to make claims against the auditor stick.

 ## SORTING OUT PARTIES AND COUNSEL

Although the intensity of the initial barrage of lawsuits may create an appearance that the class action litigation will proceed with ferocity, that appearance will quickly change as the case gets bogged down right from the outset. There will ordinarily be several reasons but foremost will be the need for the plaintiffs and their law firms to sort themselves out. Typically, any number of plaintiffs and law firms will have filed complaints, but theoretically only one plaintiff (or group) under the law is to become the lead plaintiff and only one law firm (or group) is to become lead counsel. The filing of class action complaints, therefore, will be followed by a series of discussions among various plaintiffs' law firms as to which will emerge as the leader. Given the potential fees at stake for the lead plaintiff's law firm, this is one of the two most important negotiations that will take place.

For the defendants, the resulting hiatus will provide a welcome respite. The initial class action complaints will arrive within days of the initial press release, a time during which the defendants will already be preoccupied with operational and financial difficulties. More than that, the defendants will have some sorting out to do among themselves. Among other things, they will want to sort out their own representation.

A complicating factor in arranging for the defendants' representation will be that not every defendant will have precisely the same interests as every other. At one extreme, for example, will be those defendants by whom the accounting irregularities were perpetrated. At the other extreme will be those defendants who are entirely blameless. Those two groups—and others that fall somewhere in the middle—may not share precisely the same interests on every issue. Accordingly, the need for different lawyers to represent different groups of defendants will soon become apparent. At the same time, any outside professionals who have been named as defendants will in all likelihood seek their own representation.

The initial weeks of class action litigation, therefore, will be largely occupied with the plaintiffs, the defendants, and their new lawyers trying to sort themselves out.

THE CONSOLIDATED COMPLAINT

At one point, both sides will have successfully coordinated among themselves to the point where they are ready for the battle to begin, and it will be incumbent upon the plaintiffs to fire the first salvo. The projectile will be in the form of a "consolidated complaint"—that is, a single complaint that consolidates all of the material allegations, legal claims, and parties of the others. In essence, the consolidated complaint will reflect a distillation of the information and charges hastily thrown together into the earlier separate complaints. In drafting the consolidated complaint, the plaintiffs may decide to add claims, delete claims, add defendants, delete defendants, expand the time frame at issue, shorten the time frame at issue, or otherwise adjust the contours of the plaintiffs' contentions. Although the particulars of any consolidated complaint will depend on the circumstances, certain claims are more likely than others. Such claims may include the following:

- *Section 10(b).* The one claim that is sure to be a fixture of any financial fraud class action is a claim pursuant to Section 10(b) of the Securities Exchange Act of 1934. Directed against fraud in the secondary market of publicly traded securities, Section 10(b) makes it unlawful for any person directly or indirectly "to use or employ, in connection with the purchase or sale of any security," any "manipulative or deceptive device or contrivance" in violation of SEC regulations. In substance, Section 10(b) makes it unlawful to deliberately say anything of consequence that is false or misleading in connection with the purchase or sale of a security. Among the data subject to the prohibitions of Section 10(b) are significant inaccuracies in a company's financial statements that are filed as part of its Form 10-K or Form 10-Q.

  Although Section 10(b) is broad in its scope, a critical prerequisite of a claim limits its applicability. Section 10(b) imposes liability only on those who acted with *scienter*—that is, with "intent to deceive, manipulate, or defraud." In other words, Section 10(b) does not impose liability on those who accidentally make false or misleading statements, even where the person who made the statements was negligent.

  Exactly what is needed to plead and prove "intent to deceive, manipulate, or defraud" is an issue that plaintiffs' and defendants' lawyers have been arguing about for more than 25 years—ever since the U.S. Supreme Court declined to reach the issue in the famous footnote 12 of its 1976 decision in Ernst & Ernst v. Hochfelder. The key point is that Section 10(b) does not impose liability for mere accidents or negligence.

- *Section 20.* A claim pursuant to Section 20 is frequently a companion to a claim pursuant to Section 10(b). Section 20, also a provision of the Securities Exchange Act of 1934, operates to impose liability on those who control another person who makes a significant false or misleading statement in SEC filings "unless the controlling person acted in good faith and did not directly or indirectly induce the act or acts constituting the violation or cause of action." Thus, for example, a consolidated complaint might allege that a large shareholder should be equally liable with the company. An inside director or high-ranking officer may also be alleged to control the corporation. The actual circumstances that constitute control under Section 20 are frequently an issue of dispute.

▪ *Section 12(a)(2).* Unlike Sections 10(b) and 20 of the 1934 Act, Section 12(a)(2) of the Securities Act of 1933 does not apply to false or misleading statements in connection with secondary market purchases or sales of securities. The role of Section 12(a)(2), rather, is much more limited: It applies only to false or misleading statements that are made in a prospectus, which has been interpreted to mean that only shareholders who bought in a public offering may sue under this statute. Although Section 12(a)(2)'s scope is more limited, proving a violation of Section 12(a)(2) is easier for a plaintiff than proving a violation of Section 10(b), because a Section 12(a)(2) claim does not require proof that the false statement was deliberate.

▪ *Section 11.* In some respects, Section 11 of the Securities Act of 1933 (applicable to registration statements) is the most draconian of them all. It potentially imposes liability on every person who signs a company's false or misleading registration statement, every person who is a director of such a company, every accountant who prepared or issued a report on a part of the registration statement, and every underwriter of the security at issue. In substance, Section 11 operates to make each of these potentially liable where the registration statement contains materially false or misleading information, although everyone except the company has a defense to the extent they conducted a reasonable investigation and had "reasonable ground to believe" that the registration statement was true, which they have the burden of proving. (The law also recognizes that it is easier for nonexperts to justify the reasonableness of their beliefs as to those parts of the registration statement prepared by an expert, such as an auditor of the financial statements.) Under Section 11, the company can be held liable whether it had reasonable ground to believe in the truthfulness of the statements or not.

▪ *Section 15.* Analogous to Section 20, Section 15 of the 1933 Act operates to impose liability on "every person who . . . controls any person liable under Section 11, or 12."

While each of these provisions is relegated to a particular context of the securities markets, their collective thrust is the same: It is unlawful to make significant false or misleading statements. Where a significant false and misleading statement has been made, liability may potentially be imposed on the company; those who control the company; and the company's officers, directors, underwriters, and accountants.

LIABILITY IMPLICATIONS OF THE INITIAL PRESS RELEASE

These provisions obviously pose a particular problem where a company has issued a press release announcing the discovery of accounting irregularities. The press release by itself could operate to establish some of the key elements of a securities law claim against the company and individuals directly associated with it, the most notable of which is the fact that a significant false statement has occurred. One reaction to the company's press release would be that, once it is issued, there would seem to be very little left to argue about.

However, the imposition of liability under the securities laws, even after issuance of a press release conceding that accounting irregularities have taken place, can give rise to exceedingly vigorous litigation. There are several reasons, including the fact (as discussed more fully ahead) that the amount of damages allegedly suffered by the plaintiffs' class will be vigorously disputed. Another is that, even after a company's confession of false financial statements, the various individual defendants associated with the company likely will fall into one of three categories. One category is those who will be perceived as plainly guilty. A second category is those who, when the facts become available, will be perceived as plainly innocent. The third category is those who could go either way.

Some of the most significant battles in the class litigation will revolve around those who should fall into the third category. The reason is that often this third category is where the money is. As to those individuals in the first category—those who are plainly guilty—they may not have personal assets worth pursuing. And they might end up ineligible for coverage under the company's director and officer (D&O) insurance policy, insofar as D&O policies generally exclude coverage for deliberate acts of fraud. For the plaintiffs, therefore, those individuals who are plainly guilty may be of limited financial interest.

Of even less interest will normally be those falling into the second category—those who are plainly not guilty. Though the legal system may be somewhat inefficient, it nonetheless ultimately serves to impede the prosecution of claims against those who did nothing wrong.

That naturally leaves the third category—those individuals who may or may not bear some blame. True, their financial assets may be no more substantial than the plainly guilty. However, the D&O insurance policy will treat them somewhat differently. The absence of unequivocal evidence establishing their guilt at the outset will in all likelihood cause the D&O insurer to begin financing their defense. At the same time, the D&O insurer's mindset will shift to acceptance of the proposition that these individuals are not deliberate defrauders but instead those who are at worst guilty of reckless fraud—something for which the D&O insurer will probably pay. The battle over the liability of those falling within this third category of defendants, therefore, is largely a battle over the proceeds of the D&O policy.

Of those directly associated with the company, that leaves one defendant: the company itself. A key to assessing the company's vulnerability will obviously involve those facts to which the company has already admitted in its initial press release. As mentioned earlier, the company will probably have admitted a misstatement of fact insofar as it is precisely such a misstatement that has triggered the need for a press release in the first place. Moreover, to the extent the company has announced the discovery of accounting irregularities, it will have revealed that at least someone within the corporate enterprise has deliberately misstated financial results.

It does not necessarily follow, however, that the company will be the principal target of the class action plaintiffs. Keep in mind that many of the class action plaintiffs will still be shareholders and, to the extent that they use the judicial system to extract a cash payment from the company, they are in a sense simply taking money from one pocket and placing it in another—through a judicial vehicle involving enormous transaction costs, insofar as a significant percentage of each dollar thereby extracted goes to the class action lawyers. On the other hand, to the extent that the class includes those who are no longer shareholders, their reluctance to seek a cash payment from the company will be significantly less pronounced. Another complicating factor, results from the fact that, where accounting irregularities have surfaced, the company's cash position may be somewhat tenuous. As discussed in an earlier chapter, for example, the company may be in violation of debt covenants. To the extent that cash is not available, the interest of the class action plaintiffs in the company as a defendant correspondingly decreases.

In any event, with the consolidated complaint having been prepared and filed, the ball is now in the defendants' court. It is incumbent upon the defendants to respond. The preferred vehicle is through a motion to dismiss.

MOTION TO DISMISS

A "motion to dismiss" is a document filed with the court that assumes as its predicate (as it must) that key allegations of the consolidated complaint are true. Nonetheless (the motion goes on to contend), the plaintiffs may not prevail because the law provides no remedy based on the pleaded and assumed facts. Thus (the motion will conclude), the lawsuit should be judicially terminated without further ado.

The precise defenses to be raised in such a motion depend on the circumstances. One defense in particular, however, will normally be included. Where Section 10(b) claims have been alleged—as they almost always are—the defendants will call into question whether, as to each separate defendant, the consolidated complaint has adequately alleged a sufficient awareness of the facts to render that particular defendant culpable. In the technical jargon of the procedural rules, the defense will be presented that the consolidated complaint does not adequately allege scienter.

The need to adequately allege scienter stems from the fundamental principle that Section 10(b) imposes liability only on those possessed of an "intent to deceive, manipulate, or defraud." Federal procedural requirements—designed with the goal of protecting innocent citizens from baseless allegations—require a plaintiff seeking to allege a Section 10(b) claim to set forth with specificity the precise circumstances making clear that such an "intent to deceive, manipulate, or defraud" did exist. Thus, the complaint must allege, for example, participation in a conspiratorial meeting, receipt of a telltale memorandum, or other circumstances laying a factual predicate for the allegation that an "intent to deceive, manipulate, or defraud" was possessed by each defendant.

Whether a consolidated complaint does or does not adequately plead scienter is something that, in a typical financial fraud case, plaintiff and defense lawyers may end up arguing about for months. Among the issues of contention will be such things as the legal requirements of a satisfactory complaint (the courts disagree with each other), the types of factual allegations that will satisfy those legal requirements (as a practical matter, the court has a great deal of discretion), and the extent to which a plaintiff failing to include adequate allegations should be given the opportunity to amend its consolidated complaint in order to make another try. By the time the adequacy of the complaint's allegations is ultimately resolved, more than a year may have gone by.

This passage of time, though, is not necessarily to the disadvantage of the defendants. Under tort reform legislation of the mid-1990s, during the pendency of the motion to dismiss, the plaintiffs' pretrial investigation may not proceed. The filing of a motion to dismiss, therefore, largely puts the class action litigation on hold and gives the defendant officers and directors time to deal with other pressing business problems.

PROSPECTS OF AN EARLY SETTLEMENT

Throughout the initial stages of the litigation, one thought that will never be far from either the plaintiffs' or the defendants' minds is the possibility of an early resolution of the case through a negotiated settlement. Logically, an early resolution would seem to make sense. If a material accounting irregularity has surfaced, then both sides should theoretically recognize the extent to which shareholders have been harmed. The principal remaining obstacle would seem to be the calculation of resulting damages under the law and the negotiation of an appropriate settlement amount. Neither would seem like an insurmountable obstacle.

Strategic considerations would seem to heavily favor an early negotiated resolution. For the plaintiffs, an early settlement can maximize recovery by tapping into the reservoir of D&O insurance when it is at its fullest point (i.e., before it is depleted by the expenditure of defense costs) and can result in a recovery for shareholders before the incurrence of substantial legal fees. For the defendants, an early settlement brings a prompt end to the unpleasantness and helps individuals of questionable complicity keep their reputations intact. A particular advantage of an early settlement for the company stems from the removal of the horrific distraction of time-consuming litigation at a time when the company has more important operational and financial issues on which to focus.

Nonetheless, although some preliminary discussions of settlement may take place, an early resolution of the litigation is by no means assured. The reasons are not particularly profound. Usually the plaintiffs want more money than the defendants (or, more precisely, the defendants' insurance companies) are willing to pay. That is not to say that early settlements never happen, but they are the exception rather than the rule.

THE PROCESS OF DISCOVERY

In the absence of a settlement, the court will be given the time it needs to resolve the motion to dismiss. Although, with resolution of the motion, some or even most defendants may find themselves dismissed from the case, some defendants may remain. For those remaining defendants, the next step is to begin the pre-trial investigation known as "discovery."

The process of discovery has two main components. One is that the parties will request each other's documents as well as the documents of nonparticipants in the litigation who may have interesting information. The other component involves taking sworn testimony through depositions. Discovery involves other investigative techniques as well, such as written questions, but the production of documents and the taking of depositions are the two main vehicles for gathering information.

Unfortunately for the defendants, in a class action, discovery tends to be mostly a one-way street. It is largely a process in which the plaintiffs investigate the defendants. The reason is straightforward: The plaintiff shareholders tend to have less information of importance to the case. One securities defense lawyer has analogized the role of a defendant in a class action to that of a punching bag. You take punch after punch but get to give very little in return.

 ## THE PRODUCTION OF DOCUMENTS

The first step in the discovery process will normally be a document request. This consists of a list of documents to be made available to the plaintiffs. The list will normally seek documents such as board packages, board minutes, internal financial reports, monthly financial statements, and less generalized documents pertinent to the particular accounts at issue.

It is often during the process of collecting documents that the defendants are given the first opportunity to experience remorse that the case did not settle during the pendency of the motion to dismiss. Something unfortunate almost always seems to turn up. This is not to fault the diligence of the directors at the time of the operative events. It is merely a consequence of the fact that, with the benefit of hindsight, ostensibly wholesome financial reports or operating documents may contain clues that did not stand out at the time.

Still, such documents must be turned over to the plaintiffs who will then scrutinize them for exactly that kind of information. That is not to suggest that the defendants' lawyers will turn over all requested documents without a fuss. Compliance with some requests for documents may be so burdensome, disruptive, or seemingly redundant that the defendants will formally refuse, thereby giving rise to another dispute to be resolved by the court. The process of requesting, producing, and arguing about documents may be expected to take another few months.

The plaintiffs' request for one document in particular may be expected to give rise to especially vigorous litigation. That is the plaintiffs' attempt to obtain the investigative report of the audit committee if a written report has been prepared. Such a report may include a detailed discussion of what happened, how it happened, which financial statement items were influenced, the reasons behind the accounting irregularities, and the varying degrees of guilt of each of the potential participants. Extraction of such information through the discovery process—in which witnesses will inevitably be more guarded and less candid—could take years.

However, the defense will probably assert attorney-client privilege, meaning access by the plaintiffs will likely involve the court. The extent to which the plaintiffs should be entitled to such a report has been the subject of extensive judicial rulings, not all of them consistent. Resolution of this issue, too, can be expected to take months.

 ## ADDITION OF THE OUTSIDE AUDITOR

As the investigation continues, plaintiffs' counsel will inevitably be on the lookout for evidence that would sustain a claim against the company's outside auditor. For the company, the prospect of inclusion of its outside auditor as a defendant presents dilemmas that are both significant and strategically difficult to sort out. At best, the company's reactions will be mixed. On one level, the addition of a deep pocket to the group of defendants may be perceived to offer the prospect of a reduction in the damages that will be sought from the original members of the defendant group. To that extent, addition of the auditor as a defendant would seem to work to the company's advantage. Countervailing business considerations, though, may strongly militate in the other direction. While the litigation is proceeding, one of the company's most important goals will be to procure restated audited financial statements, and the most efficient way to get restated audited financial statements is to stick with the existing auditor. If the auditor is named a defendant, that can complicate things.

As one examines the issue more deeply, moreover, the strategic complications only get worse. Some of the more removed outside directors may feel betrayed by the auditor insofar as the auditor failed to discover and expose the fraud. For them, the thought of claims against the auditor might seem to make sense. Those closer to the center of wrongdoing, in contrast, may have a sense that, in truth, it was the company and its personnel who actively conspired to defraud the auditor. If anyone has a claim against anyone else, they might surmise, it is the auditor who has a claim against them. On close inspection, even the benefit of an additional "deep pocket" as defendant may not operate to the company's advantage. Statistical evidence suggests that, where the auditor is included as a defendant, the portion of the overall now-increased settlement amount paid by the company actually increases.

Mercifully, whether the auditor ultimately gets named as a defendant is not a decision the defendants will get to make. It will be up to the plaintiffs and, after that, to the judge on the auditor's motion to dismiss. If the auditor is to remain a defendant in the case, experience teaches that the minimization of hostilities among defendants will work to all of the defendants' advantage.

 ## THE TAKING OF DEPOSITIONS

As the process of document discovery draws close to its conclusion, the parties will turn to the second phase of the pretrial discovery process: the taking of depositions.

Any number of senior executives or outside directors have been through the process of a pretrial deposition. Basically, it is the process by which one sits in a conference room while the plaintiffs' lawyer asks questions and a court reporter transcribes both the questions and the witness's answers. Throughout the deposition, lawyers will interpose objections to particular questions being asked. The parties will normally want to videotape the entire process.

The deposition process usually offers a second opportunity for the defendants to regret that the case has not settled. The process itself is fraught with peril insofar as potentially incriminating documents from previous years can be extracted from the files and a witness quizzed about their content as if he or she saw them only yesterday. The opportunities for failed recollection, inadvertently inconsistent testimony, or simply honest mistakes exist at every turn. Although corporate defendants will normally be exceedingly well prepared for the process, the process by its nature inherently presents risk.

 ## DYNAMICS FAVORING SETTLEMENT

As the case proceeds further through discovery, for everyone the prospects of a negotiated resolution will begin to look more attractive. "Everyone," by the way, may include not only the defendants and their insurance companies but also in all likelihood both the defendants' lawyers and the lawyers for the plaintiffs (who at trial would actually be at risk of losing the contingency fee). As the case proceeds, therefore, the dynamics between the opposing parties will gradually shift in the direction of a pretrial resolution.

The biggest catalyst for a pretrial resolution, though, may not come from the lawyers for the plaintiffs or the defendants but from the trial judge itself. Generally speaking, a federal judge of normal temperament may view a multimonth jury trial about generally accepted accounting principles (GAAP) as about as much fun as a root canal. More than that, such a trial may upset the court's calendar, distract the judge from urgent judicial business, and overwhelm the judge's staff with paperwork.

At a propitious moment in the discovery process, therefore, the judge will likely convene a settlement conference. The ostensible purpose of the conference will be for the judge to use his or her authority to try to move the parties to a mutually acceptable resolution. Attending the settlement conference will normally be attorneys for the plaintiffs, attorneys for the defendants, and attorneys for the insurance carriers. In fact, only one group will not be in attendance: the actual plaintiff shareholders. They are left out of the process completely.

The settlement conference itself proceeds in a fairly predictable way. Once the assembled attorneys and clients have settled down (they may fill almost to capacity the judge's courtroom), the judge will normally begin by asking to speak privately with the plaintiffs' lawyers. In that meeting, he will dutifully listen to the plaintiffs' carefully rehearsed presentation, write down their damages estimate, and then tell them what a terrible case they have. Next, the judge will ask to speak privately with the defendants' lawyers. He will then listen to *their* carefully rehearsed presentation, write down *their* damages estimate, and then tell them what a terrible case *they* have. He will then reconvene a meeting of everyone in his courtroom and announce that the prospects of settlement are dim because the parties appear to be very far apart.

Indeed, they will be. Before the settlement conference, each side will have hired a damages expert, essentially an economist schooled in calculating damages to be as high (for the plaintiffs) or as low (for the defendants) as the confines of the numerical evidence will allow. At this stage in the litigation, it is not unheard of for the estimates of the plaintiffs' expert and the defendants' expert to be hundreds of millions or billions of dollars apart. At an initial settlement conference there will typically exist a wide chasm between the plaintiffs and the defendants to be closed.

SECURITIES LAW DAMAGES

The underlying explanation for the disparity in damage estimates lies in the fact that the estimation of damages for securities law violations—and, for this purpose, we will discuss principally Section 10(b)—is not entirely a precise exercise in mathematics. Under the securities laws, the amount of damages essentially involves the difference between the falsely inflated price a shareholder paid and the true value of the stock.

For a single share of stock purchased on a single day, this would be difficult enough. In a typical accounting irregularities case, however, at issue typically will be millions of shares of stock purchased and sold over a period of years at wildly different prices through industry ups and downs. Trading patterns among plaintiff shareholders will have varied dramatically. Included as part of the class of shareholders may be momentum investors (who arguably paid little or no attention to value), day-traders (who may have traded hundreds of times a day), mutual funds (whose trading patterns would have varied depending on their stated objectives and goals), and institutional investors (who may not have traded at all). Throw into the mix warrants, options, and short-sellers, and there is much to argue about.

The correct estimation of damages almost always turns into a battle between economists. Issues of dispute often include the nonfraud value of the stock, the impact upon stock price of industry or other business matters, the number of shares that were "damaged," the materiality of information, the trading patterns of various categories of shareholders, whether some shareholders actually benefited from the fraud, and the correct interpretation of the law applicable to all this. For most, the economists' testimony is simply mind-numbing. Still, everyone has complete confidence that the jury would easily figure it out.

 ## ULTIMATELY A SETTLEMENT

For all of these reasons, no matter how determined the parties, it is an unusual class action that settles in the first settlement conference. In fact, the parties may choose a process of mediation in which they split the cost of a nonparty mediator to see if some kind of negotiated resolution can be forged. While the parties may start out far apart, a skilled mediator can be pivotal in getting the parties to move toward each other.

In the great majority of cases, the parties will finally come to a settlement number. A form of settlement agreement will be extracted from one of the law firms' computers (probably in a form that these very lawyers have used many times before), marked up to reflect the precise terms of the resolution, and signed. The most difficult part will be over.

Successful execution of a settlement agreement, though, will not completely end the matter because, to this point, one group will have remained completely unaccounted for. That group is the plaintiff shareholders themselves. The normal process of resolution will have left them uninvolved and, although the law presumes their interests have been protected by their counsel, the danger always exists that their lawyers' concern with the anticipated contingency fee may appear to cloud their judgment as to what's best for the shareholders themselves. The law thus imposes an additional procedural device to protect the shareholders. That device is the requirement of court approval, after notice to the shareholders, of any settlement terms.

The next step once the settlement agreement has been signed, therefore, is to give notice to all shareholders so that each can individually decide whether to participate in the settlement. Among other things, the names and addresses of the class member plaintiffs need to be ascertained, the class notice must be distributed, a hearing on the settlement terms must be held, class members will be called on to submit proofs of claim setting forth the particulars of their stock purchases and sales, and these proofs of claim must then be scrutinized to isolate those for which a recovery is genuinely warranted.

This process, too, can add several months. Once the settlement terms have been agreed upon, though, these procedural requirements are left largely to the plaintiffs' attorneys and their retained administrators to work out. For the defendants, it will be time for them to lick their wounds and vow never to let it happen again.

PART FOUR

The Future

CHAPTER FOURTEEN

The Future of Financial Reporting

W E HAVE AT THIS POINT LOOKED at fraudulent financial reporting from almost every angle. We've looked at its origin. We've looked at prevention. We've looked at detection and its aftermath, including investigation, the SEC, criminal implications, and class action litigation. Seemingly, the entirety of the subject has been explored.

But there is another question left: *Why?* Why is it that, over the last twenty years, we have seen such a dramatic increase in fraudulently reported financial results? And a good follow-up question is: Have we adequately addressed the problem?

The answer to the first question has more to do with the nature of financial reporting systems than anything else. The fact is that we have entered a period in which financial market demands for information are not being met by the financial reporting system that happens to be in place. On the one hand, financial markets are demanding instantaneous, nonstop financial information. On the other hand, our financial reporting system is designed to provide information only periodically—once a quarter at best. The consequence is misreported financial results.

As to whether we've adequately addressed the problem, the answer is: Probably not. The same basic financial reporting system problems that gave rise to an upsurge in fraudulent financial reporting still exist. And, while new laws and regulations may impede fraudulent financial reporting, there is only so much that we can realistically expect the law to accomplish. If the financial reporting system encourages fraudulent accounting, the law can do little more than put fingers in the dike.

So now we dig into our financial reporting system to unearth the fundamental inadequacies giving rise to fraudulent results. With a deeper understanding of the problem comes the hope that, while we can never eradicate financial fraud, certainly we should be able to improve systems so that things get better.

A REAL-TIME WORLD

To come to grips with the fundamental problem with financial reporting systems, let us first spend a moment on the demands of today's financial markets. In particular, let us first address the insatiable thirst of financial markets for nonstop information.

In substance, financial markets today are functioning in a real-time world. Financial markets want to know what is happening *now*. And innovative entrepreneurs are working hard to give financial markets what they want. Companies such as Bloomberg, Dow Jones, Yahoo, and any number of creative upstarts flash financial and business information around the world the instant it's available. Traveling executives transport miniaturized communications centers so that they may instantaneously receive and act upon the latest events. Anyone with access to the Internet (i.e., everyone) has ready access to financial information that in another era would have been available to just a highly select few.

The impact of this onslaught of information on financial markets is nothing less than extraordinary. If something happens at the German Bundesbank with the potential to influence U.S. financial markets, we might expect no more than several minutes to elapse before trading on the New York Stock Exchange is affected. Indeed, it seems that almost no corner of civilization, no matter how ostensibly isolated in locale or tradition, can escape the demand for immediate information of a real-time world. Even the courts, with their explicit exclusion of electronic communications devices, are not immune. When an important court decision is rendered, strategically placed individuals, through a carefully designed system of hand signals, find a way to get the information within seconds to the outside world so the information can be electronically transmitted and put to use.

A 1930S FINANCIAL REPORTING SYSTEM

Our financial reporting system was not designed with any of this in mind. The basics of today's system were, after all, designed in the 1930s. It was a time when carbon paper was viewed as a technological innovation. The dominant concern at the time was not the speed of transmission of reliable financial information but the objective that reliable financial information be available to begin with. It was natural to assume that the information itself would be transmitted almost entirely on paper.

At the core of this Depression-era system, moreover, was the concept that financial information need be available only periodically. No one had reason to think that someday technological innovation would collapse the time needed to assemble and report financial information to days or even minutes. The underlying concept of the 1930s was built on the notion that the financial results of operations were to be assembled by a heavily populated accounting staff, packaged for management, and ultimately—every so often—provided to the public. The public in turn could make its investment decisions in due course.

Hence, the original public reporting requirements of the Securities Exchange Act of 1934 contemplated the filing of financial information only once a year. Over time, the laudable objective of encouraging efficiency in financial markets caused this requirement to be changed to semiannually and quarterly. At root, though, the system remained a periodic one. In other words, the underlying premise of the system continued to be that financial information would be made available only periodically. Today's system is thus an anachronistic remnant of the technology (i.e., carbon paper and the printing press) that existed when the system was designed.

True to its historical underpinnings, the core of today's financial reporting system continues to be a financial report that comes out once a year. That report is the set of annual financial statements that is audited by an outside accounting firm and included within the company's annual Form 10-K. Think about how those financial statements are put together. First, we wait for the year to end. Then we wait for the auditor to comb through the company's books and records. Then we wait while the data is assembled, typed, and printed. By the time users of the financial information have received it, the most recent information is months old. At some companies, it still takes longer than it took Columbus to discover America.

It is true that, under encouragement from the SEC, the financial community has taken big strides forward. Thus, we have the development of the Electronic

Data-Gathering, Analysis, and Retrieval (EDGAR) system of electronic SEC filing and companies placing their Forms 10-K and Forms 10-Q—as well as press releases, product information, and background data—on their websites. Although this is a big step in the right direction, it continues to be intellectually hindered by the periodic concept of the 1930s. That is, basically all we are doing is taking periodic information from paper and placing it on the computer.

Thus, a vacuum in financial reporting exists. It is a vacuum between the real-time financial information that financial markets demand and the inability of our creaky, sputtering financial reporting system to deliver information more frequently than once a quarter.

SO ENTER THE ANALYSTS

It is the miracle of a capitalist system that such a vacuum does not last for long. Hence, an entire population of entrepreneurs have rushed in to provide to financial markets the updated financial information they so earnestly desire. Those entrepreneurs are the community of Wall Street financial analysts.

For it is not the case that a user of financial information has access to financial performance only once a quarter. Instead, a user has available the more up-to-date information provided by financial analysts—in the form of readily published earnings expectations. This analyst information may be right or it may be wrong, but it possesses one virtue that the official financial data does not: It is available.

It is thus that we find ourselves in the peculiar position of having in place a carefully structured and painstakingly built formal financial reporting system that is being largely ignored by everybody. And a fair argument can be made that today's system is indeed being largely ignored. The annual filing of a Form 10-K does not move financial markets. By the time the 10-K comes out, the information at best is ancient history and has been factored into the stock price for weeks. Many have heard the story of a food manufacturer that, as a test of the usefulness of its annual financial statements, offered shareholders a choice: a glossy copy of the company's annual report or a free pound of cookies. Most shareholders went for the cookies.

Although unaudited quarterly statements play a more important role, rarely do even quarterly statements move markets. That is to say, rarely do quarterly statements move markets when they are consistent with already existing analyst expectations. When they are not consistent with analyst expectations, they can move markets quite a lot.

That takes us to the crux of the matter. What moves financial markets is not an annual 10-K or even a quarterly 10-Q. What moves financial markets is the published expectations of Wall Street analysts. In substance, the published expectations of Wall Street analysts are perceived to establish within a very narrow margin the parameters for the upcoming actual financial results. Analyst expectations have become in effect a company's reported earnings.

A CONSEQUENCE IS FINANCIAL FRAUD

What does all this have to do with financial fraud? The elevated importance to financial markets of analyst expectations has resulted in a financial reporting environment in which, for a number of public companies, the preoccupation of financial reporting is not accurately depicting the financial performance of the enterprise. Rather, the preoccupation of financial reporting is seeing to it that analyst expectations—one way or another—are fulfilled.

For public companies faced with this preoccupation, its fulfillment can be a nightmare insofar as no legally satisfactory way exists by which the accuracy of analyst expectations can be controlled. That is not for lack of trying on the part of analysts. Analysts earn their living, and if they're lucky get famous, providing investors with estimates of public company future financial performance. The easiest way to formulate such estimates is to ask a company's CFO what he or she expects.

Such an analyst inquiry would seem like a golden opportunity for a CFO to get accurate information out on the street and to keep analyst expectations from varying from the truth. However, the law, as a result of its understandable paranoia about the leakage of inside information and its laudable desire to protect equal access to information, tries to keep precisely that from happening.

Here's what can end up taking place. The analyst needs to get updated financial information. He telephones the CFO. He gives the CFO, say, his latest guess as to how the quarter is going to come out. And he asks the CFO, "Am I right or wrong?"

There is no completely satisfactory way for the CFO to answer that question. Basically, the CFO has two choices. First, he can try to steer the analyst into a more accurate prediction or simply tell the analyst he is right or wrong. However, the CFO himself may not have a firm sense of how the quarter is going to come out and may end up inadvertently creating an expectation that can be neither fulfilled nor easily corrected. Worse than that, providing up-to-date financial results to a single analyst creates the risk of violating fair disclosure regulations and giving out inside information. If the information is material, and it probably will be, that sets up the CFO for a subsequent charge of violating SEC regulations and being a participant in insider trading. Insider trading is a felony.

The second alternative is for the CFO to keep his mouth shut. Here, the problem is a different one. If the CFO keeps his mouth shut, and the analyst goes forward with the publication of incorrect expectations, then the actual quarterly results, when they come out (by preannouncement or otherwise), will potentially wreak havoc. If actual results exceed analyst expectations, then shareholders are all the happier and no real harm results (beyond extraordinary inefficiency in information dissemination). If, however, actual results are significantly below street expectations, the result for the stock price can be significant. So-called "momentum" investors may flee the stock. The stock price may collapse. And the company—as well as the CFO, the CEO, and any number of inside and outside directors—may very well end up defendants in class action litigation.

Either way, our hapless CFO is at substantial risk that an incorrect earnings estimate will create a street expectation that cannot be fulfilled or painlessly corrected. If an incorrect estimate takes hold, then, as quarter-end approaches—and with it the inevitable day of reckoning—the pressure mounts. And so does the incentive to exploit those hazy areas of generally accepted accounting principles (GAAP) that would allow the company ostensibly to make up for the earnings shortfall. (See Chapter 1.)

It is, therefore, the vacuum resulting from what financial markets want, which is immediate financial information, and what the present structure of financial reporting systems enables companies to deliver, which is quarterly and annual reports, that has contributed so handily to the financial reporting environment that lies at the core of the recent increase in accounting irregularities. The vacuum is filled by analysts, and analyst expectations in turn create enormous pressure on a company to see that they are fulfilled. Financial fraud, of course, doesn't start with dishonesty. It starts with pressure.

 ## OTHER CAPITAL MARKET INEFFICIENCIES

Still additional problems result from the vacuum created by the real-time demands of financial markets and today's periodic system of financial reporting.

One such problem is the resulting volatility both in individual stock market prices and in the market as a whole. The underlying causes of that volatility are numerous. A big cause, though, stems from the market gyrations that come about during "earnings season," when companies announce or preannounce quarterly results. For an individual company, the fallout can include a collapsing stock price, a demoralized work force (whose stock options may now be under water), anxious lenders, and class action litigation (even in the absence of an accounting irregularity problem). An announcement of a weak outlook by IBM resulted in a one-day loss of market value of $39 billion. Three months later, Lucent Technologies' announcement of an anticipated failure to attain analyst expectations (it said it expected to miss them by about 15 cents) translated into a market capital loss almost twice as large—$64 billion.

But the fallout is not limited to the management and the shareholders of the particular company that happens to disappoint. When Intel preannounced disappointing earnings for the first quarter of 1998, it reportedly triggered a collapse in securities markets around the world. Unpredictable volatility in the securities markets is something that investors have just learned to live with.

But they don't live with it for free. Volatility means risk. And risk means investors want a higher return on their capital investment. An important consequence of the volatility that necessarily results from our periodic financial reporting system, therefore, is the additional premium investors require from the securities markets to compensate for the increased risk. Here, again, the cost is not limited to the company or investors of a particular company that happens to disappoint. To some extent it is shared by the stock market as a whole.

Operational inefficiencies from a periodic reporting system follow as well. Manufacturing companies, on going public, have perceived a change in the buying patterns of their customers, owing to their customers' awareness of the manufacturers' need to attain a certain level of quarterly revenue. One such company, for example, found that, after going public, purchases by distributors tended to become clustered in the third month of each quarter. As the company went into each third month, its nervousness over a prospective failure to make its quarterly numbers led to increasing levels of discounting, which only increased the incentives for the company's customers to hold off their purchases as long as they could. After several years, the company found its assembly lines less active in the first month of each quarter and then working overtime in the third. Shipping problems developed as the physical limitations of the loading docks could not accommodate quarter-end peak demand. The problem was exacerbated insofar as other manufacturing companies in the geographic vicinity seemed to be going through the same thing and all were simultaneously seeking to line up available trucking. On top of everything else, quarter-end also presented a shortage of independent truckers.

Such logistical problems can lead to breakdowns in accounting systems. One staff member of the SEC's Division of Enforcement encountered a public company that he suspected had turned back its computer clock as a result of a logistical failure to ship all merchandise during a quarter-end peak. Faced with seemingly corroborative documentation from the independent trucker showing that shipment had ostensibly taken place by quarter-end, the SEC official on a hunch telephoned the trucker only to learn that the trucker, at the request of the manufacturer, had back-dated the shipping documentation. Nor did the trucker view the request as particularly unusual. The trucker went on to volunteer that, at the end of each quarter, he received literally hundreds of similar requests from other companies.

The problems do not stop there. Still another results from inefficiency in the way that critical financial information ends up being transmitted to the public through the intermediary of financial analysts. Mechanically, the present system works something like this: The typical CFO at a public company has sitting on his desk a computer. That computer is plugged into the company's management information system, which provides information that is sufficiently reliable for fundamental operational and financial decisions. It tells the CFO, and for that matter anybody who's plugged into it, financial performance to date and, by inference, to some extent where the company will be at the end of the quarter.

Now let's consider a Wall Street analyst whose office happens to be in a building across the street. He has sitting on his desk a computer. It is the analyst's fundamental mission in life to find out what's on the CFO's computer and to get it into *his* computer. He'll take whatever information he can get, put it into his own computer, and thereby generate an earnings forecast.

To find out what's on the CFO's computer, the analyst uses one of the most up-to-date of technological devices—the telephone. Nervously aware that he may be at the edge of legal permissibility, he telephones the CFO to extricate whatever clues and insights he can gain about the company's financial performance.

For reasons already discussed, the law heavily discourages the CFO from selectively providing important information. So the two may end up speaking in code. The analyst may say something like, "I'm predicting EPS of $.32 for the quarter—how comfortable are you in that area?" The CFO, having been cautioned against expressing a view on analyst expectations, at most allows himself to talk about the past. He accordingly might respond with something like, "How can you be at $.32 when this quarter last year we came in at $.25, as we have, in fact, for the previous 17 quarters." At some point, our analyst gets the message and, sure enough, puts out his new earnings forecast: $.25. Although both possess the most efficient means of electronic communication in the history of civilization, our CFO and Wall Street analyst have digressed into a communication system of winks and nods over which cuneiform would be an improvement.

And that's without even getting to company incentives to talk down analyst expectations to less than actually foreseen, or to the potential incentive by analysts to issue favorable reports owing to preexisting relationships between the company and the analyst's investment bank. All of these amount to extraordinary inefficiencies in the dissemination of financial information to the investing public.

Our Depression-era periodic system of financial reporting even creates inefficiencies from the perspective of financial management. The chairman of one company once observed that his internal financial reporting systems were sufficiently sophisticated that every day he, like other senior executives, received on his email a report of revenue on the previous day's shipments. It so happened that the nature of the company's business was such that its margins were fairly consistent. Thus, receipt of shipping information in terms of revenue yielded in substance daily information on earnings and, by inference, earnings per share. The information was reliable and always up to date. Unfortunately, such was the terror instilled in the chairman by virtue of the federal securities laws, that the chairman (who wanted periodically to sell a portion of his stock holdings) became paranoid about having access to such timely information when the public did not. He accordingly had himself disconnected from the company's email.

 ## THERE'S ANOTHER WAY

So that's where we are. Our periodic system of financial reporting creates enormous pressure for fundamentally honest people to perpetrate accounting fraud. It creates unnecessary volatility in the stock market. It requires rational investors to demand a premium for securities investments. It gives rise to operational inefficiencies. It results in enormous inefficiency in the transmission of information from public companies to financial markets. It even creates an incentive for corporate managers to disconnect themselves from up-to-date information.

There's got to be a better way. And in fact there is. Members of the financial community are increasingly acknowledging the need for an evolution beyond the financial reporting system of the 1930s into an era of nonstop information of the sort financial markets want. In other words, there was an alternative available to our chairman who disconnected himself from the company email, though we can hardly blame him for not thinking of it. He could have stayed connected to his email. In fact he could have let the email go out to the analysts and the investment community at large. That is to say, he could have reported his company's financial results on a real-time basis.

Now an understandable reaction on the part of CFOs might be unmitigated terror. Anyone familiar with the agony of putting out a quarterly press release has reason to flee from the concept of fundamentally doing so at least once a day. How would the information be checked? What controls would there be on reliability? What happens if there's an honest mistake?

Those are all good questions, and not all of them have perfect answers. But the accelerating pace of innovation in technology and financial reporting systems will make increasingly apparent the need to move beyond the periodic system rooted in the technology of the 1930s. In other words, it is time to unshackle the transmission of financial information from the chains of outdated Great Depression technology. It is time to think less in terms of a periodic system and more in terms of a real-time system in which financial information is transmitted not long after the underlying transactions take place.

If there is to be such a shift from a periodic to a real-time financial reporting system, there needs to be a fundamental change in attitudes toward financial reporting. That is, those who report and inspect financial information will need to change their focus from methods by which the numbers themselves are checked (in other words, an audit as we know it today) to methods by which the reliability of the *system* that generates the numbers is evaluated. As a company's financial reports go whizzing out the door on a real-time basis, there will not be time for an audit of those numbers in the traditional sense to take place. Thus, the internal control system over financial reporting will gain a level of prominence that it never had before.

Viewed in this context, the real-time provisions of Sarbanes-Oxley are both better understood and recognized for what they are—a step forward in the evolution of financial reporting. Most prominent among these is the highly controversial Section 404 mandate that companies and auditors report on the reliability of a company's system of internal control. True, the early experience with Section 404 reporting has not been flawless, and some of the early criticisms—excessive documentation, liability concerns giving rise to unnecessary testing, overly vague regulatory guidance—may have been justified. But none of that should be allowed to cloud the fundamental importance of internal control reporting or the stride forward that Section 404 represents. Reporting on internal control is the wave of the future. If we are to move beyond the periodic system of the Great Depression, we need to find a way to make it work.

Other real-time provisions of Sarbanes-Oxley similarly seek to move us beyond the 1930s. Hence the acceleration of the deadlines for the filing of Forms 10-K and 10-Q. Given the need to make such filings sooner, companies may have no choice but to streamline their internal control systems and increase the reliability of them in the process. A comparable modification is found in Section 409, which requires "real-time issuer disclosures." Under this section, companies are to disclose on "a rapid and current basis" significant information regarding "changes in the financial condition or operations" of the company. All in all, these innovations—Section 404 system reporting and accelerated deadlines—should serve to refocus attention from numerical data to the speed and reliability of the system by which the data is gathered and reported.

Should financial reporting successfully make the transition from a periodic to a real-time system, the resulting efficiencies could be remarkable. Among other things, real-time financial reporting would free corporate America from its economically nonsensical preoccupation with quarterly results. There is absolutely no economic justification for focusing on a quarter as the economic unit in which to take stock of financial performance beyond the fact that that's what's written in the law. Making available financial information on a real-time basis would almost require users of financial information to discard the quarter as a unit of measurement and to adopt a unit that made sense for each particular business and industry. For some companies and industries, that unit might be a week, a month, a quarter, semiannually, or a year. The point is that users would have the freedom to adopt a time period that actually made sense rather than the one-size-fits-all period decreed by federal law.

A more fundamental advantage, moreover, would be the opportunity for increased efficiency in financial markets as investment would be allocated not according to quarterly results or the "best-guess" estimates of financial analysts, but by reliable financial information provided directly by the company all the time. A collateral but equally significant benefit would be the decrease in stock market volatility insofar as discrepancies between market expectations and actual results would never develop or, having developed, would be corrected in modest amounts every day rather than in one large correction at the end of each quarter.

Still another advantage would be the practical elimination of the principal incentive for—and perhaps the mechanical ability to perpetrate—financial misreporting in the form of accounting irregularities. Gone would be the brooding omnipresence of quarterly analyst expectations and, accordingly, the pressure to manipulate results in order to meet them. More than that, also largely eliminated would be the mechanical ability to perpetrate accounting sleights of hand, insofar as financial information would be publicly available automatically before any of the (at least traditional) manipulations could be put in place. Of course, real-time financial reporting would not eliminate financial fraud for all time. We all know better than that. But it would take us a big step in the right direction.

None of this is to suggest that anyone is proposing that the totality of a company's internal reporting system be opened up to the outside world. Public companies will inevitably want to limit access to information to that which is reliable and can be reasonably transmitted on a regular basis. In addition, the transmittal of any such information would presumably be accompanied by appropriate caveats and warnings directed to the extent of the information's reliability. Before any of this can happen, moreover, financial reporting systems would have to be improved to the point where the real-time transmission of key information is possible. Companies would have to follow the example of companies such as Microsoft, which has sought to collapse the time it takes to assemble and report financial results to achieve a "continuous close" where information is accurate and current every day of the month.

Nevertheless, the real-time needs of financial markets are dragging today's financial reporting system in the direction of increased frequency of financial reporting without anyone really focusing on the broader implications. At the same time, the SEC's Regulation Fair Disclosure (FD), in clamping down further on the selective disclosure of material information to analysts, has given public companies a stark choice: Make information available to everyone or keep it to themselves. To its credit, the SEC has also indicated a willingness to allow companies to use more immediate and direct forms of communication through "social media," thus bypassing much of the 1930s periodic system.

Increasingly, companies are choosing broader and more frequent disclosure. An increasingly common example is earnings preannouncements when actual results are diverging significantly from analyst expectations. According to one survey, 72 percent of Fortune 500 CFOs have decided to pre-announce or provide early guidance on earnings, presumably as a consequence of the downside of waiting for the end of the legally mandated quarter. Other examples include companies that regularly report mid-quarter results, retailers that post on their websites updated sales figures, hotel chains whose websites include updated occupancy rates, and newspapers whose websites include updated circulation figures. In a sense, the mid-quarter announcements of collapsing fair values as the bubble burst in the 2008 financial crisis was an illustration of more frequent financial reporting. Granted, it is not always fun to have up-to-date information on what's happening. But we've always known that ignorance is bliss.

The good news, therefore, is that, although fraudulent financial reporting will never be eliminated, the pressures giving rise to the upsurge of the last 20 years will foreseeably dissipate. Change rarely comes easily, and we can expect earnest debate and startling innovation as financial reporting systems evolve. Some will inevitably long for the days of carbon paper. But others will find a new era of financial reporting exhilarating.

About the Author

Michael R. Young is an internationally recognized expert on the causes and prevention of fraudulent financial reporting. He assisted the U.S. Congress in formulating amendments to the federal securities laws to combat financial fraud and has been a leader in helping companies to investigate and correct the consequences of some of the largest frauds of the last three decades. He lives in New York City and is a partner of Willkie Farr & Gallagher LLP where he chairs the firm's Securities Litigation and Enforcement practice.

Index

Printed and bound by CPI Group (UK) Ltd, Croydon, CR0 4YY

23/04/2025

14660992-0002